Effective Pupil Personnel Services

Effective Pupil Personnel Services

Glenn G. Dahlem

The Center for Applied Research in Education, Inc.
New York

© 1972 by

The Center for Applied
Research in Education, Inc.
New York

Library of Congress
Catalog Card Number: 72-76485

Printed in the United States of America
C-1971-5

Dedication

Shortly before this book was written, three prominent counselor-educators died within a few months of one another. They were Edward Roeber, Buford Stefflre, and Wray Strowig. The ideas and professional example furnished by all three of these scholars have influenced this writer. In addition, Wray Strowig served as the author's doctoral major professor and thus had numerous chances to influence his metamorphosis as counselor and counselor-educator. It is to these three men, for whom it was not God's will to live to see this book a reality, that it is dedicated.

About the Author

Glenn G. Dahlem, Ph.D., obtained his master's degree at Winona (Minnesota) State College, then returned to his alma mater, the University of Wisconsin, to earn his doctorate in counseling and guidance. He has served as a school counselor for eight years and a college educator for three. His counseling experience spans all grade levels from kindergarten through senior high school. As head of guidance for the Marshall, Wisconsin, schools, Dr. Dahlem founded an area counselors' association. He has also worked as a counselor for a Head Start program and has authored many articles in professional publications such as *School Counselor, Counselor Education and Supervision, Journal of Educational Research, School Management, Instructor,* and *Nation's Schools.*

Dr. Dahlem is presently Assistant Professor of Education at Regis College in Denver, Colorado. He is active in Phi Delta Kappa and the Professional Counselors' Assocation, and is a member of APGA, including its ASCA, ACES, and SPATE divisions.

Using Personnel Services
to Promote Student Growth

This book has a dual mission; one part of its job is to be
very practical, nitty-gritty, and occasionally even pedantic. The other part of its job is highly philosophic and
intellectual. Incompatible, foolishly chosen bedfellows?
No, not at all, when what is proposed for the guidance
field in the following pages is considered carefully. For
in this book, many "nuts and bolts" guidance techniques
are suggested for counselors—but every procedure proposed is based upon a logically built theory of personality development and counseling rationale. As far as the
author can determine, no one has tried to "marry" a
counselor's more mundane duties to counseling before—
so here goes!

Some counselors feel that practice of pupil services is a necessary
evil that goes with their profession. They look upon occupational-
educational, appraisal, and referral activities as second in importance
to individual and group counseling. A purpose of this book is to
demonstrate that the two parts of a secondary counselor's job—
personnel services and counseling—are co-equal, inseparable
components of the professional role. Good counseling leads to more
effective personnel services, and efficient pupil services set up
numerous opportunities for counseling. A modern secondary counselor must do both parts of his job well to be optimally effective.

Probable cause for relegation of personnel services to an inferior-
to-counseling status is the lack of an orderly philosophic approach.
Almost every counselor follows a rationale during counseling. Not so
for personnel services. In most cases, these are just tasks that have to
be done, while counseling is looked upon as the more intellectual
half of the job. So another purpose of this book is to propose a

practical yet intellectually-based rationale for practice of pupil services, one that introduces maturity-building events into the school careers of adolescent boys and girls. In such an approach, pupil services reinforce the psychological gains made in counseling.

A problem for counselors in the practice of pupil personnel services has long been the numerous sub-professional, mundane clerical chores that accompany them. This is quite likely a major cause for the inferior status which pupil services have in many counselors' minds. This book contains a proposed solution to the sub-professional work-load problem. Perhaps youngsters themselves can shoulder a greater share of work connected with pupil services performed on their behalf. However, shunting busy-work onto unsuspecting teen-agers is not the author's intention. This is unprofessional and inexcusably naive. Rather, it is suggested that adolescent counselees become involved in pupil services as volunteer aides, in ways that will be of therapeutic benefit to their personalities. If student involvement is so approached, it becomes highly professional indeed, and ties in closely with the counseling portion of a counselor's work.

A cry for greater general student involvement in education is also being heard from another quarter. Today's secondary students more and more are picking up the call for relevancy from their college-age counterparts. The young, always restless and impatient, wish to be involved more fully in educational planning and decision-making. What more appropriate place is there for this than the vocational development area of pupil services? Teen-agers will not need much urging from a counselor to help him place their peers in jobs and in colleges. Principals have long been aware that students more readily obey codes of conduct drafted by themselves. This portion of young people's demands for participation has been granted, with benefits to all concerned. Counselors would achieve greater cooperation from their adolescent clients if they too followed this pattern, and included students in planning and operating personnel services.

A universally held tenet of the profession is that the goal of counseling is to help clients help themselves. Counselee manipulation is frowned upon; rather, a good counselor assists clients in becoming less dependent on himself and other adults. This primary goal of counseling is based upon the psychological principle that maturity and emotional growth result from increasing ability to accept and resolve problems on one's own. Teen-agers grow up through coping with various situations, not from having others solve their problems for them. This principle, universally observed in counseling, may and should be applied to pupil personnel services as well. If counseling and pupil services are both looked upon as based on this premise, they become two complementary parts of the same basic process. This outlook toward personnel services is far superior to a view which regards them as sub-professional step-children of counseling.

The major premise on which this book is based is that pupil personnel services are a potential vehicle for student personality development, just as is counseling. A second, more pragmatic contention is that much time now wasted by counselors on sub-professional aspects of pupil services can be saved by having students perform these things. Of course, student involvement must be approached in an ethical manner (specifics are described in the various chapters which follow). Student willingness to volunteer for work as personnel service aides will be high—provided that such participation is couched in terms of the relevancy and involvement which the young are demanding for themselves in all segments of modern education.

A secondary emphasis of this book concerns greater personnel service involvement of two other publics of counselors, the school staff and the community at large. These two important groups, like the student body, can and should play an expanded role in practice of pupil services. Good personnel services help principals and teachers perform more efficiently. Parents, employers, and tax payers also benefit from improved vocational, appraisal, and consultative efforts of their school's counselor. Many members of these two groups are eager and ready to help the counselor in practice of pupil services.

When performing pupil personnel services that also include fellow staff members, the counselor functions as quarterback of the guidance team. Each professional educator contributes to the guidance process from the standpoint of his or her specific frame of reference. The counselor, acting as catalytic facilitator of interchange among the staff, coordinates their pupil service contributions. If the counselor has cooperated with his colleagues, helping them with their problems whenever ethically permissible, they'll be happy to assist him in personnel services when called upon.

In seeking reciprocal cooperation from members of the community, the counselor assumes a school-community liaison role. Because he is the one staff member hired exclusively to help students, the counselor's potential public image lends itself ideally to community interaction. If he's doing a good job in the opinions of parents, employers, and taxpayers, many of these folks will be only too happy to join him in helping the young. As was the case for school staff members, each community pupil-services participant enters into such activity from the standpoint of his or her specific frame of reference.

In summary, it is necessary to state what this book is *not*. It's not a manual on how to get others to perform the counselor's work, so he may "goof off." Rather, it's a framework for ethically involving others, students, staff, and citizens, in keeping with interests and competencies, in a joint effort for improved pupil services.

The book is also not an attempt to downgrade the importance of individual and group counseling and replace these counselor functions with greater emphasis upon pupil services. Instead, it advocates professional escalation of personnel services to a position of parity with counseling. A theoretical argument that counseling and pupil services are inseparable halves of one basic process is advanced. The author believes that good personnel services complement good counseling, and vice versa, and that pupil services, like counseling, are a potential vehicle for client emotional growth.

Glenn G. Dahlem

Table of Contents

neglecting PR . How student volunteers can help with PR . Tips for news media relations . Some sample news releases . How good PR results in professional advancement.

Nature of the counseling relationship . Overview of the philosophic rationales for counseling . Uniqueness and commonalities in counselor behavior . When to be "hard-nosed" and when to be sympathetic . Good counseling leads to better personnel services, and vice versa.

A bibliography of cogent readings for active members of the counseling and guidance profession, organized topically by various personnel service areas, for easy reference.

ONE

Building and Running an Effective
Occupational-Educational-Information Service

A potentially dry and unexciting place, the counselor's information service, becomes a fascinating focal
point for client vocational development and emotional
growth. Even administrators, teachers, and parents find
opportunities for dynamic involvement. Just what may a
counselor do to create an information service like this?

A DYNAMIC, EVOLVING PROCESS,
NOT A FEW DUSTY SHELVES OF PAMPHLETS

The information service is the easiest of all pupil personnel services
to maintain at a mediocre level, and the most difficult to operate at a
superior level. Like all other collections of things found in society, its
built-in potential weakness is a proclivity toward "dryness." Just as a
few of their cousins, the libraries, have, some high school information services have fallen prey to dryness. This leads to poor student
image of the service, and thus to little usage. Some counselors
contribute to low pupil regard of the information service by their
own attitudes. "Collecting booklets and filing them on shelves or in
drawers is subprofessional and trivial; I'm a master's degree-level
educator," paraphrases their sentiments. When a counselor displays
this feeling toward his information service, who can blame pupils and
teachers for failing to use it?

If the information service was actually supposed to be a few
monographs, catalogs, and books, lying around on shelves or thrown
into drawers, it would be a subprofessional, dry entity indeed! This is
definitely not, however, what a modern secondary school informa-

tion service should be. Nor can it be, if the guidance program is to function effectively. An information service is not a *collection* of anything; rather, it's a *process,* continually evolving to meet the needs of today's teen-agers. An information service is based upon activities of people, not upon inanimate materials. Of course, great quantities of relevant monographs, books, films, sound-filmstrips, and posters are constantly entering the service and being utilized within and without its physical confines. These materials are not an end in themselves. They are not the information service; they are only the tools that enable its various activities to function. Analogously, these materials are to the different informational activities as a textbook is to a teacher.

Subsequent chapters of this book discuss possible informational activities, such as college visitations, career consultant visits, and poster contests, in detail. Therefore, Chapter One focuses upon acquisition, management, and utilization of informational materials, and the physical area in which they are housed. Even when the collection itself becomes the focus, however, it is still human activities that are of paramount concern. For example, filling out and mailing a postcard occupational monograph request could be as important to a student's vocational development as reading the monograph when it arrives. Cooperatively decorating the counselor's outer office, where informational materials are housed, may do more socially for a group of teen-agers than all the socio-personal literature in existence. In short, continuous human involvement is necessary before a collection of materials, no matter how commodious and up-to-date it is, can begin to do any good.

MAKING THE PROCESS WORK—STUDENT PARTICIPATION

Volunteer aides use their talents to become deeply involved.

Every junior and senior high school abounds with pupils who eagerly wish to engage in meaningful co-curricular activity. Most teen-agers still retain a spark of the enthusiasm for school that once burned as a bright fire when they entered first grade years before. The counselor, by involving boys and girls in relevant vocational development projects, can, for some, fan that spark back into flame. Too many times, in too many places, this natural inclination of students to participate has been either cruelly suppressed or channelled into senseless frivolity. When the young demand "relevancy" in their school curricula, they are not rebelling; they are only claiming a birthright descended from the proud traditions of America's educational past.

Just how does a counselor go about obtaining student volunteers to assist him in building the information service? Basically, the call is best spread in an informal, person-to-person manner. Teachers, administrators, counseling clients, and parents are told that the counselor has several two- or three-periods-per-week volunteer jobs that pupils may wish to try. For example, the business education teacher will promote opportunities for his pupils to practice their office skills. The principal will seize the chance to challenge the discipline problem who promised to behave in school "if only I had something practical to do." Counselees, already sold on the benefits of a guidance program, will seek to become more involved and to interest their friends. Parents, eager for their children to obtain optimum benefit from their school experience, will pass the word to them.

Every school has a few boys and girls who, regardless of whether they have problems or not, seek out the counselor as a person with whom to spend some time. It's only natural that these youngsters become involved with the information service. Still other persons— students, faculty, and parents—drawn to the warm, hopefully humanizing personality of the counselor, will become familiar with the service during contacts with him.

Most boys and girls will volunteer, despite lack of pay, as there are several benefits to be gained from such work. First of all, factual vocational learnings and insights result from helping to build and run the information service. Such future job possibilities as file clerk, typist, receptionist, librarian, cabinetmaker, mail clerk, and interior decorator are related to the duties that aides perform. Secondly, by assuming esponsibility for a school program's operation, teen-agers are given opportunity to demonstrate their maturity. There aren't too many school-connected activities, sad to say, that afford such a chance. Third, the psychological feeling of belonging, and of making a worthwhile social contribution, is sought by all normal individuals. The chance to give of one's talent to further vocational opportunities for his peers is an honor and a privilege. Last of all, serving as a volunteer aide has the somewhat negative but real benefit of allowing an escape from the regimentation of study hall. Many otherwise well-behaved students find study halls repugnant—and educational psychology is on their side. Not a few boys and girls find equally disgusting the blocks of free time found in the modular scheduling system prevalent in many schools. These teen-agers look upon free time as a bribe to behave, and regard it contemptuously. In either case, becoming a volunteer aide offers an escape from a psychologically inferior situation. Of course, there's something in it for the counselor, too. When students take over sub-professional aspects of his role, such as ordering occupational monographs, it frees him for more intensive commitment to a higher level duty, such as individual counseling.

Pupils assist the counselor in acquiring materials.

As volunteers arrive and are put to work by the counselor, two important principles must be observed: (1) Don't expect a child to be a trained adult; start each boy and girl off on a relatively easy task. Later, each aide will work up to a difficulty level commensurate with his intellectual endowment. (2) Allow volunteers to work in their aptitude areas as much as possible. Don't put the industrial arts student who wants to make a bookcase to work typing letters.

One of the biggest volunteer jobs in any school's information service involves identifying, ordering, cataloging, and disseminating free occupational, educational, and socio-personal literature. This is a good position for an office practice student, and will keep at least one aide busy throughout the school year. One approach to filling this position is to write a job announcement and description, and publicize it through the business education department. An example of such a notice is shown in Figure 1-1.

In a large high school, the information Service Clerk II job may be split into two positions, if necessary. When this is done, job duties (a) and (b) are performed by one student, and (c) and (d) by another. Basically, the job is done in the following manner: The aide is instructed in finding sources to write for various occupational, educational, and socio-personal published materials available to schools. These sources, on file in the information service, include appendices in counselor education textbooks, published directories of further educational institutions, direct mailings to guidance departments, armed forces publications, filler announcements in professional journals, state education department bulletins, and lists included with commercial guidance service subscriptions.

After the aide has identified a source, she orders the complimentary material, using one of two elite type, mimeographed form

---

NOTICE OF VOLUNTEER GUIDANCE AIDE OPPORTUNITY

JOB: Information Service Clerk II

OPEN TO: Seniors Enrolled in Office Practice

TIME REQUIRED: 2 Double Modules Per Week

RESTRICTION: Must Maintain "C" Average or Above in Office
Practice

INTERVIEW WITH: Mr. Jefferson, Counselor

DESCRIPTION:

(a) Look up titles and addresses of free literature sources in books
and magazines provided by school.
(b) Fill out, post, and mail postcards ordering this literature.
(c) Stamp, catalog, and file literature when it arrives in mail.
(d) Announce arrivals of new literature to student body and
faculty on posters and in guidance newsletter.

OFFICE SKILLS USED:

reference searching
addressing
mail distribution
filing
technical reporting

The job may include supervision of a junior high school Clerk I
during second semester.

Figure 1-1

postal cards designed for this purpose. These cards are best made on
8½ x 11 white or light yellow card stock, two each to a sheet of four,
and cut apart with a paper cutter. One card is used to order
occupational and socio-personal materials, the other, educational
materials. One side of each card is left blank; on this side the aide
prints the material source name and address, and places a 8¢ stamp.
The other side, illustrated in Figures 1-2(a) and 1-2(b), is designed
for easy completion by the aide.

As various requested materials arrive in the mail, the aide opens their envelopes, rubber-stamps them as belonging to the information service, and assigns each an appropriate D.O.T. code number, or catalog number. She files them eventually in a D.O.T.-organized, or subject-headed file cabinet, but first may wish to display new arrivals on a bulletin board or in a pamphlet rack. Whenever copies of materials related to a particular teacher's subject field arrive, the aide routes a copy to the teacher with a "thought you'd be interested" memo attached. Another good idea is to post a listing of newly arrived titles in a specified spot on a hallway bulletin board. If the counselor issues a periodic guidance newsletter, the aide prepares a typed list of new arrivals for its student editor.

Acquisition of informational materials shouldn't be restricted to a formal procedure, however. As boys and girls become guidance conscious, and develop rapport with the counselor, they may be encouraged to be on the lookout for valuable materials to bring to school. For example, a teen-ager whose father is an engineer might talk dad out of some trade publications and company engineering

---

Gentlemen:

Please send us the following material(s) that you have available to high school guidance programs:

amount(s)   *title(s)*

_____   _____

_____   _____

_____   _____

_____   _____

_____   _____

We learned of this material   Very truly yours,
in: _____

_____

Thank you very much.   Information Svc. Clerk II
                           Guidance Office
                           Anytown High School
                           123 Main St.
                           Anytown, Pa. 10632

(Card used to order occupational and socio-personal materials.)

Figure 1-2(a)

brochures. A teamster's son might bring in a copy of union by-laws, and a sample cargo manifest. A girl whose big brother attends a large university might con him into getting some surplus registration packets for practice use. A student who worked for a large corporation during the past summer might bring in samples of its employee orientation literature. A young man whose brother is serving in the armed forces could possibly obtain a discarded field manual for counselee reference. Such pragmatic materials are often equal in value to occupational monographs and college catalogs for use in vocational counseling.

Another semi-formal free literature acquisition program is solicitation of used magazine donations. Parents, faculty, and pupils are eager to contribute discarded periodicals for school use. A notice in

Dear Admissions Director:

Please send us the following materials available from your institution, for use in our guidance program. We need only those for which an amount is indicated.

amounts(s)   *title(s)*

_____ Latest Catalog

_____ Bulletin of . . . .

_____ New Student Brochure

___ _____ Admission Application

__ _____ Financial Aid Application

_____ Scholarship Application

_____ Housing Information: men's ( ), women's ( )

_____ Varsity Sports Schedule

_____ Summer School Brochure

_____ Other: . . . .

Thank you very much.   Very truly yours,

. . . .
Information Svc. Clerk II
Guidance Office
Anytown High School
123 Main St.
Anytown, Pa. 10632

(Card used to order educational materials.)

Figure 1-2(b)

the guidance newsletter, school bulletin, or local weekly newspaper usually brings in a flood of magazines and journals. Local merchants and professionals are a good source of trade publications, which have innumerable educational and occupational tie-ins. Some trade associations, in fact, will even put the guidance program on their mailing list if such a request is made by the counselor. A volunteer aide position, that of Information Service Periodical Librarian, may be created to expedite cataloging and use of collected periodicals. Since "censoring" of a few donated magazines occasionally is needed (due. to "girlie" pictures, etc.), special consideration must be given to the aide's maturity and judgment. Because library-type skills are involved in the aide's duties, it's usually best to recruit her from the school library club, or somehow to involve the school librarian in the selection process. An Information Service Periodical Librarian collects, catalogs, displays, and checks out publications, just like her "real life" counterpart.

Boys and girls take over running the service.

As the word spreads, and pupils recount benefits of serving as aides, student body interest snowballs. In smaller communities, where junior high and elementary schools are located in or near the same building as the senior high, requests to serve as aides often come from pupils at those levels, as well as from senior high-schoolers. The younger boys and girls may be used, provided that their principal and teacher(s) concur, and that they are not placed on equal footing with the older students. A good system is to create Information Service Aide-Trainee (bottom level) positions for elementary volunteers, and Aide I positions for those in junior high. Trainees and Aide I's work under direction of the Aide II's, who are juniors and seniors. Of course, some promotional flexibility is maintained, so younger volunteers may aspire to advancement with age and experience. This not only provides valuable orientation to the adult world of work, but also keeps the counselor furnished from year to year with a continuous supply of trained aides. Figure 1-3 delineates a hierarchy of information service aide positions, showing duties, eligibility requirements, and promotional paths.

Of course, pupils are still pupils, and lack the maturity to handle certain responsibilities. Therefore, a counselor must "keep an eye on things," and clearly reserve true professional duties for himself alone. The purpose of student aides is not to enable the counselor to loaf, but to release his valuable time for higher echelon activity. Once a

JOB TITLE (all prefaced by "In. Svc.")	MINIMUM ELIGIBILITY REQUIRED	HOW CHOSEN	DUTIES PERFORMED	RESPONSIBLE TO
Manager III (one pos.)	senior with 2 years' svc.	application; interviewed by counseling staff	supervise work of Aide II's	counselor
Librarian II (one pos.)	junior or senior; 1 year of service	application; recommendation of school librarian	supervise ordering, collection, dissemination, & publicization of occupational, educational, & socio-personal materials	Manager III
Clerk II (one pos.)	"	application; recommendation of office practice teacher	supervise ordering, collection, dissemination, & publicization of occupational, educational, & socio-personal materials	"
Receptionist II (one pos.)	"	application; recommendation of home economics or office practice teacher	make & receive telephone calls, assist visitors to counselor's office, do superficial clerical duties as time permits, handle non-confidential mail	"
Typist II (one pos.)	"	application; recommendation of typing-shorthand teacher	type forms, take dictation & type letters, operate photo-copy, mimeo, & ditto machines	"
Technician II (one pos.)	"	application; recommendation of A-V Coordinator or industrial arts teacher	maintain A-V & office equipment, assist students with equipment operation, build simple furniture & apparatus	"
Librarian I (several pos.)	gr. 7-12 status; (permission of principal)	volunteer through school librarian	perform library-type duties under Librarian II	Librarian II
Clerk I (sev. pos.)	" + typing ability	volunteer through a business education teacher	perform clerk-type duties under Clerk II	Clerk II
Receptionist I (sev. pos.)	" + typing ability	volunteer through a business education or home econ. teacher	perform receptionist-type duties under Receptionist II	Receptionist II
Typist I (sev. pos.)	" + typing ability	vol. through a bus. ed. teacher or directly to counselor if typing skills learned outside of school	perform typist-type duties under Typist II	Typist II
Technician I (sev. pos.)	"	volunteer through A-V Coordinator or indus. arts teacher	perform technician-type duties under Tech. II	Tech. II
Aide-Trainee	grade 2-10 & principal's permission	H.S.: volunteer directly to counselor; JHS & Elem: volunteer through principal	perform lower level general helping tasks as directed by Aide II or Manager III	Aide II designated by Mgr. III

Figure 1-3

hierarchical system of aides performing specific jobs and responsibilities is implemented, everyone will be amazed at what youngsters can do, if only given the chance.

SELLING THE SERVICE—RELEVANT BENEFITS FOR EVERYONE

Everybody wants to be where the action is.

Each public of the information service, pupils, teachers, administrators, and parents, derives definite benefits from using the materials found there. Each public also has a role to play in the on-going informational activities and programs of the service. The counselor, acting as facilitator and catalytic agent, sees that each public knows what the information service offers, and understands how using it will complement its specific role, i.e., student, teacher, administrator, or parent. Each has something to gain from the service, and by participating in its evolving, active processes, something to contribute, too.

When many people become actively involved in using the information service, the physical area in which it is centered, generally the outer office of the guidance suite, becomes a busy place indeed. This is good; utilization is contagious, and the service soon acquires the image of a place where things are happening. Building such an image is the key to running a successful informational program—persons are attracted to what is being frequented by others. If the information service is giving tangible aids to the publics it serves, this image soon results.

Students get the facts they need, and grow up in the process.

The largest and most important public of the information service is, of course, the students. The most obvious way in which they participate is checking out and reading, viewing, and or listening to various materials. Occupational materials are used as aides for career planning, educational materials to expedite choice of further schooling, and socio-personal materials for facilitating various emotional growth experiences. While this general statement describes an important pupil activity, individual use of monographs, books, catalogs, films, filmstrips, posters, etc., it doesn't begin to cover the spectrum of possible involvements. The following tables (Figures 1-4 and 1-5) list a series of specialized projects, both within guidance office confines and extramurally, in which boys and girls may engage. Of course, these activities overlap with other personnel services, and some with school programs completely outside the guidance area. Their inclusion here points up their importance as instruments for conveyance of developmental learnings and insights. Each table lists activities, materials needed, student benefits, and adult roles played.

In all pupil participations, whether check-out and use of printed or audiovisual materials, or engagement in an informational activity, a psychological climate conducive to maturation should prevail. This is achieved by encouraging students to seek out and use materials and join activities on their own initiative, with a minimum of adult direction. While such a laissez-faire policy can be overdone, and stressed to the point of seeming indifference, even that is a lesser evil than over-protective client manipulation. A counselor who spoon feeds informational materials and activities to a counselee does him no favor. This counselor unwittingly defeats the very purpose for which such endeavors exist; he impedes client maturity and responsibility development. To succeed in a chosen vocational or personal growth venture, a youngster needs the psychological capacity to decide for himself, as well as factual knowledges about his postulated course. This capacity evolves from experience in personal decision-making and acceptance of accountability. This doesn't mean, of course, that existence and availability of materials and activities should not be made known to students. The counselor, working through the school staff and his corps of volunteer aides, has an obligation to publicize the information service. Once this is done, however, it's up to individual boys and girls, tomorrow's adults, to carry through for themselves.

Teachers appreciate enrichment materials and experiences.

Classroom teachers use the information service to both complement their teaching and further their professional careers. Occupational materials may be used as reference sources for students preparing class reports, papers, and projects. Not only may pupils read monographs and books to find facts about various career fields, but they can also bring films and filmstrips into the classroom to audio-visually support oral presentations. Sometimes teachers, as well as students, seek summer and part-time employment to supplement personal income and strengthen insights related to their subject fields. There is no reason why they cannot use occupational materials to help them in personal planning, as do pupils. By participating in such activities as job field trips, staff members gain valuable know-

STUDENT INFORMATIONAL PROJECTS OPERABLE WITHIN THE GUIDANCE OFFICE

Activity	Materials Needed	Student Benefits	Adult Role(s)
ordering, previewing, deciding whether to purchase guidance films & film-strips	projection equipment, mail-ordered films & film-strips	vocational learnings, experience in budgetary decisions & in responsibility (for returning unpurchased material)	counselor supervises spending of school money by students
inviting, listening to, & interacting with career consultant, admissions counselor, or recruiter	conference room in guidance suite	vocational learnings, small group interactive skill proficiencies	representative of career field, educational institution, or military service
check-out & reading of road maps, travel brochures, etc.	road maps; road atlases; travel literature; air line magazines; Sunday newspaper travel section	easing transition into new school, college, or armed forces geographical environment	exit or entrance interview, or career counseling by counselor, as appropriate
preparing reports, themes, & papers on vocational or psychological topics for classes	occupational or socio-personal materials on the specific chosen or assigned topic	enrichment of curricular experience, obtaining supplemental references to those found in library	subject teacher grades the student's effort
ordering, publicizing, showing, & returning noon-hour or activity-period films on jobs and colleges	Projection equipment, room that can be darkened, films	vocational insights for audience; experience in putting on a commercial entertainment for the student committee	counselor or A-V coordinator in charge, but does very little supervision
decorating guidance suite	paint, varnish, wood, tools, furniture catalog or inventory of district supplies	skills in interior decorating, painting, art-display, etc.	counselor or principal keeps eye on things
operating want-ad clipping bureau & placement service for part-time job-seekers	subscription to daily newspaper, scissors, etc.; telephone	clerical & human relations skills for student placement officer; help in job-seeking for clients	counselor helps get it started, then supervises minimally

Figure 1-4

**STUDENT INFORMATIONAL PROJECTS HEADQUARTERED IN GUIDANCE OFFICE,
BUT TAKING PLACE ELSEWHERE**

Activity	Materials Needed	Student Benefits	Adult Role(s)
*community occupation survey, including planning, executing, & utilizing of the survey	survey sheets, community map, card file of jobs, special reports	discovery of part & full-time job opportunities; human relations & clerical skills; social studies learnings	counselor supervises guidance aspects; social studies teacher supervises academic aspects
job & college field trips	transportation facilities	vocational learnings & insights, social skills	counselor, related field teacher, parents act as chaperones
"helper" programs	assigned monographs on job in question; physical work setting of assisted staff	vocational learnings & insights; feelings of worth & belonging	counselor orients; involved staff member supervises
work-study programs	preliminary reading-assigned monograph on job in question; physical work setting of co-operating community employer	vocational learnings & insights financial remuneration; feelings of worth & relevancy	counselor &/or distributive education teacher, as appropriate, directs program; employer supervises student
tutorial programs	assigned socio-personal monograph on helping relationship-preliminary reading; small area adjacent to elementary classroom setting	experiencing a one-to-one helping relationship; vocational learnings & insights	counselor orients; cooperating elementary teacher supervises

*For specifics of conducting a community occupation survey, consult one of several popular counselor education texts.

Figure 1-5

ledges of the world of work and of their students' needs. A counselor who includes his colleagues in such endeavors not only strengthens them professionally, but also earns added rapport for himself and his program.

Educational materials are as helpful to teachers as to pupils. In this day of increasing necessity for educators to continue their in-service and graduate education, a collection of college catalogs, bulletins, and application blanks is needed as much by faculty as by students. The number and nature of state, school district, and accrediting agency regulations, as well as college graduate programs and workshops, is too vast for anyone to retain in his head. The information service is a haven for teachers faced with a multiplicity of programs and options. By inviting colleagues to join educational activities, such as college field trips, the counselor builds good will bridges and gains some chaperoning help. He also gives teachers the chance to acquire insights for their own future professional escalation.

Socio-personal materials frequently fill a void in training and skills for staff members who wish to assist their students in emotional growth. Teachers conducting home room group guidance and related activities may use the workbooks, open-ended stories, and filmstrips from the information service. Sometimes, too, a teacher wishes to privately assist a youngster needing help with a minor problem, such as making friends or building study skills. This concerned educator may quietly obtain the needed reference for his friend from the information service, with no questions asked. Adult-level references from the service orient teachers to the minimal levels of quasi-counseling competence needed to conduct low-key group discussions of common pupil problems. Such references are also valuable in helping teachers acquire classroom practices conducive to improved mental health. A counselor must see that faculty members know of the availability of socio-personal materials. Their use by teachers is not usurpation of the counselor's prerogatives, but is instead highly complementary to the individual and group counseling on a deeper emotional level that takes place exclusively within a guidance program.

Administrators need to know things, too.

Many times, pupils, parents, and other educators expect school principals to be authorities on every school problem that arises. This is unrealistic, and while the "head man" has ultimate responsibility for what goes on in a school, he cannot always be fully knowledgable on all aspects of education. A counselor can provide vital informational help in many instances, help that means the difference between a good administrative decision and a poor one. It's especially crucial that a counselor and his principal have a good working relationship, understanding each other's problems and concerns. Then, when factual help is needed, it becomes a little easier for the administrator to make his need known.

One specific informational need of principals in the occupational area is determining what types of repairs and services may be rendered to the school building by different service workers, and at what costs. The counselor, as vocational specialist, may advise his administrator of various options open to him in different remodeling and repair situations. The D.O.T. and occupational monograph collection can be a valuable source for planning efficient and economical physical plant maintenance or modification. Educational materials often prove invaluable in hiring new teachers. College catalogs indicate what majors and specialities are offered by education schools; accreditation information and college placement office addresses may also be learned from them. The socio-personal collection is a resource for assisting a principal in understanding various personality and learning disabilities that sometimes befall pupils. The counselor should have adult-level references available on various youth problems. A principal who understands the nature of a behavioral disability is much more apt to make a good decision regarding a child who has one.

Some administrators may wish to become involved in various informational activities, but are reluctant to ask, as this could appear to be unduly directing the counselor. Because a principal stands to gain valuable insights from occasionally accompanying a job or college field trip, for example, the counselor might well invite him to come along. Such participation strengthens an administrator's comprehension of the guidance program and builds his student body rapport.

Parents get positive benefits from their school.

No one, this writer included, would suggest that a school information service is obliged to keep pupils' parents supplied with occupational, educational, or socio-personal materials, nor could the school involve large numbers of parents in its informational activities on a regular basis. A sensible policy for parental participation is one which encourages them to avail themselves of the service when they feel it beneficial to their own or their children's lives. Parents who know that *their* school (after all, they do pay school taxes and elect board of education members) offers them meaningful, relevant informational help when needed, become positive, constructive guidance program boosters. Moreover, many parents have skills and interests to contribute to the program's functioning and will serve as career consultants, field trip chaperones, and donors of informational materials. Thus, parental involvement becomes anything but an all-take, no-give relationship. By showing willingness to help out a parent here and there with informational needs, the counselor not only builds good will, but also sets the stage for innumerable reciprocations on behalf of his program. Also, neglect of parents can lead to a negative effect upon the school in general, and guidance in particular. Persons tend to become suspicious of what they regard ambiguously. If the counselor's program remains a mystery to parents, chances are they will develop suspicions, and display hostility toward it.

What, then, are some specifics of parental participation? The first step is to insure that they are aware of the information service's existence (don't assume any prior knowledge whatsoever), and have rudimentary knowledge of what it contains, and why. This is accomplished through publicity techniques. For example, an issue of the periodic guidance newsletter, sent home with all students, may contain a feature story on the information service. A talk before a P.T.A. meeting, in which the counselor uses various informational materials as props, might prove effective. A series of explanatory articles and pictures in the local weekly newspaper often works well. Informal publicity measures are very important, too. Word-of-mouth contacts, both directly with parents during community interaction and chance meetings, and indirectly, through counselees, teachers, and administrators, are often the most valuable message-conveyors of all. The next step is to constantly foster development of the image of a helping relationship as the governing principle of all guidance programs. "The counselor is there to help people help themselves," and everyone must know this. Such a message cannot be adequately conveyed by a formal publicity program. Rather, this attitudinal communication is passed along by example. In all his dealings with all his publics, a counselor must constantly display qualities of a true helping relationship—reflection, positive regard, and empathy. As this message sinks in, parents will seek to use the information service, and will offer their assistance to help implement its activities.

What are the mechanics of parental involvement? Use of informational materials falls into two categories, not always differentiable (nor need they be) by the counselor. Parents might request materials (1) for their own needs, or (2) to better understand and assist their children with theirs. Frequently, a counselor has no idea which purpose a parent has in mind, and it's usually best not to inquire. The main thing is to see that an appropriate occupational, educational, or socio-personal source is made available. Since it's unwise to have numerous adults using the information service during school hours (although an occasional visitor should certainly create no problem), the counselor encourages parents to make telephone or written inquiries. If appropriate materials are available, these may be sent home with the child, picked up, or mailed, as good judgment dictates. If a parent does not wish to discuss why a particular item is needed, the counselor shouldn't ask. For example, job changes are sometimes embarrassing to an adult, and the counselor's eagerness to help may not be appreciated. If a parent makes it known that he wishes to use borrowed materials to assist his child, this leads naturally to consultation with the counselor. A policy of *professional informality* is a good rule of thumb for loaning or giving materials to parents. This policy can be expressed as, "Avoid too stringent an observance of library-like check-out regulations, etc., but also stress the information service's role as official school repository of occupational, educational, and socio-personal factual assistance."

Parental participation in information service activities grows naturally as what's going on, and why, is learned. Parents serve as career consultants, job and college field trip chaperones, and donors and collectors of free materials. Occasionally, an enterprising father may even contribute his painting, carpentry, or welding know-how to build or repair a piece of furniture or equipment in the guidance office. A mother conceivably could lend a little stenographic or filing expertise to supplement the efforts of a relatively inexperienced student aide. Of course, before non-staff adults are ever allowed to perform duties within the guidance office, administrative approval must be forthcoming. A counselor should sound out his principal regarding this before broaching the matter with a parent. A few adults, sad to say, have ulterior motives for entering a school building. The counselor, by developing numerous informal contacts with parents, forms opinions relative to the feasibility of involving them in guidance activities. These opinions will certainly be sought by a principal before granting anyone permission to become identified with a school program. This is as it should be, and a counselor who has good community rapport can advise his principal intelligently.

PROFESSIONAL STEP-CHILD NO MORE

When an information service acquires a school and community reputation as the place where people do things to learn about jobs, colleges, and emotional growth, a highly professional personnel service must be operating. An information service which houses a large collection of materials and sponsors numerous activities, all the while approaching its mission with a policy of building helping relationships, will acquire that kind of image. Such a process impresses all who encounter it as something of vital, relevant importance for success in today's complex world, so they use it, and sing its praises. Students, educators, and parents wish to use it, and become identified with its programs, because they perceive it as worthwhile, helpful process for themselves and others. When a part of the guidance program attains that plateau, all concerned know that its mission is a professional one indeed. There's nothing dry or sub-professional about this type of information service, and it proudly assumes a role of equality in stature with appraisal, referral, articulation, and other personnel services.

TWO

Facilitating Maturity Through
Teen-Age Job Placements

Part-time jobs can mean far more to teen-agers than spending money sources. A counselor may adapt his work placement service into a plethora of invaluable counselee growth experiences, in addition to monetary gains. How does the counselor go about reaping psychological benefits from student quests for employment?

WHY KIDS WANT TO WORK

Everyone knows why high school boys and girls seek after-school, weekend, and summer jobs. They want to earn money, of course! They want to save for future needs, such as college or marriage, or to satisfy immediate needs, like the purchase of a party dress or motorcycle. After all, no one knows the value of money better than a teen-ager!

Indeed, high school students do work for the money it brings them, as does everybody else. However, in addition to this factual, cognitive reason for taking gainful employment, there are two emotional, conative, often sub-concious factors in adolescent employment. These subtle reasons are usually overshadowed by the obvious dollars-and-cents one, and overlooked. The complex intertwining of emotional and factual aspects in almost every personal counseling case is well known to counselors. The teen-age job placement personnel service also contains this conative-cognitive interaction. The two emotionally tinged aspects most frequently encountered are (1) the client's desire to demonstrate maturity to self, peers, and family, and (2) his exploratory, often unsure feelings about the need to eventually make a definite vocational choice. A counselor who operates a part-time job placement service must, to be optimally successful in this venture, take cognizance of both factual and emotional dimensions of such activity.

SETTING UP THE SERVICE

Let the students know what you're there for.

Many high schoolers have no idea that a counselor will help them obtain a part-time job. In fact, a goodly number expect him to oppose the idea, on the somewhat unrealistic grounds that a job reduces available study time. Use of public relations procedures by the counselor, slanting the message to his student public, sets the record straight. Some message-spreading activities are listing part-time job vacancies on a bulletin board and in the periodic guidance newsletter, announcing appointment of a volunteer student aide as placement assistant, inviting students to accompany the counselor on visits to potential employment situations, making his interest known during talks before pupil and adult groups. Such measures serve to inform the student body of the counselor's job placement interest, and are prerequisite to actual placement efforts. They are especially crucial for a counselor new in a given school, as his predecessor, if there was one, may not have been active in this area.

There's a way to kill several birds with one stone; namely, inform all pupils of the part-time placement service, prepare them for eventual gainful employment, and procure each a student number, valuable for a variety of school administrative purposes. This is done by requesting each to apply for a Social Security Number upon admission to high school. This is accomplished by distributing U.S. Treasury Department Form SS-5 (12-64), available at any post office, through homeroom teachers. A counselor's volunteer aide collects, posts, and mails the completed forms. If handled properly— that is, accompanied by a message explaining why this step is taken—applying for one's own SSN becomes for many a maturing experience, and a builder of rapport for the school as a whole, as well as being an efficient administrative measure.

Answer any objections right at the onset.

Whenever a counselor moves into the area of part-time work

placements, some well-meaning soul, usually a teacher or parent, raises the question of jobs encroaching upon student study time. This point almost always is presented in a sincere, helpful context, and the counselor should treat the complainer as a helpful friend, not a detractor. Basically, major arguments in favor of teen-agers working, with the counselor's blessing, are: (1) Certainly, too much time spent on a job is detrimental to any student, and would cut into needed study time. This is the very reason a counselor involves himself—so pupils, who would work whether the counselor was a factor or not, won't commit themselves for too many hours or to tasks of an overly taxing nature. (2) It's unrealistic to assume that adolescents would invest more hours in study if they were not working. More likely, they'd only while the time away. (3) Boys and girls need the maturity and vocational insight that job experience gives, as well as the factual knowledge study gives, if they are to become optimally successful adults. (4) Some youngsters, not academically gifted, need recognition from a job well done, just as honor students need recognition for school work well done.

Know your state's child labor laws.

Before engaging in any vocational activities or counseling with students, obtain a copy of child labor laws from your state industrial commission, and read it. Failure to do so can cause obvious problems later on. The following rules of thumb are only generalizations, and should not be substituted by the reader for perusal of his state's regulations:

(1) Almost all states exempt children working in parental businesses from child labor laws, and take a relaxed, tolerant view of baby sitting and residential lawn-mowing, regardless of age.
(2) Many states allow children over 12 to work on certain agricultural type jobs, provided that permits are obtained and rigid hours restrictions observed.
(3) Some states allow children to perform certain other jobs, with restrictions, when age 14 is reached.
(4) Most states allow teen-agers with permits to perform a wide variety of adult-type jobs—with certain restrictions, such as forbidding night work—once they turn 16.
(5) Most states forbid minors to work in occupations considered hazardous or unwholesome for the young, until age 18 or 21 is reached. In addition to state laws, many employer insurance policies bar full-time employment for persons under 18.

Some schools in some states have become issuing authorities for youth work permits. Whatever your state's rules and procedures, your area industrial commission representative is a good man to know.

Avoid stepping on toes of colleagues running similar programs.

Many large high schools, and not a few smaller ones, operate work-study programs for terminal students of limited scholastic ability. Many of these are organized under federal-state funded LVEC (local vocational- educational coordinator) or DEC (distributive education coordinator) auspices. Some other schools have elected to organize work-study programs on their own, foregoing outside funding. In some cases a regular counselor is designated LVEC and/or DEC; in others, a special education, industrial arts, or marketing teacher fills this slot. Another staffing pattern has been to hire a counselor-specialist whose sole duty is operating these programs. A few school districts have made released time arrangements similar to work-study for highly gifted pupils. In these, students spend time at a local technical industry or college, performing tasks commensurate with their intellectual level and interests. If your school has any such programs, directed by persons other than yourself, Mr. Counselor, coordinate your own part-time placement activities carefully with the appropriate colleague(s). Failure to do so leads to student and faculty rivalries. A good way to minimize problem occurrence is to restrict your efforts to after school, rather than released time placements, and to avoid soliciting employers already committed to a released time program.

Let student volunteers run the placement service.

The best part-time job placement service is one of, by, and for the pupils themselves. The counselor, a professional in the vocational development field, utilizes his time more profitably in training student aides in placement techniques, and in vocational counseling, rather than actual telephone and leg-work aspects of the service. There are two exceptions to this rule of thumb: (1) When beginning a placement service, the counselor may wish to make some initial employer contacts. (2) Whenever a job field trip or visitation requiring student transportation is undertaken, a certified professional educator must be present. Volunteer aides are usually eager to perform job-placement efforts on behalf of their peers, as such endeavors, related closely to the adult working world, smack of maturity and responsibility. In addition, a counselor may point out to a potential volunteer placement aide, the receptionist, filing and stenographic skills performed are great preparation for an office career. They may also be used in a college placement office, helping finance further education.

OPERATING THE SERVICE

Develop a standard operating procedure,
but keep it flexible to meet individual differences.

When a boy or girl comes to the counselor's office and informs a volunteer aide receptionist of interest in a part-time job, the aide initiates certain clerical procedures. The client is asked to fill out one side of a 5 x 7 card (see Figure 2-1), and to prepare a rough draft resume, a simplified version of that shown in Chapter Three. Later, a client work history record is chronologically kept on the back of the card. However, such an impersonal approach should never stand in the way of the client seeing the counselor, if such a desire is expressed. It's normally preferable for a prospective part-time job applicant to receive factual briefing from a fellow student, in this case the aide. The reason for this is that such a spread of job information is analagous to the passing on of labor know-how in the adult world. Nevertheless, this standard operating procedure must never prevent a client who wishes to see the counselor from doing so as soon as possible. A few counselees each year approach the counselor ostensibly to discuss a minor vocational or scholastic

---

NAME . . . . S.S.N. . . . .
ADDRESS . . . . YR. IN H.S. . . . .
TELEPHONE #. . . . . D.O.B. . . . .DATE . . . ., 19 . .
What kind of work do you want to do? 1st choice . . . .
2nd choice . . . . 3rd choice . . . .
When do you want to work? (Check as many as you want.)
after school ( ), weekends ( ), summer ( ), during . . . .
vacation ( )
Do you have a state work permit? no ( ), yes ( )
If "yes," what is its number? . . . .

Figure 2-1

matter, but in reality they are troubled by a more serious psychological problem. To allow an impersonal clerical process to delay or prevent these cases from seeing a counselor is a tragedy that must not occur. The opposite side of this coin is that many students really mean it when they say they desire part-time employment. For the counselor to see them all only dilutes the time available for interviews with more seriously troubled counselees, and denies the student aide a valuable growth experience.

No attempt should be made by the counselor or aide to check a pupil's past employment references, as these are not a school-connected matter. The responsibility for checking a potential employee's background lies with the employer. Nor is it the counselor's job to determine whether a young job aspirant has his parents' approval for his quest. One of the earmarks of maturity is willingness to face the consequences of one's actions. The adolescent who takes a job, only to be forced to quit by his parents, demonstrated immaturity by taking an action for which he knew there would be adverse consequences. For a counselor to snoop into such an outcome in advance only reinforces the very client immaturity that counselors seek to diminish. A different situation along these lines develops when a client asks the counselor to intercede with parents who will not allow part-time work for their offspring. In this case, a counselor frequently may wish to go to bat for the student, provided that the child has first discussed the matter with his parents himself. In such cases, the counselor must approach parents politely, justifying his intervention on grounds that the boy or girl has asked him to become professionally involved. The counselor must respect the parents' concern for, and right over, their child, and not assume a superior attitude. It is not reinforcing immaturity to intercede for a pupil in this type of case because the teen-ager has faced reality by not taking an action for which a counter-reaction (parental opposition to job taking) would occur. The child has also first attempted to solve the dilemma himself by discussing the matter at home, so the counselor cannot be said to be fighting a youngster's battles for him.

When the young job-hopeful has filled in his card, and developed, with the aide's help, an acceptable resume, the aide's first chore is to duplicate the resume, a copy of which will be taken to job interviews by the client and presented to each potential employer. The aide then informs the client of possible employers whom he may contact. In so doing, the aide stresses the fact that while she and, if necessary, the counselor, will provide factual tips and emotional support, it's up to the student to sell himself to an employer, and win a job. (This includes the implication that a similar philosophy applies to holding a job once one is obtained.) If school policy allows sending the applicant to an interview during school hours, it's wise to have such permission, and any restrictions on it, come directly from the principal's office.

How does the aide learn of job possibilities? Initially, she has recourse to the telephone and the Yellow Pages, calling potential employers in expressed student interest categories. After the job-placement service has become established, employers begin to call in their needs to the counselor's office, simplifying the aide's quest. Frequently, employer needs don't match pupil preferences, and boys and girls are faced with taking a less desirable job, or none. Such a situation is not as bad as it might seem, and it is ripe with maturational implications for adult life ahead. Some adolescents, not familiar with job duties and eager to earn money, tell the aide that "any job is o.k." When confronted with such a situation, recourse is made to employment categories traditionally known to need ample young help. Examples are drive-in restaurants, conventional restaurants, nursing homes, horticultural nurseries, and supermarkets.

When calling, the aide keeps paper and pencil handy, and proceeds along the lines of the following hypothetical telephone conversation:

> Hello, may I speak to the manager, please? . . . What was his name, again? . . . Yes, I'll hold. . . . Hello, Mr. Smith? This is Judy Simpson at Central High School. Mr. Jefferson, our counselor, asked me to call you. We have three boys here at Central who are interested in supermarket work after school, and on Saturdays. . . . Yes, two are already 16, and the third will be 16 next month. Could the boys come over and have an interview with you? . . . When would be convenient? . . . Sure, next Monday, right after school, is fine; I'll ask the boys to get there as soon as they can. . . . Oh, Mr. Jefferson said to tell you to call him if you have any questions. Our number is 625-3900. . . . Any time during school hours is fine. Thank you a lot, Mr. Smith, we really appreciate your giving our boys a chance. . . . Goodbye.

Once an employer has indicated willingness to hire a pupil, the aide completes a 5 x 7 file card on that specific job situation. One side of the card is used to record basic work information, the other to briefly list past hirings and separations of students who worked there. As the card file grows, student aides and counselor use it as a placement reference. Such a file eventually proves helpful not only for part-time placements, but also for terminal, career ones, as well as for helping teachers and former clients now in college find summer jobs. It may even assist a counselor in helping the jobless parent of a student find urgently needed work.

Figure 2-2 shows both sides of a typical file card reference.

EMPLOYER .City Hospital............... INITIAL DATE: .9-14..,19....
ADDRESS: .....613. 4th Ave., Anytown... PHONE: .238 - 5020. Ext 313
CONTACT PERSON(S): .Mrs. Sheila Jones.... TITLE(S): Personnel Manager

TYPE(S) TEEN JOBS	APPROX. #
Candy - Stripers (unpaid) (girl or boy)..	...5. at once.........
stock room boy... (boys only).........	......1 or 2.........
lunch room waitress (girls only).....	.....3 to 5.........
lunch room food helper (summer only)...	..........1.........

RESTRICTION(S): must have health exam with family doctor before employment, paid workers must be 16

REMARKS: .like to give former candy-stripers first chance at jobs when they turn 16.

STUDENT WORK HISTORY NOTES	DATES
1. B. Brown, J. Cohen & P. Fiore were candy-stripers	9-68
2. J. Robinson - stock boy - until graduated	1-69
3. B. Brown & J. Cohen worked in lunch room	summer '69
4. J. Simpson & P. Moore - candy-stripers	9-69
5. B. Robinson - stock boy - quit after one month	9-69
6. J. Simpson - waitress	summer - '70
7. M. Miller & J. O'Grady - candy-stripers	9-70
8. J. Banks - stock room boy	10-70
9. J. Banks - offered full time at graduation, took it	6-71
10. J. O'Grady - stock room	9-71
11. M. Miller - waitress	summer '71
12. J. O'Grady - transferred to lunch room for ...	summer '71
13. Hired J. Robinson home from college as orderly	" "
14. S. Klein, M. Smith, M. Pignorem - candy-stripers	9-71
15. J. O'Grady, transferred back to stock room for ...	71-72
16.	
17.	
18.	
19.	
20.	
21.	
22.	

Figure 2-2

Cooperate with employers without revealing client confidences.

Occasionally, when a hiring official inquires of the counselor about various students, a conflict of interest threatens in which counselor is torn between pupil and employer. Most frequently, this occurs when a hiring official seeks personal information about prospective young job applicants, especially in the area of honesty and moral character. A less frequent but equally serious conflict threatens when students consult the counselor about an employer—for instance, an employer about whom the counselor possesses potentially derogatory confidential information, such as impending bankruptcy. While no two interest-conflict cases are alike, and each must be handled as a unique instance, there are certain rules of thumb that this author wishes to propose:

1. *The counselor is a professional educator, therefore, his primary obligation is to the clients he serves, and the school district which employs him.* He also has a series of secondary obligations to his various more removed publics, one of which is the employers of the community in which the school is located.

2. *Pupil confidences may not be revealed to anyone, unless death or injury is preventable by so doing.* This tenet, borrowed from the field of clinical psychology, is absolutely essential if counselors are to enjoy appropriate respect and trust of counselees. It obviously precludes telling a child's personal problems to an employer.

3. *It's sometimes wise to urge a student to reveal private problems to an employer himself.* Frequently, a counselor realizes that a student problem will surface at some future time, causing possible job dismissal or embarrassment. Consequently, he suggests that the boy or girl involved avoid trouble by informing the hiring official in advance. An example is an adolescent who has claustrophobia, and who wishes to work in a hotel equipped with elevators. More than likely, the employer would hire the student anyway, respect his confidence, and assign him work as a bus boy, where elevators are not a factor.

4. *A counselor may reveal and discuss commonly known school information relative to client differential abilities and aptitudes with employers.* At his discretion, a counselor may talk over with hiring officials the relative suitability for various jobs of different boys and girls, provided that his opinion has been solicited. Variables like approximate intellectual endowment and educational achievement level, as measured by the school's standardized testing program,

school grades, and apparent interest areas, etc., may be discussed when such information is relevant. In so doing, a counselor must be objective as possible, and request that the employer treat this information professionally. When discussing test scores, it's preferable to use verbal rather than numerical terms—for example, "On this test, John showed he has well above average intelligence," not, "John has an I.Q. of 120."

5. *Employer inquiries regarding pupil honesty and disciplinary record should be referred to the principal.* Should a potential hiring official wish to discuss a child's moral character, the counselor is bound by the ethic of confidentiality not to reveal private matters. The high school principal is the person in charge of school discipline, just as the counselor is the person in charge of discussing problems with students. Therefore, those wanting discipline-related pupil information should be informed that school policy establishes the principal as the appropriate person to see.

6. *Undesirable working conditions that are part of public record should be discussed with students in a professional way.* If an employer has been convicted of a criminal offense, filed for bankruptcy, been successfully sued in a business-related civil action, or found guilty of an unfair labor practice during an N.L.R.B. investigation, these things are public record. If a counselor deems it unwise for his clients to work for such an employer, he may point this out to them during counseling, and sometimes, if necessary, to his principal and to parents.

7. *Undesirable working conditions known to the counselor but not part of public record may not be told to pupils, but the counselor is within his rights in discouraging their taking jobs at the establishment in question.* Occasionally, a counselor learns of certain job-connected events that he deems unwholesome to minors. This information, however, is private, and not part of public record, or even of public knowledge. While it's wrong for the counselor to defame an employer, it's also wrong to allow unsuspecting adolescents to work in such an environment. Perhaps the best way to do justice to both parties is to avoid listing job vacancies at such an establishment in the first place.

8. *A counselor must not favor one child over another in providing job information, nor one employer over another in obtaining access to potential student workers, except as stated in thumb rules 6 and 7.* The counselor is a facilitator and a catalytic agent, not a business executive. He doesn't "get" anyone a job, nor "find" anyone an employee. Rather, he makes it possible for youngsters to obtain and

hold their own jobs, and thus for employers to hire young help more efficiently. Such a helping relationship cannot exist in any other than an atmosphere of fairness. All students in the school and all ethical, law-abiding employers in the community must be accepted by the counselor as worthy, equally important persons. This tenet is mere application of good counseling philosophy to the practice of pupil personnel services.

9. *A counselor has an obligation to provide work-adjustment counseling to clients and employee-adjustment consultation to employers whenever a perceived need for this service arises among persons with whom he has been working.* The counselor just doesn't help a pupil get a job and then forget him; neither does he take a favor from an employer (a student job placement) and wash his hands of any obligation. If difficulties subsequently arise in relation to a part-time work situation, the counselor must use his professional-level counseling and consultation skills to help ameliorate the problem. Periodic informal follow-up of various job placements is a wise move; a counselor's interest in client vocational development experiences doesn't end with a student's first day on a job.

Part-time work can become a vehicle for educational and social escalation of disadvantaged and minority group pupils.

Holding down a job has several potential benefits—educational, social, psychological, and financial—for minority group youngsters.

1. *Educational benefits* don't just come from school classes. To understand the educational value of a part-time job to a black, Hispano, or Indian student, a counselor must first attempt to "step into the youngster's skin," and view work from his frame of reference. A job is a vehicle for upward social mobility, and the white, Anglo majority has often used discriminatory practices to keep the better jobs for itself. School, the place where subjects are learned so pupils may someday hold jobs, is thus somewhat irrelevant. The so-called better jobs it prepares one for have largely been closed to minority persons. This syndrome, coupled with the fact that many minority neighborhood schools have been inferior in quality to other schools, has created de facto educational inequality. A part-time job in some cases is a better tool for compensatory or catch-up education than is a formal academic program in a school building. The ghetto school is still the same old educationally deficient stereotype of enforced inferiority to many black students and parents, notwithstanding recent money influxes from on high. For example, it may be more realistic to expect a weak-reading,

minority youngster to seek to improve his reading skill because his part-time job requires some reading, rather than through an educational program he considers irrelevant, held in a school building for which he has low regard. A counselor, using a little imagination, and working closely with employers as well as with other educators, can build a whole series of educational reinforcements into the lives of disadvantaged clients via part-time work. Such learnings are more likely to be retained by the student, because they enter his perceptual field from a favorably regarded source—the world of work, with its new-found promise of upward social mobility.

2. *Social benefits* of part-time work are tied closely to racial integration problems of modern American society. Polarization of racial issues has spawned apprehensions and mistrust among the populace that have trickled down into high schools. Research has repeatedly shown that ignorance of an ethnic group leads to suspicion, and ultimately to prejudice toward this group. Of course, it's unrealistic to assume that having adolescents rub shoulders with persons of other races during part-time job participation is going to cure the racial ills of society. Were it so easily done, counselors could solve all social ills with ease! Realistically, however, it is suggested that teen-agers of all ethnic backgrounds stand to gain improved racial attitudes through interaction during job experiences. Having to cooperate with persons of other backgrounds, in order to produce mutually profitable outcomes, is a growth experience which all adolescents should have.

3. *Psychological benefits* accruing to minority children from vocational experiences center around improvement of the self concept. Academicians have pointed out that many minority persons experience sub-concious feelings of self-hate. These, it is said, are engendered by the realization that one's blackness, Puerto Ricanness, etc., appear to automatically condemn him to unequal life in white, Anglo society. Many disadvantaged youngsters are dubious of the fact that they or any counselor can find a job situation, other than an extremely menial one, for which they'll be accepted. Considerable ego-reinforcement may be necessary before a student will consider attempting to obtain a job. After all, "Who wants me, man? I'm black!" A counselor faced with this situation may wish to begin such a client with internally procured volunteer jobs, using the counselor's aide system for this purpose. Later, as the student's confidence improves, and he observes that a measure of social acceptance is occurring, he may be urged to utilize the placement service, and seek an outside, paid position. One danger must be

pointed out here. A counselor must resist feelings of sympathy that can arise when helping a minority counselee. The counselor must never seek to give such a child an unfair, patronizing break because other elements in society have discriminated in the opposite direction, for to do so only reinforces inferiority feelings and revulsions over social position, and tends to erode the minority student's pride and self-esteem.

4. *Financial benefits,* the most obvious dividend of part-time work, accrue to all students, not just to those in minority groups. However, there are certain minority ramifications of monetary work rewards that counselors should consider. Most counselors, having been teachers, grew up in so-called "upper lower class" or "lower middle class" homes, from which research has shown most teachers come. While such families are seldom rich, they also are seldom poor; the father is usually employed regularly. A counselor from such a childhood background may not fully understand the emotional impact of gainful employment upon a disadvantaged youngster, who suddenly "comes into money" for the first time. In working with these cases, a counselor must again attempt to view the problem from the client's frame of reference, not always an easy task. He should also avoid overly directive, "big daddyish" exhortations that urge the disadvantaged student to "spend his money wisely," or "save for a rainy day." (For many minority pupils *all* days are rainy!) Counselors must realize that when any teen-ager wastes money or displays inability to manage financial affairs, the causes of such behavior are emotional, not factual. Thus, cognitive exhortations are of little value in curing this problem. Of course, a counselor works with a disadvantaged client, providing factual help regarding monetary affairs, as adequate learnings along these lines are probably missing from the youngster's experiential background. Such information-giving is only done, however, in a spirit of complete counselor-counselee acceptance and positive regard. The counselor must not appear as an authority figure, seeking to "put strings" on the money his client is now earning. Instead, he's a helping friend who acknowledges the student's freedom to do with his own funds as he sees fit.

EVALUATING THE SERVICE

Part-time job placement offers ideal opportunities for counselors to do research. While there's a large body of vocational development research in existence, little has been done upon informal part-time work during high school. Such research has two purposes, scholarly and pragmatic. The former revolves, in this case, around providing greater insight into the vocational development process in youth and into employer labor practices. The latter field offers an opportunity in investigate how service given to students and employers may be made more effective and more beneficial to them and to the school. When such research is reported in educational journals, it will fill a void in the professional literature, keep other school districts and university counselor-educators posted, and enhance the professional career of the counselor-researcher who did it.

Basically, two types of research are possible on the part-time work placement function, namely research into *process,* and research into *outcomes.* Process research means looking into the ways in which part-time job seeking, choice, and performance take place among students, and/or how part-time job creation, hiring, and supervision take place among employers. Outcomes research entails comparing adolescents and/or employers who participated in a job program to those who did not, to see if the experience induced any demonstrable effects in their later lives or upon the schools or business establishments involved. Process research, because it investigates an ongoing, present-oriented phenomenon, lends itself well to controlled observation, in which the counselor-researcher collects data on how clients and/or employers go about various activities connected with part-time jobs. Such data lend themselves well to correlational studies, in which various other pupil or employer statistics are compared to their part-time job-related data to discern significant relationships. Outcomes research, being more future-orientated, is ideally suited to an experimental approach, in which a control group of non-working students or non-hiring employers is compared to an experimental group that did work or hire on a part-time basis. The dependent variable, in this case the part-time job experience, is the one criterion that differentiates experimental from control group. It thus becomes possible to identify possible statistically significant differences between the two groups, and infer that these, if they occur, are related to the job experience.

WHAT LIES AHEAD?

Some persons hold the belief that as automation and technology reduce the number of available adult jobs, teen-age part-time work should be prohibited, in the interests of reducing unemployment levels in society. The author of this book is obviously not of that persuasion. While it's true that employment trends appear to favor rising technological unemployment, as machines take over what men formerly did, more preferable ways to compensate for this trend than barring high schoolers from working also appear. One possible alternative is continued gradual reduction of retirement ages. More and more, mature workers look to a "second career" of avocational pursuits following retirement somewhere in their sixties or even late fifties. Another possibility, also an established trend, is reduction of weekly hours worked by many types of adult workers. Still another solution is reserving certain types of jobs to teen-agers, college students, and other part-timers, thus preventing their direct competition for jobs with full-timers. This approach, too, already exists to an extent.

The reason that part-time work should remain open to adolescents is the emotional-maturational one. In addition to putting money in his pocket, a job during high school years puts therapeutic behavioral activities into a student's realm of experience. This fact is becoming more and more recognized by educators and psychologists, as many young people undergo identity crises and feelings of irrelevancy in their lives. It could well be that the value of part-time work to adolescent growth and development will become more formally recognized. It is conceivable that future guidance programs will make greater provision for these and similar activities. Such a movement, coupled with reasonable safeguards against competition with full-time adult labor, could become a highly significant trend in pupil personnel services.

THREE

Enabling Students to Choose
and Enter a Career

Vocational development is a complex process, as many researchers have proved over and over again. Thus, how is the counselor ever going to get anything done in this area which will benefit pupils? There is a basic, overall strategy he may follow which will facilitate the career choice of boys and girls, regardless of the complexity of the underlying personality dynamics. There are many activities, too, which the counselor may promote which will help in this area. What, specifically, is this approach to enabling career selection?

SOME PRELIMINARY CONSIDERATIONS

Career choice is an excellent example of the inseparability of counseling and personnel services. As the high school boy or girl works with the counselor, the discussion moves back and forth between factual and emotional ends of a continuum. One moment, emotionally tinged client feelings are discussed in a counseling context; the next moment the counselor is listing job entrance requirements in the role of information-giver. Some counselors approach career choice from a Rogerian, non-directive theoretical orientation; others favor the more directive, trait-factor approach, in which testing plays a prominent part. Regardless of the counselor's philosophy, career choice is a client responsibility. The counselor is at best a facilitator of vocational decisions.

There is a dangerous trend in modern American secondary education toward stereotyping youngsters into categories at the start of high school. One finds students routed into so-called "college-bound" or "terminal" tracks, based upon such variables as IQ, past achievement, and their own or parental preferences. This tendency is generally blamed upon the "increasing complexity of modern society." It is claimed by many educators to be at worst a necessary evil. Counselors must constantly remember that stereotyping of students runs contrary to suggestions made by research findings. For example, research has shown that IQ and achievement scores are frequently unreliable, and that ninth graders usually cannot make realistic vocational choices. Another argument against rigid tracking is that social class values and motivation often make a college-bound student out of an apparently terminal one, and vice versa. Yet many schools continue to stress inflexible tracking, despite strong evidence that for many teen-agers, their "career express" has been switched onto the wrong track.

Another dangerous form of stereotyping involves client personality variables, and pertains only to girls. This is the housewife vs. career girl dichotomy. Today's complex society, in which many mothers work and some non-working wives prefer not to be mothers, has rendered the old dichotomy obsolete. In dealing with career choices of girls, counselors must remember this and avoid dichotomizing their clients.

THE PROCESS OF CAREER CHOICE

Discussion leads to action.

The counseling associated with career choice is merely a continuation of an exploration process that began in the cradle. The high school student and his counselor talk over the many facets of various careers in an atmosphere of relaxation and enjoyment. Removing tension from the counseling process does not mean, however, that the client is relieved of eventual career choice responsibility. The whole goal of counseling and personnel services in this area should be the building of emotional and experiential maturity, so a realistic client choice can result. Some counselors fall into the trap of trying to force a premature client decision—the opposite fault of deciding for him. These counselors overlook the Super and Overstreet finding which indicated that most ninth graders lack the maturity to make realistic vocational choices. Many perfectly normal and mature adolescents do not choose a career until shortly before, or even after, their graduation—and some, in fact, not until well into their college years or beyond.

Career choice is an area that offers numerous opportunities for group counseling activities in which adolescents share their feelings about vocations with each other and with their counselor. The small-group counseling approach is an area relatively untapped by counselors for vocational purposes. A counseling group is a natural starting place for seniors to initiate personnel services for themselves in the area of vocational development. For example, a group of seniors engaged in discussing career choice becomes a natural nucleus for factory visitation, sound filmstrip ordering and viewing, or sharing and discussing a particular occupational monograph.

Following one-to-one and/or small-group counseling in their junior or senior year, adolescents begin to classify themselves to an extent as college-bound or terminal. But even then, designations are at best tentative, and are not mutually exclusive. The need for continual post-high school training of many non-college educated workers makes it evident that compartmentalization of individuals is hopelessly obsolete, if indeed it ever was a valid concept.

Pupils plan and carry out exploratory activities.

It doesn't take much urging from the counselor to get high schoolers involved in career choice activities. Teen-agers yearn for the day when they will be considered adults; consequently, vocational investigation has high psychological appeal to them. All a counselor has to do is drop a hint here, a piece of advice there, reinforcing enthusiasm all over, and let the students take over. Allowing students considerable free rein in planning and execution of career choice activities is a wise psychological move. Teen-agers are always looking for opportunities to prove they are grown-up, and will jump at this chance. Also, students are much more likely to take seriously the vocational investigations they arranged themselves.

Small student exploratory groups may be set up in several ways. They may come into being as outgrowths of group counseling or guidance sessions. They might be composed of individual counselees who have authorized the counselor to reveal tentative career plans to other students, so a group of similarly interested clients can get together. They could just be informal groups of friends.

Career exploration may begin through the use of materials from the occupational-educational information service discussed in Chapter One. Though not as good as the real thing, vicarious occupational experiences play an important role in teen-agers' lives. Another starting point for vocational investigation is the sharing among boys and girls of things learned during previous part-time jobs. As important as on-the-job learnings are those connected with application for and termination of employment. Many of the activities discussed in Chapter Two become relevant once more—this time as part-time working adolescents prepare to become career working adults.

When tentative career choices are made, and possible work fields are narrowed down to specific jobs or job families, the counselor suggests that each small, homogeneous interest group invite a "career consultant" to meet with them. Career consultants may be drawn from the ranks of the school faculty and staff, parents, or the community at large. When small groups of high school students sit down to chat semi-formally with volunteer representatives of various occupations or professions, an atmosphere conducive to two-way interaction is created. Specifics of working with career consultants are discussed in Chapters Ten, Eleven, and Twelve.

This approach is far superior to the more spectacular "career days," in which youngsters are herded as captive audiences to hear various occupational representatives. Mass confusion alone tends to negate the value of many career days. Another frequent problem of career days occurs as students, regardless of aptitudes, crowd into sections led by representatives of the more prestigious occupations. This selective crowding probably results from unwillingness to admit preference and aptitude for a career considered low on the peer group prestige scale. For example, if student preference for career day speakers was an accurate indication of the true proportion of various occupations in society, there would be an airline hostess for every passenger, and a high school football coach for every athlete! And we would be living in a world devoid of cleaning ladies and assembly line workers! Another criticism of career days is that an unusually good-looking and erudite speaker may cause an audience to consider the individual and not the career in question.

In the privacy of the counselor's office, a small group of students with similar vocational aspirations can meet with a career consultant, removed from both ballyhoo atmosphere and pressure of a large peer group. While a consultant's good looks and delivery could also influence a small group, the two-way interchange of such a meeting tends to minimize such charismatic influence.

As spring of the senior year approaches, students who have been examining occupational literature and meeting with career consultants should begin more active job exploring and seeking endeavors. One or more teen-agers should visit several places of employment for the purpose of finalizing vocational choices. Each student then makes application at the place(s) of his choice. Although a counselor should always be ready to lend his advice and good offices to expedite student job visitations, he should not forget that students must assume the initiative in these ventures. He must also remember that if a student is not mature enough to take the initiative in job-seeking, he will not be mature enough to hold that job. The counselor who "spoon-feeds" his client into a job placement after graduation is doing him no favor. Rather, the counselor is probably fostering client immaturity, which could lead to unsatisfactory work performance and subsequent dismissal.

The next step in student vocational development is job visitations. These have the dual purpose of increasing client job information and building contacts for possible hirings later. One way to insure that pupils take the responsibility for arranging job visitations is to insist that the youngsters request them by letter or telephone on their own. The counselor allows the use of his name in these contacts, however. This has the dual psychological advantage of building maturity and confidence through action in self-behalf, yet providing the supportive relationship of a counselor who cares.

A typical job visitation letter and telephone call are shown here:

SCHOOL LETTERHEAD

(date)

Mr. John Jones
Personnel Manager
First National Bank
1 South Pinckney St.
Madison, Wis. 53703

Dear Mr. Jones:

Several members of our senior class are interested in clerical, stenographic, and filing careers after graduation next month. Our counselor, Mr. Sheldon Smith, has suggested that we write you.

We would like an opportunity to visit the First National Bank at your convenience to observe the type of work we plan to do. We would also like to find out what opportunities exist for us there, and how to apply for them.

If you have any questions, please call Mr. Smith at 655-2345.

Respectfully yours,

Miss Beverly Brown,
Senior, Marshall High School

(Telephone conversation)

"Mr. Jones, Personnel Manager, please. . . . Mr. Jones, this is Beverly Brown, a senior at Marshall High School. . . . Our counselor, Mr. Smith, suggested that I call you. . . . Several of us senior girls are interested in clerical type careers, and Mr. Smith wondered if you'd let us visit the bank someday to observe. . . . Oh, thank you, Mr. Jones. What day and time would be convenient? . . . Thursday, May 10th would be just fine, Mr. Jones. . . . What time can we get off from school? Well, we all have study hall at 10:00, and after that, we can count our visit as a field trip for office practice, which meets at 11:00, so from about 10:15 to 12:00 would be great. . . . Are you sure that's all right for you? . . . Thank you, Mr. Jones, we'll see you at 10:15 next Thursday, then. . . . What's that? . . . Yes, some of the girls would like to apply for work at your bank, that's right. . . . Application blanks for us? That's wonderful! . . . Thank you again. We'll remember to pick up the forms when we visit. . . . Goodbye."

The counselor assists clients in making realistic career choices.

An old cliche, but one still worth quoting is that a counselor "helps pupils to help themselves." In career selection, this means that a counselor provides an emotionally supportive and informationally rich atmosphere. But he never, never chooses an occupation for his client. The counselor who makes a counselee's choice not only fosters immaturity, but also runs the risk of being forever damned for a selection which did not work out. The client must choose his own career, and the counselor must never let him forget this.

This does not mean than an undecided or vacillating high school senior should be chided by the counselor for immaturity. Instead, a good, supportive counseling relationship must be built to help the client cope with his feelings. Many 18-year-olds are not ready to make a final vocational decision. A boy or girl who has feelings of uncertainty should be told that such emotions are normal. At the same time, the client must never lose sight of the eventual necessity for decision-making. Therefore, a counselor must be ready to discuss practical alternatives (temporary exploratory work, military service, a general college course) open to the student, as a supportive counseling relationship is provided.

In vocational counseling, the counselor proceeds along lines of the theoretical frame of reference (non-directive, rational, existentialist, etc.) in which he believes, as in any other form of counseling. In fact, vocational counseling is intricately interwoven with counseling related to classroom, personality, and family problems. It cannot be isolated from these other areas. Career choice is just another aspect of the total life style of the individual. The counselor and client focus on such variables as school grades, IQ and achievement test results, personality characteristics, part-time work experience, contact with members of different occupations, and hobbies and avocations. This last item, hobbies and avocational interests, many times becomes the most significant clue of all for a client making a vocational choice. It is all too frequently considered of minor importance by counselors.

Much has been written concerning use of so-called "interest tests," the Kuder Preference Record and the Strong Vocational Interest Blank. Professional opinions range from extremes of condemnation of these instruments as worthless psychological quackery to claims that one or the other is an extremely accurate guide for a youngster trying to choose a career. This writer takes a middle position, acknowledging the statistical-methodological shortcomings of all interest inventories, but advocating consideration of their use on a one-to-one, voluntary basis, as a possible clarifier of client career thinking.

Much criticism of the Kuder and Strong tests has come about through school misuse of these instruments. For example, there is strong evidence to support the statement that any interest inventory administered on a compulsory basis yields worthless findings, yet many schools continue to herd students into an auditorium to take these inventories. An even more serious criticism of many users of the two instruments is the age level at which they are given. A few schools still administer one or the other to their ninth graders. This is done in spite of the fact that the inventory constructors indicated that these instruments should not be used below grade 11. Also, there is strong independent research evidence that Kuder and Strong scores of 14- and 15-year-olds are of no predictive value.

One problem in using the Kuder as an aid in vocational choice is that it measures overall interest, rather than interest associated with job ability. In practical terms, this means that a paraplegic who is interested in outdoor pursuits and has read many books on this subject could score higher on the inventory's Outdoor scale than a successful forest ranger or telephone lineman. In addition, the Kuder can be easily faked. A testee who wishes to score high or low in a given area can see through most of the items, and cause a scale score to appear as he wants it.

Although the Strong has been established as a more statistically valid inventory than the Kuder, it too has drawbacks. Some of the items contain names of former public figures who have long since passed from popularity and are completely unknown to today's high schoolers. This influences the face validity of the instrument. In practice, this means that some adolescents will assume that the Strong is obsolete, not "with it," and of little value. Finally, the Strong reports scores primarily in terms of only 48 occupations; many potential careers are scaleless. Thus, score reports are of value only to students considering a particular occupation for which a scale exists.

Often the Kuder and Strong have only limited value in vocational counseling, but they can sometimes be highly utilitarian if certain rules are observed.

(1) A client should take an interest inventory only when he is honestly concerned with career selection.

(2) The instrument should be used solely on an individual, voluntary basis, when both counselor and client agree the scores would be helpful.

(3) It should never be used as the sole basis on which a client makes a vocational choice.

Occasionally, Kuder or Strong results provide valuable new insights into vocational aptitude, but more often than not they merely confirm what the client, his parents, his teachers, and the counselor already strongly suspected.

Despite all that has been said regarding client responsibility for vocational choice, there is one area in which a counselor must be alert to protect students and their parents. They must be defended against unscrupulous salesmen from some private, profit-making vocational schools. While there are many highly ethical, fully accredited training institutions, there are a few private, post-high school vocational schools that are neither. Salesmen from these have been known to visit students and their parents at their homes, without informing local high school authorities, attempting to sell various courses at their institutions. Many fantastic claims are made for these schools. One is known to have guaranteed airline hostess jobs to all female graduates, despite repeated airline statements that the only hostess training they recognize is their own. These salesmen often pressure clients into making, and parents into signing, applications for admission which are legally binding contracts. They also require large non-refundable downpayments.

In 1968, the state of Minnesota, under the leadership of Governor Harold Levander, enacted regulatory legislation that may well become a model for the other states. This law is aimed at curbing abuses of private vocational school recruiting, and provides controls against fly-by-night operators. It should serve as a guide for counselors in advising parents. A copy of this bill may be obtained by writing the office of the Governor, State Capitol, St. Paul, Minnesota 55101.

The counselor helps pupils land that job.

After a student has made sincere and strong efforts on his own but failed to get an interview, it sometimes becomes necessary for the counselor to obtain an employment interview for him. When failure to obtain an interview occurs because of lack of client sophistication, rather than a lack of motivation, it is not psychologically damaging for the counselor to lend a hand. A sample letter and telephone call that may appropriately be made by a counselor are presented here:

SCHOOL LETTERHEAD

(date)

Mr. Donald Doe
Personnel Manager
Union Electric Company
P.O. Box 529
St. Louis, Mo. 63166

Dear Mr. Doe:

Several of the senior boys have asked me to help them apply for the Lineman-Labor Grade I (trainee) positions that are open with your company. They learned of this opportunity from a recent advertisement in a local paper.

Would you be willing to look the boys over? Each will graduate next month, and will have completed our full four-year industrial arts sequence. None has ever been involved in any disciplinary problems. If you wish, send me a supply of application forms, and I'll see that the fellows fill them out to bring to their interviews.

If you have any questions, please call me at 739-5000, extension 66.

Very truly yours,

Joseph Jefferson, counselor
Pattonville Senior High

(Telephone conversation)

"Mr. Donald Doe in personnel, please. . . . If at all possible, let me speak to Mr. Doe in person. . . . Hello, Mr. Doe? . . . This is Joe Jefferson, counselor at Pattonville High School. . . . Some of the senior boys tell me they've been pestering your poor secretary with phone calls. . . . They saw your Lineman-trainee ad in the Post last week. . . . These are pretty good young men, Mr. Doe; They've all gone through our four-year shop course with passing grades. None of them have discipline problems, either. . . . When could they come down to interview? . . . Next Saturday? Great. What time do you want them? . . . 8:30, and that's at the Jefferson Street Office, isn't it? . . . Good. I'll see that the boys report Saturday, 8:30, on Jefferson, and ask for. . . . Mr. Anderson, assistant personnel manager—got it! . . . Oh, say, tell you what. Send me some application blanks, and I'll see that the boys fill them in and bring them along. . . . Put your secretary on, and I'll dictate the address to her right now over the phone. . . . Thanks for everything, Mr. Doe. . . . Goodby." (Talks to secretary.)

After an appointment has been made for a client, the counselor should be sure that the client has his resume ready. Details of building a resume are contained in Chapter Two. Again, a counselor should refuse any help until the student has shown an inclination to help himself by getting a rough draft resume on paper. After this is done, the counselor may go over the draft privately with his client, making tactful suggestions for improvement. He should never dictate changes. The task of resume writing should always rest where the task of holding a job will soon be resting—right on the student's shoulders.

In keeping with the general philosophy of building client maturity through his assumption of responsibility, a counselor should not be directive in counseling students on interview demeanor and conduct. But prior to the time for an interview, a counselor should refer his counselee to grooming and interviewing literature contained in the occupational-educational information service. This puts the burden of knowledge of appropriate grooming on the student. Another approach for facilitating favorable client interview behavior is nondirective depth counseling in this area. Most teen-agers have enough basic knowledge of good manners and courtesy to make considerable self-discovery of good job interview behavior possible during such counseling.

The filling out of employment application forms is another task that can be turned into a client learning experience and maturity-builder. One procedure is to suggest that students get an extra application blank; if this is not feasible, make them a duplicate on the school photocopy machine. The extra copy becomes a work-sheet, to be filled out first in pencil. The counselor insists that each client have his work-sheet completely filled in before any assistance will be forthcoming. When this is done, each student goes over his work-sheet with the counselor, who leads him to self-discovery of why given wordings should be changed, etc., if necessary. This process is another example of the inseparability of counseling and personnel services. The typewriting of resumes and employment applications is a student responsibility. In the case of those who do not type, this is an excellent assignment for a student clerical assistant.

Occasionally a counselor encounters what appears to be unwarranted fear regarding fitness for a particular job in a normal, well-adjusted counselee. When this happens, sometimes a counselor takes it upon himself to decide that a certain job is "just right" for the client. But when he makes this kind of judgment, he makes it from the counselor's frame of reference, not from the student's. Such a judgment is never justified. In cases of serious client doubts or fears, extensive probing or depth counseling is needed to resolve the conflicts. Attempts made to uncover the causes of the inner conflict and doubt are in order under these circumstances. Counseling of this type often follows Analytic, Neo-Analytic, or Non-Directive lines.[1]

There are other times when client fears appear to be little more than superficial teen-age jitters. If the counselee's job selection is his own, and is in full accord with demonstrated interests and aptitudes, chances are these jitters are not serious. If someone else, such as parents or teachers, pressured the student into his job choice, it's quite likely that the jitters will grow into serious fears.

A good way to determine the seriousness of expressed client fears is to compare his intelligence, training, and personality to these same factors as they occur in successful holders of the job in question. If the client resembles the successful job holders in terms of these factors, he should be told that there is little reason to be fearful.

---

[1]Readers wishing to investigate various theoretical rationales for counseling should read *Theories of Counseling and Psychotherapy* by C.H. Patterson (New York; Harper & Row, 1966) and pp. 221 - 475 of *Fundamentals of Counseling* by Shertzer and Stone (New York; Houghton-Mifflin, 1968).

With these cases, a counselor might apply the Positive Thinking school of counseling. This approach emphasizes building a client's ego-strength by stressing the fact he can procure and hold the job in question, as long as he believes he can. Other schools of thought frequently applied to such cases are the Neo-Behavioral and the Existentialist. Neo-Behaviorists use counter-conditioning to desensitize fears, while Existentialists stress the individual's freedom and responsibility to make a choice which is his and his alone. Regardless of which theoretical rationale for counseling is used, the important thing is to emphasize the normality of job interview jitters, and to label them as what they are.

The counselor interacts meaningfully with other personnel specialists.

A modern, effective secondary counselor must display gregariousness in his dealings with fellow personnel workers. Personnel managers of business firms and governmental offices, state employment service counselors, and military recruiters all have a certain commonality of interest with school counselors. Therefore, it behooves a high school counselor to develop meaningful professional and social interactions with these fellow personnel specialists. The time always comes when intimate cooperation with these persons is necessary. The counselor who has developed amicable associations will see these contacts pay off, with his high school students the ultimate beneficiaries.

In professional dealings with personnel managers, the counselor must remember that his high school is not the only one that wishes to place its graduates in good jobs. Personnel managers frequently find themselves in the enviable position of buyers in a buyers' market, and therefore are in no hurry to hire students. When this situation occurs, the counselor may use a "squeaky wheel with dignity" approach. This means that he continually communicates with hiring officials, reminding them of the availability of his graduating seniors who are awaiting action on their job applications. Yet in so doing, he maintains a decorum suitable for a professional person. The counselor avoids a hucksterish, undignified image by keeping his letters, telephone calls, and personal visits formal and proper. But he also keeps them frequent!

A few counselors have gotten themselves into a conflict of interest position by being overly friendly with certain personnel managers. These counselors have endeavored to steer the cream of the graduating manpower crop to their friends' firms, excluding other hirers from a chance at these seniors. This is unethical counselor behavior, and is never justified. It becomes especially despicable when seniors are pressured to make vocational choices that benefit the favored employer, rather than themselves. In a democracy, all employers who have demonstrated that they provide just wages and acceptable working conditions, and do not engage in unfair labor practices, should have equal opportunity to attempt to hire whom they wish. Of course, it is perfectly proper to be on close terms with personnel managers, provided that there is no playing of favorites at hiring time.

Another group of persons with whom a counselor should have good relationships are labor union officers and state industrial commission personnel who oversee apprenticeship programs. These people are well versed in the needs of business and industry, and can often give valuable tips which can be relayed to youthful job seekers. Still another fellow personnel worker who is a *must* to know is the local state employment service counselor. Many school counselors recommend that graduating seniors register with their SES as a matter of policy. Another benefit of knowing these various fellow professionals is they can often be called upon to serve as career consultants.

Military recruiters are another type of personnel specialist with whom the counselor must deal. There was a time when recruiters frequently behaved in unethical ways in their zeal to fill the ranks, and often encouraged boys to drop out of high school to enlist. The modern recruiter is a different type; upgrading of personnel assigned to recruiting and stringent military regulations have brought this about. Today's recruiter is a top-echelon noncom with combat experience, and almost always a fine person with whom to deal. Of course, the spectre of conflict of interest always looms in dealing with military, as with civilian employers. When the question, "Should I enlist?" comes up in counseling, a counselor must place his client's welfare ahead of any positive or negative feelings about the recruiter, or the military in general. Just as in other career selection, the decision to enlist or not enlist is the client's to make.

The counselor must likewise steer a middle course in allowing or not allowing recruiters to do various things in the school building. A good rule of thumb is to allow them to meet with students in school, but only on a voluntary basis, and only during the students' non-instructional or free time. If the recruiter wishes to speak to a class or an assembly, this is an instructional, not a guidance function. Requests to do this should be referred to the principal and the teacher involved.

There are certain ultra-conservative and ultra-liberal elements in society that will cause trouble for a counselor who they feel is either hampering the recruiter's efforts on one extreme, or trying to obtain volunteers for him on the other. If the counselor steers a middle ground in his dealings with the military, he not only does the fairest thing for students, but he also spares himself a lot of grief in the form of hate mail and other extremist harassment.

One counselor strategy for dealing with all fellow personnel specialists involves capitalizing on the universal human proclivity for friendly, informal talk over a good meal and a beverage. When employers, union officials, or recruiters visit the school, try to time their visit to overlap a lunch period. Suggest in advance that they plan to eat at school with the counselor and either a group of students or some faculty members. The pleasant interaction that occurs over dinner builds good will for future dealings, and often results in valuable insights gained from exposure to a new point of view.

SOME ON-GOING CONSIDERATIONS

What job a teen-ager takes after graduation is determined by three things: student characteristics, current labor market needs, and Lady Luck. This last factor cannot be emphasized enough. Occasionally a counselor concludes, after observing what happened to a particualr client, that it is by far the most crucial vocational determinant. Human behavior is multi-variate and complex, and modern society is much more so. Therefore, interference by chance variables with the smooth passage of a human being through life is to be expected. Lest he become discouraged, a counselor should consider how much worse the young person's experience would be had there been no counseling and personnel services for him.

Vocational development must not be thought of as an isolated portion of a student's life. It is not a process that operates only in a counselor's office for adolescents, and only between 8:00 A.M. and 4:00 P.M. weekdays for adults. Rather, it is inexorably bound up in the total life style of the individual. Vocational development began in the cradle, and will not cease until death is near. It operates continuously, as incoming stimuli constantly interact with the specific constellation of traits constituting a human being.

The influence of chance variables and the continuous nature of vocational development are two reasons why no two vocational counseling cases will ever be exactly alike. A counselor should not be mystified when one high school senior decides easily upon a career, while another cannot seem to make up his mind. For some students, formal vocational counseling is a short, simple process; for others, a long, complex one. There are clients who make a vocational choice while in elementary school, enter that occupation after high school, and hold this job until retirement. There are other clients who never make a career choice, and who subsequently change jobs frequently during adult life. Such occurrences are perfectly normal, and are but extremes upon an ease-of-decision-making continuum.

The professional world of the counselor is also complex. It behooves a secondary counselor to keep abreast of trends in the vocational field. This is done chiefly by professional reading, and by interacting with fellow counselors and personnel specialists. State Employment Services, the U.S. Department of Labor, and the U.S. Office of Education publish excellent periodicals. A counselor should get on the mailing lists for these, and read them. He should also see that appropriate excerpts from them are read by students, teachers, and parents. The advent of the photocopy dittomaster has made quantity reproduction of printed material easy for school personnel. Local newspaper classified ads also require at least cursory reading.

Five scholarly journals, the *Vocational Guidance Quarterly, American Vocational Journal, Journal of Vocational Behavior, Personnel and Guidance Journal,* and *The School Counselor* contain numerous vocational articles, with the first three exclusively devoted to that topic. Also, the book reviews in these journals can guide a counselor in acquiring professional books on career choice.

Reading is not enough, however, if a counselor plans to keep abreast of the world of work. He must enhance his comprehension through interaction with fellow counselors from other schools. He must also rub shoulders with the related personnel specialists previously discussed. When the counselor stays current with the complex, fluid vocational situation, it is his clients who benefit most.

FOUR

Helping Students Select
Appropriate Further Education

A stunning sequence of vexing questions faces high school seniors: "Should I go on to school or not?" "If so, what kind of institution is best for me—trade school, university, business college, nursing school, liberal arts college, etc.?" "And then, when I've finally selected a specific institution, what course of study should I take when I get there?" What are some counselor strategies and activities for helping clients with these quandaries?

SOME PRELIMINARY CONSIDERATIONS

Many educators, including some counselors, tend to over-simplify the process of student choice of further schooling past high school. Basing their judgments largely on IQ scores or high school grades, these educators pursue a naive, simplistic form of "directive" guidance: "The 'dumb' ones go to work, the 'not-so-dumb' ones take vocational training, the 'sort-of-smart' ones attend a state college, and the 'smart' ones go to a large university." This caricaturized rule of thumb aptly sums up their philosophy for choosing further education. The tragedy in such nonsense is that many educators and parents seek to force graduating seniors into a mold based on this system.

Choice of further education is a complex, multi-variate process, interrelated with the more general process of vocational development. Such variables as IQ, achievement, motivation, social class values, marital plans, financial status, college enrollments, and geographic location are but a few factors to be considered. Moreover,

67

each client is an individual, functioning within a unique constellation of traits and factors. Therefore, every boy and girl must be treated as a specific counseling case and cannot be lumped into any stereotyped category based on subjective judgments and value systems of others.

In fact, it's highly unwise for a counselor to attempt to choose for any student, no matter how objective he seeks to be, and no matter how well he is able to ignore his own personal values. Choice of further schooling, like all other personal decisions, rests on client shoulders. The counselor facilitates client decision-making by providing a supportive counseling relationship, giving needed factual information, and making effective personnel services available.

The preceding statements are not meant to be a proposal to reject all measurements such as test scores and grade point averages, and to rely solely on a psychological counseling process in choosing further education. Rather, it is suggested that many little scraps of information be introduced during counseling as the client seeks to arrive at a realistic choice. For example, both the American College Testing Service and College Entrance Examination Board provide highly useful freshman class test score profiles of member colleges. These profiles give a prospective applicant an approximate idea of the intellectual level of student functioning at various institutions. Yet, armed with this information, a counselee must still decide if he is willing and able to compete with his peers at this or that college.

Even if the many non-academic variables—financial, social class, matrimonial, geographical, etc.—are ignored, a counselee is still faced with a complex picture when choosing further education. This is due to the interaction of three personal academic characteristics possessed by all students. These are ability, knowledge, and motivation. *Ability* is known to counselors and their clients largely from intelligence test scores. *Knowledge* is known both through achievement test scores and past school grades. *Motivation* is known only through subjective opinions. Our ability to measure the first two variables is fair, but somewhat circumscribed by such shortcomings as standard errors of measurement and human variability. The latter characteristic is wholly unmeasureable. This in itself should warn all those who would choose college on the basis of test scores alone. If there is any rule of thumb for use in college choice, it is that we should emphasize the importance of motivation in future success. Or, with apologies to Holy Writ, it might thus be paraphrased, "There be these three, ability, knowledge, and motivation, and I say unto you, the greatest of these be motivation!"

THE PROCESS OF CHOOSING FURTHER EDUCATION

Activities early in high school start students thinking.

Boys and girls do not acquire information about or positive feelings toward further education all at once. Instead, bits and pieces of the total picture are constantly trickling into their frames of reference throughout childhood and adolescence. By the time the average elementary school pupil has passed into junior high school, he already possesses a considerable, but unorganized, jumble of facts and feelings about various institutions of higher learning. Teachers, parents, peers, the news media, and chance contacts of various kinds are all sources of information. For most grade school children, the principal source of information about colleges and universities is news media sports reports of various collegiate athletic teams. This source is not so poor as one might assume, as the positive feelings almost all children have toward sports readily transfer to the institution as a whole. To the average grade schooler, a university football team *is* the university, and an adored all-American athlete is little different from all his fellow college students. While it may be argued that sports occupy too large a place in most youngsters' value structures, it can also be said that this phenomenon makes the vast majority of American youth aware of and favorably disposed toward higher education.

It is up to junior high and middle school counselors to see that this favorable childhood attitude is nurtured and not lost. It's also their job to see that early adolescents receive other information about higher education to go with the sports knowledge they already possess. One such source of information is the collection of occupational, educational, and social references maintained by the counselor. This so-called information service must contain attractively presented monographs, books, posters, sound-filmstrips, and movies in the area of careers and further education. Moreover, these materials must be available for semi-formal and browsing use by pupils during study halls or unstructured blocks of school time. Teachers must also be encouraged to borrow these materials for curriculum enrichment. Some counselors even loan materials to parents and various community groups.

Another exploitable source of further educational information for counselors is visits to the high school by former students now enrolled in post-secondary institutions. These visits include exhibitions by collegiate performing groups, such as musical ensembles; one-act play casts; and debate teams, one or more members of which are alumni of the high school. Also included are appearances at school assemblies by graduates who have distinguished themselves individually at college by earning recognition for scholastic honors, student government, or athletics. When such visitation occurs, it should include opportunities for high school boys and girls to meet the college students informally, following their formal meeting as part of an audience at a speech or concert. Informal contacts might include bull sessions in the counselor's office, impromptu classroom appearances, and eating school lunch together at a reserved table.

Sometimes the visitation process is reversed, and a counselor arranges for high schoolers to attend an event at a nearby college. Usually a teacher is also involved, generally one in whose teaching area the affair being attended falls. Examples include performance-type events, such as rock concerts or football games; workshops for high school pupils, such as cheerleading clinics or school newspaper seminars; and various college get-togethers open to teen-agers, such as science fairs and dances. Here again, opportunities for informal contact between high school and college students, especially those who are alumni of the visiting high school, should be arranged whenever possible. Most colleges bend over backwards to accommodate school groups, providing reduced fare admission, student guides, free overnight visitors' housing, and other inducements. Counselors and teachers can set up all sorts of beneficial visitation activities for their students by keeping communication channels open with appropriate college faculty, such as admissions counselors, high school relations officers, and athletic directors.

No matter how informative and enjoyable inter-school visits become, they must not be considered vehicles for immediate college choice by younger adolescents. The decisions as to whether to go on to school or not; if so, to what institutions; and if so, to major in what, come later. Research has shown that early adolescents are not yet capable of realistic career choices. College exploratory activities of junior high and early senior high youngsters are just that— exploratory. They serve to build a child's background information and a realm of personal experiences, so that he will be able to make a more realistic choice of further education when his senior year rolls around.

Parents and teachers become involved in the choice process.

Other adults besides counselors are interested in further educational plans of teen-agers. This is to be expected, and in certain ways encouraged. A few counselors resent attempts by parents and teachers to facilitate educational planning by children. These counselors claim that career choice is rightfully their own area of professional involvement, and that parents and teachers are often misinformed regarding many aspects of college attendance. While this is indeed true, it's nevertheless unwise for any counselor to discourage such interest. After all, parents are emotionally involved in their offspring's lives, and teachers are many times seriously concerned with the future success of various pupils. Counselor attempts to get a parent or teacher to "lay off" a given client's educational planning will only result in friction which could hinder, rather than help, the student in question.

A more sensible strategy for a counselor faced with parent or teacher involvement in child's educational decision is to enlist the adult's aid in a joint team effort on behalf of the youngster. Since the other adults in the student's life are going to be concerned in any case, it's a wise move to channel their interest into avenues that are beneficial to him. Basically, counselor strategy in such a problem is first to obtain client permission to discuss the matter with parents and/or teachers. Then the counselor sends various relevant materials, such as college catalogs, home to the parents or to the teacher's classroom, using the student as courier. Finally, he seeks personal liaison with the parties involved. This is sometimes best done by asking the client to suggest that his parent or teacher make contact with the counselor. On other occasions, a counselor may deem it best to initiate the contact himself. Sometimes he invites the concerned adults to accompany him on a college visitation, or to come to his office to view a pertinent movie or meet a visiting admissions counselor. If rapport has been established in such a manner, the counselor is in a much better psychological position to discourage any unwise parental or teacher influence on the client that might arise.

At the opposite pole from the overly concerned parent is the apathetic or indifferent one. Occasionally a client tells his counselor that his parents could not care less what the client's post-high school plans are. There is no rule of thumb for dealing with these cases, as some appear to stem from emotional problems in the home, while others possibly result from social class values or the parents' intellectual levels. The nearest a counselor can come to formulating a general strategy for dealing with these situations is always seek to explain the values of further schooling in meaningful terms. For example, if hostility exists between parent and child, it might be wise to suggest that further schooling can facilitate an adolescent's leaving home to begin a life of his own. Or, if over-attachment is the problem, a discussion of apron string cutting as essential to gaining maturity could be in order. In dealing with non-emotional aspects of parental lassitude, economic arguments are often effective. Many parents who had limited schooling themselves do not realize the financial horizons open to college degree holders. Factual information from the counselor on this may open parental eyes. After all, who can quarrel with future riches for their offspring? Of course, at the same time that he is attempting to influence parental attitudes by information-giving in meaningful areas, the counselor must build a supportive counseling relationship with the client. A counselor frequently stresses the importance of client decision-making during such counseling. For if emotional support for further schooling is not forthcoming from parents, a client must be prepared to accept this fact. While a counselor might attempt to manipulate parent attitudes on behalf of a student, both counselor and student must face the fact that each person's life is his alone to lead.

Another way in which parents and teachers become involved in the choice of post-high school education is through alumni representatives. Many colleges, business colleges, finishing schools, and universities use their successful former students as volunteer recruiters and high school contact persons. When these people also happen to be parents or teachers of current pupils, the counselor has a prime opportunity to involve them as resource specialists. Of course, he might be careful when so doing not to show favoritism toward the institutions these teachers and parents represent.

Still another way that counselors may use parents and teachers in personnel services pertinent to college choice is as institutional visitation chaperones. Frequently, collegiate and other open-house type programs are scheduled in conflict with one another, and the counselor can accompany only one student group. When this occurs, an interested teacher or parent may wish to transport a car load of youngsters to a nearby campus. If such trips are taken on school time, questions of legal liability may arise, and school district policies relative to transporting pupils must be rigidly observed.

In all conversations with parents and teachers regarding a student's further educational choice, there's one area which counselors cannot emphasize enough, namely, informal learning and independent exploration. Hobbies and avocational interests of boys and girls frequently provide meaningful insights into potential college majors and life careers. Today's 14-year-old raising hamsters may be tomorrow's zoologist, that 16-year-old bus boy may some day manage a motor hotel, and the little girl who colored with her baby sister might teach a future kindergarten. While good high school grades and study habits are vital in preparing for college admission, and later in achieving general academic success, leisure-time learnings probably play a bigger part in choosing and excelling in the major study field. Many parents and teachers don't realize this, see only the values of formal education, and may even disparage hobby-type activities as frivolity. Counselors must set the record straight on behalf of their clients.

The second important aspect of avocational endeavors is their potential for teaching perseverance, a quality many college educators insist is paramount in academic success. Just like going on to college, these informal activities are voluntarily chosen by boys and girls. Therefore, attractive possibilities exist for using these activities as examples of rewards accruing from hard work, ingenuity, and perseverance. Because hobbies are of their own choosing, children are apt to respond positively to adult encouragement not to abandon them when discouraged or impatient. The analogy to pursuance of further schooling is obvious. Some counselors feel that parents cannot be advised strongly enough to (1) allow children to widely explore various hobby-type endeavors, and (2) insist on perseverance in carrying these projects to fruition. For in childhood hobbies counselors see, in symbolic miniature, choice of and success in future further education and lifetime careers.

Students plan and carry out meaningful selection activities.

In their last two years of high school, students begin to formulate tentative further schooling plans. The decisions whether to go on to school, if so where, and to major in what, are individual decisions and are each pupil's personal responsibility. However, despite the necessity to ultimately decide for one's self, it's highly beneficial to include in the choosing process supportive interpersonal relationships. These include one-to-one individual counseling with the counselor, and loosely structured, voluntarily organized group counseling sessions with peers. These small (three- to-eight member), informal groups are composed of students with similar problems regarding post-high school educational plans. The counselor sometimes acts as group counseling leader, but his presence should never be strongly felt. Group members have the final responsibility for arriving at problem solutions and should use the counselor's catalytic influence sparingly, and only when they deem it absolutely necessary. It's best if each group contains pupils that have as many interest commonalities in the further schooling area as possible.

The first step for these counseling groups is to discuss the general problem at hand, as members perceive it. For some groups this will be whether to go on to school or not; for others, institutional selection, course of study choice, or obtaining adequate financial support. The benefits that accrue to group members are supportive relationships developed by helping and being helped by others (emotional level), and increased comprehension of various confronting situations (factual level). These sessions differ little from other forms of group counseling practiced in school settings.

Small student interest groups do more than discuss further educational problems. Pupils work to plan activities which aid in decision-making. For example, they may order and view films and sound filmstrips on various colleges, invite admissions counselors to appear at group meetings, and write letters and make telephone calls to arrange campus visitations. Groups can also facilitate execution of more pedantic yet absolutely essential details of college admission, such as preparation for the A.C.T. and College Boards, interpretive study of catalogs and bulletins, and filling in of applications.

Because groups contain any students with similar further educational plans, their utility is not restricted to preparation for college and university careers. Since good group counseling practice requires groups to be set up on a common problem basis, students considering beauty, nursing, business, and preparatory schools can also hold sessions to help resolve their further educational conflicts. Regardless of where group members consider going on to school, final decisions must be made by each student. The small-group process is an aide in choosing, but never a crutch. The counselor must remind boys and girls that while it's his job, and that of the group, to assist in further educational planning, ultimate decisions are always individual responsibilities.

A caution is in order in the area of student college choice activities. Seniors must be warned not to obtain a false impression of an institution through exposure to it under abnormal or distorted conditions. Erroneous ideas frequently result from two phenomena, (1) the "student week-end," at which hordes of invited area high school seniors descend on a college campus, and (2) the "college night," at which numerous institutional representatives visit a high school to compete for students on a mass production basis. The danger in both these situations is that high schoolers receive biased impressions of institutions, caused by the unnatural, carnival atmosphere usually surrounding both types of events.

While attending a gala student week-end is certainly a proper fun activity for teen-agers, it's not a means for arriving at realistic college choices. A far better approach is for a small group considering several colleges to first study the literature of these schools, then invite a representative of each to visit the high school on a semi-formal basis. Sometimes a college will send an admissions counselor, others give this job to teaching faculty or students. The more geographically distant schools generally have local alumni who answer such calls. Informal, small-group interaction with an institutional representative in the counselor's outer office, followed by eating school lunch together, is usually highly beneficial to all concerned. The next step for the student group is campus visitations. It's highly advisable that such visits take place on regular school days, and include stops at places which later will figure prominently in college life. These include a freshman course lecture, dormitories, the library, financial aids office, and eating facilities. A counselor, working through the proper contact persons, can arrange such an itinerary. After the visit, it's a good idea for the student group to compare impressions and critique their experience.

The same criticisms of career days, made in Chapter Three, apply with little change to college nights. The visitation procedure outlined in the previous paragraph is a far better approach to college exploration than either student week-ends or college nights. In fairness to college nights, it is true that in some rural areas where high schools are small and widely spaced, and colleges are distant from many communities, a college night at a centrally located high school is perhaps a necessary evil. Under such conditions, a college night does make possible the exposure of many seniors to a considerable number of institutional representatives at minimal travel cost and time for all concerned.

The counselor facilitates selection of realistic higher education.

It is impossible to separate counseling about further education from the practice of personnel services connected with going on to school. As senior high boys and girls work with their counselor, they both probe feelings about further education at the emotional level, and tackle problems related to Scholastic Aptitude Tests, admissions blanks, visitations, etc., at the factual level. Good counseling facilitates better personnel services, and good personnel services develop insights for more effective counseling relationships.

Counselors must realize that client problems connected with more schooling after high school cannot be divorced from other problems. Too frequently, the decision to continue in school is looked upon as a narrow, academic matter, influenced only by past scholarship. This is unrealistic, as the whole life style of the individual, including the effects of social class values, feelings, and financial capacity all affect the choice process. Counselors need to rely heavily on a good information service when dealing with college choice problems at the factual level. Beauty, vocational, nursing, and business schools all publish brochures explaining their programs to prospective students. Colleges and universities print a whole series of booklets designed to inform potential students about various aspects of their institutions. They generally issue a catalog, which lists rules, regulations, and courses of study; bulletins of various divisions, which list individual course and curriculum descriptions; and new student, housing, financial aids, and summer session brochures. Descriptive materials emanate from testing agencies, too: the National Merit Scholarship Corporation, American College Testing Program, College Entrance Examination Board, Association of Accredited Schools of Business, and National League for Nursing. Some life insurance companies provide college cost summaries and/or occupational monographs. Commercial producers of guidance materials include all sorts of higher educational choice aids in their school services. A counselor must not only see that the information service is well stocked with these things, but must also take steps to guarantee that clients are using them. This is best done by making materials readily available to students, and explaining their practical utility, so students will seek to inform themselves. The counselor must be ready to furnish counselees with explanations of unclear points found in such literature, provided that the students have first made attempts to comprehend these independently.

While pupils should take leadership roles in ordering materials, inviting institutional representatives, and arranging visitations, a counselor sometimes must assist them. Adults occasionally insist on dealing with other adults, the students in question may lack the experiential maturity to handle certain details, or legal liability problems can make counselor intervention prudent—these are reasons for helping students directly. When the counselor does intervene, there must always be a good reason. A counselor who spoon-feeds his clients, performing personnel services they themselves could manage, does them no favor. Unnecessary intervention deprives them of growth experiences and erodes the very maturity they will need for future educational success.

At all times, the counselor should foster a favorable climate for client consideration of further educational options open to them. Wall posters, informal bits of information conveyed to pupils and their parents, and invitations to college faculty and students to visit the high school are some means of doing this. However, in these and other familiarization activities, the counselor must seek only to inform persons about further schooling and its implications, never to impose his own values. Let the benefits of higher education speak for themselves; if certain high schoolers "should" go on to college or other training, they'll get the message!

The preceding also holds true during individual counseling. Even if a counselee appears to be making an unwise decision, it's far better strategy to lead him to see this himself, than to seek to dissuade him. Imposition of values leads to trouble, no matter how sensible the counselor's views apparently are. Discouraging the unconvinced client from a course of action invites future blame, no matter how unfairly rendered, when something goes wrong.

The counselor helps clients implement their choices.

To be optimally effective in practicing personnel services related to further schooling, a modern counselor must cultivate communication channels with fellow personnel workers at post-high school institutions. Nothing takes the place of one-to-one personal contact—just as a counselor must maintain good counseling relationships with students, so must he nurture dialogue with admissions officers.

The further-education picture is changing all the time, and it's impossible for a secondary counselor to stay abreast of the situation by reading. By being on close terms with his higher education counterparts, the high school counselor learns of admissions policy changes before they happen—in time for the information to be helpful to his clients. Moreover, having the ear of college officials gives a counselor opportunity to pass on ethically interpretive academic information about students. Data that cannot always be accurately stated on paper can mean the difference between a student's admission application being accepted or rejected.

Basically, counselors have four different opportunities for developing contacts with admissions personnel. These occur when:

(1) admissions officers are invited by students to the high school as institutional representatives,

(2) the counselor accompanies pupils to the institution on a campus visitation,

(3) both counselors and admissions personnel attend conferences, such as work-shops, teachers' conventions, and college nights,

(4) each party is a member of the same chapter of a professional organization, such as Phi Delta Kappa, American School Counselors' Association, American Personnel and Guidance Association, a regional guidance organization, or the American Federation of Teachers.

Informal contacts made during such get-togethers are vital to counselors, and often more important than more formal group meetings, such as admissions conferences and workshops. Of course, an up-and-coming counselor participates in these group experiences too, as many valuable insights into the admissions picture are often developed there. During both informal, one-to-one contacts and group contacts, a good tip for promoting helpful interaction is to use the mutual meal effectively. Whenever like-minded professionals get-together, extremely significant dialogue often occurs over lunch, dinner, or the coffee cup. Frequently, what transpires during informal refreshment periods is more significant than what is said at more formal portions of a meeting.

It might seem incongruous to some that a counselor who insists that clients decide for themselves, and who does not impose his values on them, should lobby in their behalf when dealing with admissions personnel. However, it must be remembered that the counselor only lobbies on behalf of the decisions already made by boys and girls during individual and group counseling. While high school students must choose for themselves in making further educational plans, it's asking too much to expect them to overcome as well the road blocks of institutional politics and impersonality often obstructing their well-made plans. A good counselor, having been tough with his clients by insisting that they do things for themselves, now becomes equally tough with college officials when protecting client interests. Counselors who aren't afraid to "talk up" on behalf of students often are surprised to find admissions personnel ready and willing to listen and compromise, provided that the facts are not misrepresented. This is because of (1) the psychological principle that persons respect others who display confidence in their convictions, (2) the fact that many institutional admissions policies are guides, rather than inflexible rules, and can be modified by admissions officers if circumstances warrant. In colloquial terms, "the squeaky wheel gets the grease."

SOME ON-GOING CONSIDERATIONS

As more and more opportunities for post-high school education become available to graduating seniors, the complex further educational picture becomes more so. This behooves the counselor to intensify efforts to stay current with this constantly changing situation. This is best done by professional reading, attendance at workshops and seminars, and maintaining close personal contacts with fellow counselors and college admissions personnel. Three "must" sources of professional reading are the *Journal of the Association of College Admissions Counselors,* and the periodic reports of the College Entrance Examination Board and American College Testing Service.

A growing trend in education is the upgrading and multiplying of further educational opportunities in other than four-year colleges and universities. During the 1950's and '60's, and somewhat into the '70's, the trend has been for higher and higher percentages of high school graduates to go on to college. While this trend has undeniably been a good and necessary thing, its continued upward climb is probably not. A counter movement begun in the late '60's and continuing into the '70's has sought to temper the "college mania" found in some sectors. Spearheaded by university educators themselves, this counter movement advocates that college is not for all students, and that there's no disgrace in graduating from a vocational, business, or junior college training program. Probably by the mid '70's, college and university enrollments will experience lessened growth rates, somewhat attuned to those of the general population. On the other hand, there is no end in sight to proliferation of post-high school alternatives to college. By the 1980's almost all high school graduates will probably enter a further educational institution of some type.

The non-college bound but further-schooling-oriented counselee is a rapidly multiplying breed. Counselors need to keep abreast of the highly fluid training situation and job placement scene pertinent to these individuals. First, sources of professional reading need identification. The U.S. Labor Department is a continual producer of both periodical *(Occupational Outlook Quarterly)* and specialized literature. Other government agencies, especially those charged with the task of assisting minority groups, also publish useful materials. It's a good idea for counselors to get on the mailing list of the Superintendent of Documents, Washington, D.C. 20025, so as to be notified of new materials. A valuable private source is the B'nai B'rith Vocational Service, 1640 Rhode Island Avenue, Washington, D.C. 20036. The commercial guidance materials producers such as Chronicle, Careers, Inc., and S.R.A. devote some attention to this area. *The Guidance Clinic,* published by Parker Publishing Company, Inc., West Nyack, New York 10994, is a helpful periodical service.

Second, the counselor must keep up local and regional personal contacts with persons knowledgeable in the further-schooling-other-than-college sphere. These include admissions directors of such institutions, state and federal employment and manpower professionals, and key employers of program graduates. Third, empathy for this type of student must be cultivated. The counselor, having a master's degree or being a higher college graduate, may not readily appreciate the value structure of a counselee "smart enough to go on," who nevertheless disdains college. All persons are worthy, regardless of how closely their life styles correspond to the counselor's. This fact must be implemented by continual display of positive regard toward clients of this type.

Another trend with which counselors must be familiar is the growing reliance upon data processing procedures in facilitating college and other admissions. This trend owes its origin to the same phenomenon as the rising percentage of students going on to school, the increasing complexity of modern society. Streamlined clerical techniques are a good thing, a cutter of red tape and tremendous labor-saver for counselors and colleges alike. However, there is one deleterious influence brought about by reliance upon data processing against which counselors must constantly be on guard. This is the tendency to blame machines rather than men for mistakes and unwise decisions. "Our computer made an error," is an excuse no counselor should accept. What the person making such a statement really means is, "I'm unwilling to accept responsibility, so I'm blaming an inanimate object, which cannot be punished." One of the ills of modern society is a growing tendency to avoid responsibility for one's actions, and the poor computer is a popular scapegoat. Counselors, with their administration's backing, must take the lead in bucking this trend to shirk accountability—and one place this can frequently be done is in further educational admissions.

FIVE

Assisting in College Admission
and Financial Aid Acquisition

Getting into one's chosen college, and then being able to afford it, are two extremely serious problems for a great many high school seniors. There are certain things counselors may do—and other things they should never do—to facilitate the meeting of these perceived client needs. What are some ramifications of helping students in this area?

TO INTERCEDE OR NOT TO INTERCEDE?

The choice of further education is not only a complex and lengthy process, but is merely one aspect of the even more complex and lengthy vocational development process. Thus, decisions as whether to go on to school or not, and if so, to what institution, and to major in what, and how to finance it, are made by the client in light of a background of facts and feelings accrued over a number of years. A counselor must remember this, and not expect client decisions in this area to be made in a vacuum, or to correspond to what the counselor might do were the choices his. The counselee is responsible for his own decision-making, and the counselor, both in counseling relationships and practice of personnel services, merely facilitates. Therefore, for example, when a counselor goes to bat for a student whose initial admission application to a college has been rejected, he must only do so because the youngster himself, during counseling, has determined such assistance to be realistically advisable. In fact, some persons would never advocate counselor intercession on behalf of a student, on the grounds that teen-agers must fight their own battles. Others espouse mandatory counselor intervention, on the grounds that the counselor is hired to help students, and thus must intercede on their behalf whenever possible.

This author takes a middle position between these two extremes, namely, it's sometimes proper for a counselor to battle actively for a student's acceptance into a further educational institution, provided that the client has first done two things:

(a) He must have arrived at a decision, during counseling, that attendance at the college in question is a realistic choice. Therefore, if reconsidered and admitted, he will strive hard for scholastic success.
(b) He must first make some effort toward persuading admissions authorities to reconsider their decision on his own.

The psychological foundations of this eclectic counselor intervention policy are fostering client aspirational realism through insistence upon self-help, yet avoiding alienation-abandonment feelings, which might result from a feeling that "no one cares." From a more pragmatic standpoint, such an approach lessens chances for later counselor embarrassment caused by subsequent client college failure. Approaching the question of active counselor intervention from yet another perspective, one finds the information-giving aspect of the counselor role bearing on this question: If a counselor makes a number of cognitive aids, such as college catalogs, financial data, and scholarship testing programs available to pupils and/or their parents throughout the secondary school years, many adverse decisions will be averted in advance. While factual material cannot directly alter an affective background of a problem, continued exposure to pertinent further educational data is bound to enhance client choice realism when the moment of truth finally arrives.

PLAN AHEAD

Oftentimes, admission to a prestigious institution, or winning of a scholarship, loan, or federal tuition grant really occurs much earlier than the actual moment of decision by college authorities. A strategy worked out by student and counselor pays off in the final analysis, in terms of a high test score or favorable impression upon an admissions or financial aid director. Hard work, ingenuity, and careful planning must precede the actual test, application blank preparation, and college interview, if these endeavors are to be optimally successful. Such planning may at times even extend as far back as junior high school, and involve teachers and parents as well as pupils. Of course, when this is the case, it must be remembered that younger adolescents have been found incapable, in most cases, of realistic career choices by research. Therefore, early preparation should only encompass broad preparatory activities, such as acquiring test-taking sophistication, learning what various further educational institutions are like, and studying the basic principles of budgets and college costs.

SO THEY'LL DO WELL

Three general areas of student preparation for application acceptance are: (a) improvement of test-taking behaviors, (b) development of facility in paper-and-pencil application form completion, and (c) preparation for maturation of face-to-face application interview decorum. These three areas apply both to gaining admission to institutions, and receiving various financial aid from them or other sources. A counselor may develop elaborate programs for building client expertise in all three types of skills conducive to application-consummating, but it's up to each individual pupil to profit from them. The counselor can only provide a means for developing cognitive application skills; the counselee must furnish the conative motivational drives to acquire and use them.

**Mature test-taking behaviors result in
desired admission and sometimes in financial aid.**

Nation- and state-wide testing programs in this area fall into two categories: (a) those created to provide institutions of further learning with pupil data for use in admissions decisions and academic counseling, and (b) those set up to provide a recruitment and screening vehicle for various scholarship programs. The former category includes five nation-wide programs: those of the College Entrance Examination Board (CEEB) and the American College Testing Program (ACT), both used primarily by four-year colleges and universities; the National League of Nursing (NLN) and the Entrance Examination for Schools of Nursing (EESN) batteries, used by nursing schools; and the Personnel Classification Test, used by business colleges. The latter category also includes some nation-wide programs, and such as the National Merit Scholarship Qualification Test (NMSQT) more recently supplanted by the PSAT, and the "Talent Search" of the National Science Foundation. The Preliminary

Scholastic Aptitude Test (PSAT), while part of the CEEB program, also serves a secondary function of scholarship eligibility determination. Other competitions are held on a state-wide basis; for example, one state mathematics teachers' association sponsors a scholarship contest, using a mathematics achievement test as selection criterion. Another form of scholarship competition, found both nationally and state-wide, is the essay contest in which a subjective, rather than objective, measure is used to determine student winners.

Do coaching and practice really help?

Considerable controversy has arisen in measurement circles regarding the merit of various practice routines for improving subsequent test performances. As one might expect, testing agencies declare pre-test coaching attempts worthless, while producers of practice materials claim that vast benefits result from using their products. A considerable body of research exists in professional measurement journals, which largely points toward a somewhat in-between position. This position may be summarized as follows:

    (a) Practice test-taking can raise a test score by several points, but seldom, if ever, drastically.

    (b) This gain is probably due to increased familiarity with test item types and improved psychological confidence (placebo effect), rather than to pre-discovery of actual correct test-item responses. (That is, student test-taking expertise is what improves.)

    (c) Content improvement, that is, learning item answers, is much more likely to result from study of the subject field being evaluated than from the taking of old or simulated tests. Thus, to score higher on a science achievement test, read science books and conduct science experiments during the months prior to test-taking.

    (d) Study of practice or former tests can be mildly helpful in directing content study into general topical areas within a subject.

    (e) Practice testing helpfulness increases with resemblance to the real thing, because enhanced sophistication, rather than improved content knowledge, is its result. Therefore, taking the actual test for practice, whenever permissible, is superior to taking a simulated test under artificial conditions. For example, taking the SAT "for fun" while a high school junior will help improve a student's later, senior year SAT performance more than will studying a practice test, or taking one at school. Whenever prior "for fun" testing isn't possible, a counselor staging a simulated test using a practice book should create a testing environment as much like the actual testing situation as possible.

    (f) Any attempts to practice or prepare for a test must include definite counselor behaviors designed to lessen client anxiety over outcomes. If this is not done, the pressure to do well might lead to emotional interference, which will actually lower, rather than raise, pupil scores.

Preparation for scholarship competition may begin as early as junior high school.

While ninth graders are not yet ready to finalize vocational plans, many have already decided that they wish to attend college. Consequently, their development of test-taking expertise should begin at this level. It goes without saying that the counselor owes each youngster and his parents an explanation of *why* testing programs are important. Such a factual background usually enhances pupil motivation. Let's look at an example of prior year preparation for an actual scholarship testing program.

The Scholastic Aptitude Test (SAT) of the CEEB has an accompanying version for younger students, the Preliminary Scholastic Aptitude Test (PSAT). This test, given in schools by counselors each October, is normally available to tenth, eleventh, and twelfth graders. It serves two official functions: providing likely estimates of subsequent SAT performances, and serving as a screening vehicle for several scholarship programs, including, since 1971, National Merit Scholarship Qualification. It is also completely ethical to administer the PSAT to ninth graders, in order to better orient them to future performances on both this test and the SAT. Of course, no norms exist for this youngest age group, and their PSAT scores are thus not accurate predictors of future SAT performance. Neither are ninth graders eligible for any scholarship competitions connected with the PSAT. The value of encouraging them to take it along with the older students lies solely in providing these younger boys and girls with a chance to develop greater test-taking experience and sophistication. Such "practice" might be used to precede the more advanced, increasingly realistic step of taking the actual SAT "for fun" during the junior year and/or early in the senior year. The SAT is used by many colleges as a variable in awarding scholarships, in addition to its major purpose as a factor in determining admissibility.

Due to the changeover of the National Merit Scholarship competition from S.R.A.'s March-given achievement tests to E.T.S.'s October PSAT, more younger (grade 9 and 10) pupils will no doubt take the PSAT as "warm-up" for grade 11 NMSQT competition. Formerly, S.R.A.'s National Educational Development Tests served this purpose, as they resembled the old form of the NMSQT.

Some scholarship competitions rely upon more subjective measures, such as essays, or upon a combination of subjective measure and standardized test. For example, the Thom-McAnn Shoe Company, among others, has sponsored an essay-type competition for many years. The best way for a counselor to provide practice situations for motivated clients is to encourage them to write essays, and develop overall composition skills. Using past years' contest essay topics as models, the counselor creates practice essay questions for students to expound upon as warm-ups for the real thing. He then grades their efforts in terms of stated contest evaluative criteria, and reviews these criticisms with students. It's often advisable to involve English teachers, if willing, in such a project, as composition is one of their regular curricular sub-fields. Also, if contest essay topics have traditionally involved other subject fields, such as social studies or science, teachers from these areas may be fruitfully engaged in helping scholarship aspirants prepare.

An example of a scholarship competition which combines objective and subjective selection criteria is the annual Talent Search of the National Science Foundation. Here, seniors are asked to submit a written description of a proposed project (subjective), and to take a science achievement test (objective), which is then sent by the school to the examining body. A counselor wishing to assist a pupil in winning a Talent Search scholarship must work closely with an interested science teacher colleague. This teacher advises the student regarding project report preparation, while the counselor helps him develop readiness for the test-taking session. This latter objective is best achieved through administration of one or more standardized senior high science achievement tests, scaled to the approximate length of the Talent Search examination. Ideally, the room utilized for the practice tests should be the same one in which the real test is later given, as should be time of day, day of week, lighting and temperature conditions, and so on. A good procedure is to give two practice exams, approximately six and three weeks prior to the actual test. More testing than that is probably a waste of time which might better be spent on extra study in chemistry, physics, and the life sciences.

Numerous state and regional scholarship competitions employ tests, generally those of the achievement variety. Many times a counselor has to bring these programs to the attention of appropriate subject field faculty, who then urge qualified students to attempt them. In many cases, it's completely ethical to save copies of previous years' exams, and use these for practice sessions. Sometimes, contest rules require that test booklets be destroyed immediately after usage. When this is the case, the counselor may purchase several copies of the standardized achievement test that most closely resembles the scholarship instrument. Another possibility is for a teacher to construct a test that approximates, in his opinion, the real thing. As with Talent Search practice, rehearsal for state competitions should be made as much like the actual examining situation as possible.

In all scholarship competitions, providing realistic practice testing and essay-writing situations is only half the counselor's job. The other half consists of interesting students in such contests, and in helping them achieve, through counseling and other encouragement, a mental-emotional outlook conducive to success. Many teen-agers possess the intellectual capacity to compete, but may be overly pessimistic regarding their chances for success. Assisting boys and girls in developing proper motivation and enthusiasm for scholarship competitions is many times a highly challenging counseling assignment. And many times too, a few minutes spent in such an endeavor are far more fruitful than many hours of practice testing activities.

Two nation-wide admissions test programs
challenge college-bound high school seniors.

Two friendly competitors vie to test the hordes of twelfth graders who annually seek admission at one or more institutions of higher learning. These programs are the American College Testing Program (ACT) and the College Entrance Examination Board (CEEB). The latter is frequently called SAT by counselors and students, after the name of its most widely used test. Both programs administer nation-wide standardized examinations on specified Saturdays at numerous centers all over the nation. The ACT is given during October, December, February, April, and July, while the SAT takes place in November, December, January, March, May, and July. Both ACT and SAT programs are exactly alike in their principal function—namely, to provide colleges and prospective students, through their counselors, with meaningful evaluative data to facilitate admissions and placement decisions. There are, however, certain important differences between the two programs.

The College Board (SAT) program, the older of the two, is headquartered in Princeton, New Jersey. Its tests are produced and scored by the Educational Test Service. The College Board has close working relationships but no official connection with Princeton University. The SAT, traditionally given on the mornings of test

Saturdays, is a two-part (verbal and mathematical) scholastic aptitude or intelligence-type test. The SAT is taken by about twice as
many high school students as are all the board's afternoon offerings,
a series of about 15 subject-area achievement examinations. A
supplemental battery of achievement tests is also given on the first
Tuesday of February. Some colleges use SAT scores as determinant
variables for admissions decisions, employing a definite statistical
cut-off procedure. Others use SAT scores on a more advisory basis,
or merely to determine eligibility for various special programs.
Originally, the different college board tests were used mainly by
liberal arts colleges and private universities, and by state institutions
located mostly in the East. The ACT, on the other hand, began its
existence appealing almost wholly to state colleges and land-grant
universities, especially those in the Middle West. Today, a slight
tendency toward this original pattern remains, but both ACT and
SAT enjoy completely nation-wide usage popularity, and both are
employed by all types of colleges and universities. The CEEB's
Locater Service (CLS) is a valuable aid for students who are unsure
of which institutions best meet their needs. The ACT, headquartered
in Iowa City, is produced by Science Research Associates. Statistical
studies of its scores are done by Measurement of Research Center,
Inc. The ACT has a close working relationship, but no official
connection, with the University of Iowa. Unlike the SAT, which is a
form of ability measure, the ACT is an achievement/proficiency test
battery. Its four sub-tests, English Usage, Mathematics Usage, Social
Studies Reading, and Natural Sciences Reading, measure acquired
knowledges and skills in the four "core fields" of learning. Or, to put
it another way, the SAT more nearly measures a student's innate
ability to do school work, while the ACT more nearly measures what
he has already learned in school. Both College Board and ACT
organizations provide numerous booklets and reports to secondary
counselors, their clients, parents, and high school and college administrators. It's possible, for instance, to obtain mean score and
percentile rank data for student body classes at colleges and universities for both SAT and ACT. Thus, a high school student may
appraise approximate relative position in scholastic ability or academic preparation he would occupy among his peers, were he to
matriculate at the college in question. Even before the ACT or SAT
is taken, well-written explanatory booklets are available to orient
prospective testees. Both College Board and ACT publish excellent
periodical newsletters which belong in every counselor's office, the
College Board News and *ACTivity.*

It's likely that as more and more high schools either abandon or restrict revelation of the traditional A,B,C,D,F grading system, both ACT and SAT will increase in importance. Colleges, thus deprived of high school grade point and class rank information, the traditional best predictors of college success, will be forced to rely even more heavily upon test scores. At the present time, almost all colleges and universities require or strongly recommend either the ACT or SAT. A small number of institutions have elected to use neither, either, or both programs.

Pressure on students to do well on College Board and ACT programs has resulted in a proliferation of commercially available practice books. As stated earlier in this chapter, while practice tests have some value, their contribution probably lies in increasing pupil confidence and test-taking skills, rather than "giving away" any actual test item answers. Therefore, a counselor might wish to make use of commercial practice tests with his clients, but one simulated test session, two to six weeks prior to actual testing, is probably sufficient. A far superior method of "practice" for both ACT and SAT is to take the real test more than once during the senior year, or during the summer after the junior year, as a warm-up. Before urging any pupil to do this, however, a counselor should check with admissions authorities of the student's three indicated college choices. (Each test allows score reports of a testing session to be sent to three institutions for the cost of taking the test: additional score reports cost extra.) Some colleges allow a student to repeat the SAT or ACT several times, and count only the highest score. Others, however, refuse to do this, and only count either the initial or the most recent score. Quite a few colleges have even begun to accept junior year SAT's, a practice once discouraged. Therefore, a student who considers his first testing to be "practice" should not list his first three college choices as such during initial testing, unless his counselor has verified that the colleges in question will disregard it if a later, higher score is submitted. If the "practice run" proves to yield an unusually high score, the pupil may always have it sent to his actually preferred choices by paying the modest fee for additional score reports, and "quitting while ahead." There are numerous stories of high school seniors who have taken the ACT five times during a school year, the SAT six times, or even both. Actually, there are only two rare occasions in which any benefit could accrue from such determination, however admirable. (The practice-effect gain from repeating the tests is not a constant factor, and levels off after two or three tries.) If a student has been narrowly missing either a scholarship consideration cut-off point, or a minimum score for admittance to a college, then repeated testings could pay off, especially if the elusive plateau sought is but a standard error of measurement away. (Provided, of course, the college in question employs a rigid cut-off score system.)

Lesser known testing programs confront nursing school and business college aspirants.

It's difficult to tell whether the trend begun by some nursing schools in switching from either the National League of Nursing (NLN) battery or the Psychological Corporation's Entrance Exam for Schools of Nursing (EESN) to the ACT will continue. Possibly, as curricula leading to RN diplomas become more college-like, the ACT, primarily a college-type admissions instrument, will continue to oust the NLN and EESN, instruments developed especially for nursing schools. One can only speculate. The NLN is still popular enough to warrant consideration here, as is the slightly less used EESN. The NLN is a more formalized program than the EESN, being administered on agreed-upon nation-wide test days. The NLN consists of Level I, Form B of the "SCAT" intelligence-type test, and Reading Comprehension (higher level), Mathematics (JHS level), Natural Science (SHS level), and Social Studies (SHS level) sub-tests from the Educational Test Service's "Cooperative" series achievement tests. The EESN yields seven so-called ability and six personality-type sub-scores. The former are derived from an achievement-scholastic aptitude sub-test purporting to measure science reading and arithmetical abilities, and verbal and numerical intelligence. The latter are derived from a personality-type sub-test that is in essence an adaptation of the Edwards Personnel Preference Schedule. A counselor wishing to assist students in preparing for the NLN or EESN might administer a practice group test similar to those contained in the actual battery. Unlike the ACT and SAT, neither program has a parental financial aid inventory connected with it. These parental financial aid inventories will be discussed shortly.

Some business colleges have not yet elected to join fellow institutions in a movement to establish a nation-wide admissions testing structure. However, the trend is definitely in that direction, as more and more of these schools perceive a need to utilize a standardized instrument, from which may be derived national, regional, and local norms. The Personnel Classification Test of the Psychological Corporation appears to be slowly winning out as the battery preferred by business colleges for their purposes. It consists of mathematics and English achievement sub-tests, and is given to applicants at the discretion of each institution. Visiting high school seniors generally may be tested at a business college on certain specified test days. Counselors should inquire of business schools in their immediate area concerning client appointments. Most participating schools use test scores for both admissions and placement purposes, and allow low-scorers to repeat the test after a three-month wait. A counselor helping a student prepare for this test might have him practice taking mathematics and English sub-tests of one of several senior high level achievement batteries. There is no standardized financial aid structure for students or their parents connected with the Personnel Classification Test.

**Filling out admission and financial aid application blanks
ties in closely with the counseling relationships.**

There are two extreme approaches to pupil application form completion which some counselors unfortunately employ. Each has a serious psychological drawback. One poor method is to fill the blanks out for the student; the other is to wash one's hands of the matter, and leave the pupil 100% on his own. The former procedure is not only bad psychology, but is also fraudulent, as the standard NASSP application blank calls for a short essay written by the applicant in his own handwriting. Psychologically, filling out a blank for a student fosters dependency and immaturity; by thus lessening the client's ability to do things for himself, such a procedure is diametrically opposed to good counseling philosophy. Refusing to help at all also runs counter to proper counseling practice, as a good counselor is an empathetic helper who cares. Refusing to become involved obviously is not caring, and brands the counselor a hypocrite. A more sensible procedure is to place the burden of application form preparation upon the client, but also to discuss the operation with him during counseling. One way of implementing this eclectic approach is for the counselor to secure a large supply of surplus college forms, and to suggest to students that they prepare rough draft copies prior to a counseling interview. This makes each college-bound pupil responsible for his own decision-making, yet gives the counselor a chance to eliminate any "boo-boos" which would damage student acceptance chances. Typing non-confidential portions of finalized applications is a good assignment for a volunteer student aide. If a counselee feels that another student should not type his application, however, this task should then fall upon an adult secretary or the applicant himself.

Developing expertise in filling out applications should begin in the eighth or ninth grade, when students first become mature enough to apply in writing for various things—part-time jobs, contest entries, class work enrichment projects, etc. A counselor might do well to see that various opportunities to create persuasive written communications abound in the junior and senior high school environments, both curricularly and extra-curricularly. Also, he should seek to inform his younger counselees and their parents of the future value of such skills, including their not always obvious role in helping get into college and win subsidization there.

With the advent of numerous financial aid programs, parents have also become involved in filling out forms. Both CEEB and ACT have created a parents' financial status form, which these organizations use to provide pertinent data to member colleges. Both these forms are highly complicated, and some parents need assistance in completing them. When this is the case, a philosophy similar to that employed with student admissions blanks may be followed, allowing, of course, for parental ability levels. However, because of the highly confidential information required by these financial aid statements, some parents may not wish the counselor to become involved, at least not to the extent of seeing the finished product after all data has been entered. In many cases, this means that the extent of counselor participation will be restricted to obtaining blanks and printed accompanying information for parents, and giving them some preliminary, verbal pointers. Also for this reason, student volunteer aides may not be used for typing these forms.

When a given high school senior sits down to fill out an admissions or financial aid application for the college of his choice, there is no secret bag of tricks a counselor may use in advising him. Each applicant is an individual, with a unique constellation of personality, intellectual, and academic variables. Moreover, each college situation is unique, changing from day to day with the tides and currents of pragmatic needs, philosophic doctrines, and human whimsy. Therefore, each college application counseling case is different, and counselee and counselor must play it as they see it. This is another argument for highly professionalized practice of both personnel services and counseling by counselors, and for tight interweaving of these two counselor tasks. This situation is one of the best examples of unification of counseling and pupil services into one global, intertwined process. If the counselor had a cook book solution to give application blank preparers, he would be a sub-professional technician, not a professional educator. Each case is different, thus calling for a professional approach.

Face-to-face meeting often achieves
what test scores and written applications have not.

The modern college admissions picture is complex, probably unavoidably so. In keeping with the American concept of academic freedom, further educational institutions have considerable leeway in establishing admissions policy. This is as it should be, and the totalitarian alternative to it would result in many more student injustices than does the present system. There are, of course, certain strictures placed upon admissions policies by outside authority, even in the free American system. Public junior colleges and state colleges are the least autonomous, many being required by city ordinance or state law to accept all resident applicants, in the former case, and all resident applicants with a high school diploma, in the latter case. State universities are also subject to state law in the admissions area, but some have nevertheless been successful in excluding very low academic ranking applicants. Private colleges and universities are freer of outside controls than are public ones, but even they may find themselves subservient to a religious denomination, or to non-academic interests on their boards of trustees. Profit-making further-educational institutions, mainly the nursing schools and business colleges, are the freest from outside influences of all. Occasionally, however, these two types of schools find financial considerations rather than governmental or religious ones acting to influence admissions policies. The crazy-quilt status quo does create certain inequalities, of course, and it's this author's contention that only direct human interaction, not letters, phone calls, or even invoking of obscure rules, can straighten most of these out.

First however, let's also consider the current financial aid situation. If admissions may be termed complex, financial aid is chaotic, for all sorts of programs, funded by innumerable souces, are bandied about in as many ways as there are persons administering them! For instance, a modern college financial aid office adminsters scholarship, fellowship, tuition grant, loan, work-study, and plain old part-time job programs. These draw their funding from federal, state, foundation, institutional, and private sectors. And eligibility criteria vary widely from school to school, and less admittedly so, from administrator to administrator. This bureaucratic wonderland frequently suffers from confusion problems, as the reader might assume. This, in turn, results in occasional unfair treatment of youthful applicants. And here is where the counselor comes in. Is there any way he may help his clients achieve justice in receiving financial aid for higher education?

Before undertaking any direct intervention, or suggesting this avenue to clients, a counselor must do his homework and build his contacts. Any of several recent books on college admissions procedures and policies should be in every secondary guidance office. A subscription to the professional journal of the Association of College Admissions Counselors is a wise investment. Technical reports of the CEEB and ACT are *must* reading. Two valuable references for understanding the financial aid situation are the College Board's *A Design for a Model College Financial Aid Office,* and the ACT's *Your Financial Aid Applicants.* Knowledge of some little-known institutional policy or obscure government regulation may yield dividends later, when the counselor is able to quote it. Knowing all the programs and all the rules can put the counselor in a position of demanding admission or granting of subsidy to his client by a college. Such knowledgeability enables a counselor to combat the one evil inherent to the American academic freedom system—individual human arbitrariness.

College admissions and financial aid officers are members of the guidance profession, as are school counselors. By being active in state and local personnel and guidance association chapters (APGA affiliated), and state guidance associations (NEA affiliated), secondary counselors have occasion to interact with their college personnel counterparts. The value of both professional and social contacts that result is crucial. Attendance at college public relations functions, such as admissions conferences, is another must. Still another is the inviting of college guidance workers to workshops and meetings held by school groups.

The decision to visit a college admissions or financial aid office and plead a student's cause in person can only be made by the student himself. While the counselor must be willing to accompany the student and to help him prepare his case, it's up to the youngster to present it. This approach is consonant with the previously spelled-out rationale upon which this entire book is based: only the client can make his own decisions and take the initiative in implementing them. To alter this premise is to foster immaturity and irresponsibility. The counselor, as a facilitator and helper who cares, certainly may assist and advise the student, provided that the major premise of self-help is met. After all, if this is not the case, why have counselors? Then too, it's assumed that a decision has been made during counseling that the college in question is a reasonable academic choice for the applicant-supplicant.

When a pupil decides that an in-person interview is desirable, he and his counselor carefully plan the college visitation. With client permission, the counselor may ask other properly concerned adults to call or write the college official, bringing factual evidence to his attention. Parents, teachers, principal, the client's part-time job employer, his clergyman, etc., are good possibilities. Of course, to remain professional, such persuasive communications must not degenerate to a badgering campaign, nor should they ever resort to distortion of facts.

The actual visit, for psychological reasons, is usually best undertaken unannounced, to the office of the official in question, during his normal working hours. The counselor has first checked with the college official's secretary to avoid arriving when he is away or unduly busy. Both counselor and client meet with the personnel worker in question; a strategy mutually determined during previous counseling is followed. The client does most of the talking; at this stage, the counselor's role is largely one of emotional support. If at all possible, the three participants have lunch or at least refreshments together while their discussion continues informally. The psychological effects of bargaining over food or beverage are mystical, but they are profound! This book is not a proper place in which to suggest actual persuasive arguments for a student to employ in the situation being described. These will be shaped by the personalities of the three individuals involved, by the cognitive facts of the client's particular circumstances, and by the policies and characteristics of the institution from which admission or financial aid is being sought. Such arguments will become obvious to counselor and counselee during their discussions preceding college visitation.

WHAT LIES AHEAD?

As the college admission and financial aid picture becomes more complex due to the increased numbers of both students and programs, modern computer technology will no doubt play an even bigger role. This is good; even greater reliance upon data processing is a wise trend, as it promises to simplify personnel procedures for countless students. It also, one suspects, will lessen the frequency of unfair treatment of individual applicants. Greater reliance upon data processing means greater reliance upon statistical rules, and thus better overall fairness. Despite technological advances, however, the human element will always remain in the admissions/financial aid picture. Therefore, there will always be a need for counselors to render professional service to clients desiring assistance in this area.

SIX

Building a Utilitarian Testing Program

The mere mention of the word "testing" evokes a
flow of questions in any school: Who chooses tests?
What tests are best? How often should various tests be
given?—and so on. Are there any guidelines counselors
may use as they seek to build the best possible testing
program for their school?

WHY TEST IN THE FIRST PLACE?

In far too many school systems, the standardized testing program
has become a permanent fixture which needs no explanation or
justification. — "Why test? Why because you're supposed to, that's
why! Now get back to work and quit asking silly questions!" — This
little monologue aptly stereotypes the attitide of some school
administrators, and sadly, a few counselors as well. Testing has
become, in numerous schools, something like the uniform ten-foot
elevation of baskets in the gymnasium—an unquestioned, taken-for-
granted fixture. A few critics of U.S. education have dared to
question the validity of standardized appraisal procedures employed
in the schools. Some have even condemned testing as a part of a
communist plot to destroy the fibre of our society through promo-
tion of sexual promiscuity among the young. Other, more restrained
critics, while not condemning testing per se, have pointed out various
misuses of the process.

Had schools been more careful in their use of tests in the first
place, and taken steps to explain reasons for standardized evaluation
to their publics, testing would not have come under fire. The
counselor, as director of the testing program, has the obligation to
insure that tests are used properly, and that they are adequately

explained to students, parents, teachers, and administrators. Failure to do so not only wastes money and decreases reliability of test results, but also invites the invective and censure of well-meaning patriotic groups, who perceive tests as unwholesome influences upon the young. Why *do* we test? What rationalizations should a counselor have ready when called upon to explain standardized appraisal endeavors?

Students receive concrete evidence of their academic strengths and weaknesses.

No counselor should ever administer a group intelligence or achievement test to students without first promising a score interpretation interview to anyone who wants one. Moreover, preliminary testing remarks must spell out why a youngster should want a score interpretation in the first place. Basically, intelligence or scholastic aptitude tests may be represented as measures of how well we think or "take to" figuring things out. It's important to know this because the test scores will show how we rate, compared to other teen-agers all over the country (national percentile norms). This information will help later in planning what colleges or vocational schools to attend, and/or what type(s) of job(s) to seek, and/or what program to pursue if we enter the armed forces.

So-called achievement/proficiency type tests tell how much we know about different school subjects, or how aptly we perform various academic skills, such as mathematical computations. It's good to know these things, because it will help us plan what to take if we later go on to further education, or what more we need to learn in order to get a certain job after graduation. After all, it helps us to know more about ourselves for a number of reasons. A final caution should always be given students immediately prior to testing: namely, assurance that each testee's scores will not be revealed to other students must be made. However, it's also wise to promise that group "average" scores will be told to pupils. This will allow them to compare their collective performance to that of previous classes (local percentile norms), and it is often a motivating factor of considerable magnitude.

Parents learn where their children stand.

Parents have a right to know their own children's compulsory group testing program intelligence and achievement percentile scores. They also should be told class average scores, so they may better evaluate their own son's or daughter's relative performance. They should not be told, without client permission, test scores that result from individual appraisal during counseling. These are not part of the regular testing program. Parents utilize score information to appraise the relative intellectual and academic standings of their offspring on national, regional, and local bases. In order to do this, however, they need adequate briefing on fundamental measurement concepts. Especially important for parents to understand are what tests measure, and what is a percentile score, norm group, and standard error of measurement. Several of the large test companies publish excellent explanatory leaflets, which counselors may obtain free for use in helping to explain these and other measurement concepts to parents. When parents comprehend the values of test scores to themselves and to their children, they are more apt to be supportive of the school's evaluational procedures. It is normally unwise to reveal IQ scores to students or parents unless they possess unusual statistical expertise, and thus grasp a mean- and-standard deviation type score's correct meaning. Percentiles are generally the route to go when informing parents of pupil intellectual capacities.

Occasionally, some parents become very adamant, demanding to know their offspring's IQ score. Without getting into the many legal and public relations ramifications of this ticklish situation, it's possible to suggest a guiding procedure for handling it. When this happens, a joint conference should be arranged, with the participants being both parents, principal and counselor. It's very important that both parents be present; this rule should never be broken except when one parent is absent due to death or divorce. Whether or not the child is also in attendance must be decided by the other four participants; in some cases this is desirable, in others not.

Counselor strategy during such a meeting goes like this: "We'll be happy to tell you your son's group IQ score, if you'll first go over with the principal and me the reasons why educators normally don't like to reveal IQ's." The counselor and principal next go over the following: (1) Too many things vary for an IQ score to always be a constant factor. (a) The score itself can fluctuate over several testings, due to standard error of measurement. (b) The youngster is apt to vary—minor illness and anxieties often cause a score to be unduly low. (c) Tests themselves vary—an IQ score from a test with a standard deviation of 10 is not the same as one from a test having a standard deviation of 17. (Here, a layman's explanation of what a standard deviation is is in order.) (d) Test situations themselves vary—if the students have tonight's big football game on their minds, scores may suffer. (2) We're not sure just how closely intelligence tests measure "true" or "pure" intelligence, or even functional capacities. Consequently, an IQ is not comparable to a medical blood test, for example, which yields very accurate blood analyses. Yet lay persons, not knowing this, put so much faith in the accuracy of IQ scores that they tend to become stereotypes, leading to many family problems, etc. (3) Schools don't want parents or students comparing each other's IQ scores, as this often leads to unwholesome family, sibling, and peer group rivalries.

When this explanation has been made, tell the parents the score. Play down its importance, and caution them not to reveal it to others, because of the factors discussed. If the child has scored unduly low, offer to retest privately using a different instrument, or to have a district psychometrist administer a WAIS or BINET.

Teachers have a chance to gauge effectiveness of past approaches, and to plan for the future.

Many counselors use teachers to disseminate student test score reports and to provide general class score interpretations, via the medium of homeroom group guidance. This is a wise move, as it not only saves the counselor much work, but it also familiarizes teachers with test results. When this is done, however, teachers must be cautioned to respect the privacy of individual student score reports. A highly effective technique for application of test scores to teaching improvement is to figure separate local achievement test norms for high, low, and average intelligence sub-groups as established from scholastic aptitude test reports. Then, teachers may ascertain their relative effectiveness with each of the three student intelligence level categories. Some test companies compute such score reports for an additional fee. Teachers may also profit from comparing test scores, over a period of time. For example, did last year's chemistry students, taught via textbook, score as highly as this year's, taught by the inductive method? Test scores also help teachers plan strategies for educating future pupils. For instance, if senior high algebra and general math teachers find incoming junior high students weak in multiplication skills, as revealed on a sub-test of a mathematics achievement battery, they may plan their teaching to remedy this deficiency.

**Administrators and board members obtain
objective data for analyzing the curriculum and student body needs.**

Test scores, when viewed in overall district perspective and in historical dimension, help those charged with running the schools to spot critical trends. For example, if district-wide results reveal English scores to be above national averages while mathematics scores are below, this could suggest that a beefing-up of the math curriculum is in order. If a steady drop in intelligence test percentiles over a ten-year period was observed, this might reveal that significant changes in district population composition were occurring, and so on. Caution must always be urged by counselors when interpreting test results to superiors, especially in the realm of conclusion-jumping. For instance, a rise in achievement scores may not necessarily be due to improved instructional quality, nor is a drop always indicative of inferior teaching. Board members, not being professional educators, may need special help in fathoming score report meanings. In this regard, they may fail to understand that intelligence test scores do not rise as a person becomes learned, as might achievement test results. This misconception could lead to the erroneous conclusion that a high school student body population whose mean IQ was 95 was being inadequately educated. Counselors, in the role of consultant to administrators and board members, must use their knowledge of measurement to stamp out such inaccuracies.

PLANNING THE PROGRAM

What's been done before is not necessarily wrong—or right.

The few counselors who take positions in brand-new secondary schools, or in those which never before had a testing program, are fortunate indeed. There are no set precedents which might tie a counselor's hands as he seeks to establish his testing program. Often, what has gone before dictates what will prevail, at least for awhile, in the future. This is especially true in the financial realm, where if a large quantity of reusable test booklets have been purchased, a counselor may be under heavy administrative pressure to continue their use until worn out or obsolete. If such pressure doesn't exist, a new counselor or group of counselors may get the urge to clean house, and change the testing program just for the sake of change. Unless the tests currently used are obsolete, having been supplanted by more recent editions, they should not be discarded before careful study. If this scrutiny does point to needs for change, sometimes costs may be held down through sale or trade of unwanted reusable test booklets to nearby school districts or parochial schools. Because perceived student needs change, teaching methods and curricula change, necessitating changes in testing programs, or at least in the statistical treatments given their data. This factor, student needs, should be the prime consideration in any deliberations upon whether to change or not.

Coordination with feeder schools and sister institutions is a must—but can be overdone.

Frequently, a test-producing company will seek an entire school district's business, arguing that the interests of continuity are served by using the same tests (in different forms) at both elementary and secondary levels. Also frequently heard is the argument that all high schools in a district should use the same tests in order to facilitate district-wide data analysis and comprehension of scores of intra-district transfer pupils. Both these arguments have a certain degree of validity, the latter a bit more than the former. However, it may also be argued that if counselors, well versed in measurement concepts, are serving as consultants to their various internal publics, such vertical and horizontal continuity is not a necessity. If, for example, the feeder elementary schools of a junior-senior high school are using the California Test of Mental Maturity and Comprehensive Test of Basic Skills, while the secondary level prefers the Lorge-Thorndike and Iowa Tests of Educational Development, this is not necessarily catastrophic. The counselor, as consultant to pupils, parents, teachers, and administration, should be able to compare, through his knowledge of measurement, score profiles of incoming sixth graders to those of seventh graders, and so on.

Even if one district high school is using the SCAT and STEP, while another preferes the Henmon-Nelson and Metropolitan Achievement Tests, this is not hopeless. While direct district-wide comparisons are thus not possible, it might be that differences in student body and faculty make-up, which initially brought about the differences, are more important than unit-wide uniformity. Here again, the counselor, or in a larger district, guidance director, serving as consultant to central administration and school board, should be able to reasonably compare two sets of test scores. Some districts have sought uniformity, but with a degree of diversity, by alternating two different companies' intelligence and achievement batteries through elementary and secondary years. When this is done, generally one battery is administered in odd-numbered grades, another in even ones. While no panacea, this system has several advantages, centering around diversity without abandonment of some degree of uniformity. Generally speaking, the greater the homogeneity of pupil population, district-wide, the stronger the argument for testing uniformity becomes. The greater the school-to-school pupil heterogeneity, the stronger the argument for diversity.

The counselor must involve pupils, teachers, and administrators in test selection, and brief them on fundamental measurement concepts.

Whenever changes are contemplated in the testing program, it's best for the counselor to include those who will be effected in his decision-making. The most radical departure from tradition here is, of course, giving students a voice. Such a move is not, however, as far-out as it might first seem. First of all, there are many pupils who have the intellectual capacity to profit from this assignment. Thus, being included upon a test-planning committee is realistic, both in terms of eliciting their intellectual contributions for the task at hand, and providing them with meaningful educational experiences. Second, if students are given a voice in an endeavor, they are much more likely to regard it positively and to cooperate in bringing it to fruition. Understanding why something is done and what problems its operation entails is bound to increase their appreciation of it. Third, when a counselor cares enough about pupils to allow them a say in choosing tests, they will care enough about these tests later to help him run the program. There will be lots of test administration-connected jobs—alphabetizing answer sheets, mending reusable booklets, distributing materials, etc.—and it's nice to have a few hands helping to lighten the counselor's subprofessional work load.

Teachers have a right to be heard in test selection. They too gain from examining test results, as do pupils. Teachers need these scores to appraise their past efforts and to plan strategies to best fit specific intellectual/academic characteristics of incoming students. Consequently, they need to examine various test batteries prior to adoption, so as to determine which best meet their needs. Administrators likewise need to evaluate instructional effectiveness and to plan for future pupil needs, but in this case, it's the overall school perspective that's under scrutiny. Both teachers and administrators will be needed later during testing, the former as proctors and the latter as modifiers of bell schedules and intercom usage, to accommodate actual test administration. If these groups have had their say during preliminary operations, they'll much more willingly and knowledgeably cooperate during test administration.

In making up a committee of this type, the counselor should not choose persons for membership already known to reflect his point of view. This defeats the very purpose of the group. One procedure is to invite class officers or student government to nominate one or two pupils from each class, after first explaining to the nominators what will be required of those chosen. Each head teacher or academic department chairman is asked to name one teacher from his or her area, preferably one with an interest in measurement. The administrator invited to participate should be one officially charged with evaluation of the instructional program. In a small school this means the principal, while in a larger one it means a vice principal for instruction. Very large districts often have committees of this nature which include students, teachers, and administrators from several schools. A director of pupil personnel services, rather than a building's head counselor, then serves as organizer.

When the group is assembled, the counselor first must brief members on background facts. What tests are in use now? Why is a change contemplated? What things do we want to learn through testing? These are three preliminary points to clarify. Next, basic factual measurement concepts must be explained. What is a scholastic aptitude test? An achievement battery? Why is each needed? What are percentiles? Norm groups? Band scores? Serving as consultant to his publics, the counselor utilizes his grasp of the field of measurement to set the tone for discussions to follow.

Test company salesmen will visit planning sessions and explain their services.

When the selection committee has been prepared, it's time to invite area representatives of large test-producing companies to appear and tout their wares. In order to utilize each salesman's time most profitably, it's best to have test specimen sets and manuals sent ahead. (This is especially crucial because some tests are harder than others; a perfectly good test for one school or grade level may be inappropriate for some others.) Then, committee members will have had an opportunity to peruse materials, and have questions ready. Such ordering and inviting is usually done via telephone or mail, using the yellow pages of the nearest large city telephone directory as reference. When the meeting with test firm representative occurs, it should be held in a conference-type room, conducive to free interchange of ideas. A blackboard should be available if needed. Whenever possible, the test salesman's visit should be arranged contiguous to or overlapping a school lunch period, so the salesman may eat conveniently during his visit. Ideally, the entire selection committee brings its lunch into the conference room, so the group may gain from informal discussion and interaction while eating. This type of beginning is the soundest possible foundation upon which to build a testing program.

Are some tests better than others, and how does one tell?

A complete answer to this question would require a book-length volume. The reader is referred to the most recent edition of Buros' *Mental Measurements Yearbook* for critiques of specific tests. Any of the several books cited in the bibliography at the end of this work will provide factual learning which will enable a reader to acquire test evaluating expertise of his own. There are a few basic questions which serve to establish the groundwork for examining tests, however, which may be used as fundamental departure points for test evaluation:

(1) How old is the test? Have new educational approaches appeared on the scene since its publication, making its evaluative spectrum obsolete?

(2) What are the published reliability and validity data, as determined by scientific investigation? That is, how consistently does the test measure, and how well does it measure what it purports to measure? (Publishers' technical manuals and articles in the several measurement journals listed in Chapter Fourteen provide references.)

(3) Upon what kind of norm group was the test developed? How large was the group? Were all kinds of youngsters included—regionally, ethnically, intellectually, and from both public and private schools?

(4) Does the test serve the needs of the school? Does it yield data wanted by students, teachers, administrators, and counselors?

(5) What about costs?—How do this test's costs, relative to what is gotten out of the test, compare to costs of other instruments, on both long and short term bases?

(6) How about ease of administration and consumption of school time? Considering the quality and quantity of data yielded, is this battery more difficult to administer than its competitors? If so, is the added trouble worthwhile? How do the data yield and costs per lost class period measure up? Could another instrument give us more and consume less school time for testing?

A TYPICAL PROGRAM

In the strict sense of the word, there's no such thing as a "typical" testing program, as each school's selected appraisal instruments have been chosen to meet specific local needs. However, there are certain identifiable commonalities among all measurement programs. These include types of tests used and various basic problems connected with the *hows, whens,* and *whys* of using them.

There are four families of standardized appraisal instruments.

While innumerable measurement instruments are offered for sale by over 30 companies and agencies, tests may be broken down into four general types. The first test family contains so-called ability, or intelligence-type measures. These are tests which measure innate ability to perform intellectually, although no standardized ability measure yet devised is completely free from the effect of prior learning. These instruments are subdivided into two major categories, both of which contain individual and group tests. (Individual tests, more accurate than group ones, are more expensive to administer, as only one client may be tested at a time, by a highly trained examiner.) The two subdivisions of ability tests are the so-called "pure" or "general" intelligence tests, measuring ability for its own sake, and "aptitude" tests, which seek to measure ability to perform a socially envolved area such as school work (applied intelligence). The former category is often further subdivided into two components found in almost all intelligence tests, verbal and non-verbal. Verbal intelligence test sub-scores are derived from items containing words, and non-verbal ones from items employing numbers or symbols. The latter category also has two subdivisions, namely, so-called scholastic aptitude tests, which measure ability to do academic school work, and special aptitude tests, measuring adeptness in mechanical, artistic, musical, and similar areas. The following outline graphically portrays this breakdown of ability measures, listing several better-known tests in each category. An important point must always be kept in mind when considering ability tests: there's no fine line between general intelligence-type tests and scholastic and special aptitude-type tests. Operation of human mental faculties is a complex process, and no one has yet been able to fully differentiate between manifestations of innate and applied ability. (Note: This is not a comprehensive list of tests, only an illustrative one. Many fine instruments are not listed below due to space limitations.)

    I. Ability tests
      A. Intelligence
        1. individual
          (a)   Stanford-Binet
          (b)   WAIS
             (1)   verbal
             (2)   non-verbal
        2. group
          (a)   Otis-Lennon
          (b)   Henmon-Nelson
          (c)   Lorge-Thorndike
             (1)   verbal
             (2)   non-verbal
          (d)   Kuhlmann-Anderson
             (1)   verbal
             (2)   non-verbal
          (e)   Miller Analogies
      B. Aptitude
        1. scholastic aptitude
          (a)   DAT
          (b)   SAT
          (c)   SCAT
        2. special aptitude
          (a)   GATB
          (b)   Orleans-Hanna Algebra Prognosis
          (c)   SRA Mechanical Aptitudes
          (d)   Seashore Measures of Musical Talents

A second great family of standardized appraisal instruments are knowledge tests. Whereas ability tests measure innate capacity to learn *before the fact* (prognosis), knowledge tests try to ascertain what has been learned *after the fact* (diagnosis). This family includes both test batteries, or groups of tests designed to measure overall school attainment, and specialized tests aimed at appraising one area only, sold separately for this purpose by test companies. Knowledge tests are subdivided into two categories, namely, achievement tests, which measure the amount of factual material known, and proficiency tests, which measure the ability to perform certain academic skills, such as mathematical multiplication or English sentence diagramming. All knowledge test batteries used in high schools contain both achievement and proficiency components, with the former measurement concept predominating in social studies and science, and the latter paramount in mathematics. It must be noted here that there is no complete separation of what is measured in scholastic aptitude (ability) tests and in achievement tests, nor is there complete separation between special aptitude (ability) tests and proficiency tests. This unavoidable overlap does create a flaw in pure theoretical approaches to measurement, but it is somewhat pooh-poohed by pragmatists, who point out that if test scores are utilitarian for school purposes, so what? The following outline lists some knowledge tests widely used at the secondary level. Here again, the list is illustrative, not comprehensive, and many excellent instruments are omitted for brevity's sake.

II. Knowledge Tests
  A. Achievement
    1. batteries
      (a) STEP   (mostly achievement content)
      (b) ITED   (..   ..   ..   )
      (c) NEDT (..   ..   ..   )
      (d) ACT   (..   ..   ..   )
    2. specialized tests
      (a) Nelson Biology Test
      (b) Cooperative Science Tests
      (c) MLA Cooperative Foreign Language Tests
  B. Proficiency
    1. batteries
      (a) STEP (math portions)
      (b) ITED (certain language and math portions)
      (c) NEDT (math portions)
    2. specialized tests
      (a) Nelson-Denny Reading Test
      (b) Blyth Second-Year Algebra Test

The third family of measurement instruments are the so-called interest inventories. These measure testee inclinations toward various fields of endeavor. Much has already been written in this book

(Chapter Three) on the two best-known interest inventories, the Kuder and the Strong, so a somewhat cursory coverage will be undertaken here. Basically, interest inventories used to be called aptitude tests, an incorrect term, as they neither measure aptitude nor are they "tests," in the strict sense of the word. (Aptitude connotes relative facility in doing something, whereas interest merely connotes degree of concern for doing it.) A true test appraises a relative amount of some quality (intelligence, achievement, etc.) inherent to a person, while an inventory assesses his area of inclination, regardless of facility.

Interest inventories represent a transitional area between measurement of academic traits (ability and knowledge) and measurement of the affective domain (personality). While not tests, interest inventories make use of the same statistical concepts, such as percentile scores, reliability and validity coefficients, and norm groups, and for this reason may be considered standardized, objective measures. The common interest inventories, suitable for senior high usage, are listed below. (This author takes the position that interest inventories are not statistically valid for use in junior high schools.)

    III. Interest Inventories
        A. Brainard Occupational Preference Inventory
        B. Gordon Occupational Check List
        C. Guilford-Zimmerman Interest Inventory
        D. Kuder—(four related, separate inventories)
        E. Minnesota Vocational Interest Inventory
        F. Strong Vocational Interest Blank (two forms, boys and girls)

The fourth family of appraisal instruments is the affectively oriented group which contains so-called personality tests, attitude inventories, and projective techniques. These seek to measure testee emotional dimensions, and for this reason should never be administered on a mass, compulsory basis. They do have a place in the high school testing program, however, *provided that the counselor is qualified to administer and interpret them.* Their usage should be confined to individual counseling situations. Basically, these affectively oriented instruments are divided into two categories, objective tests and projective techniques. The former are composed of definite test items, with scores reported in terms of percentiles, as are ability and knowledge tests. The latter, generally administerable on a one-to-one basis only, involve a highly trained examiner who categorizes client responses to pictorial stimuli. Because of the greater problems of objectivity and reliability inherent in projective techniques, their usage is largely restricted to clinical settings where supplementary diagnostic information is also available. There are many, many personality and attitude tests, inventories, and standardized techniques. The following outline is therefore only illustrative.

    IV. Affectively Oriented Measures
        A. Objective Personality tests and attitude inventories
           1. MMPI-MCI
           2. California Test of Personality
           3. Eysenck Personality Inventory
           4. Gordon Personal Inventory
           5. Mooney Problem Check List
        B. Projective Techniques
           1. TAT
           2. Rorschach Ink Blot Test

All testing programs contain compulsory and voluntary components.

Every secondary school in America probably uses some standardized appraisal battery which is required of all students. Almost every counselor keeps in his desk or file cabinet some extra, specialized tests which are given only as need arises during counseling. Compulsory testing takes place for several reasons beside counseling: curriculum improvement, instructional evaluation, and district assessment. It generally, at both junior and senior high levels, contains at least one ability measure, and a yearly knowledge measure, usually in the form of a so-called achievement battery. Specialized tests are required as need arises, such as an algebra prognosis test to help eighth graders choose between ninth-grade general math and algebra, and a GATB to assist twelfth graders with career decisions. The compulsory aspect should only contain group ability and knowledge measures. Individual ability tests, interest inventories, and affectively oriented (personality) measures should be administered on a private, voluntary basis, if and when need for them becomes apparent during counseling. To do otherwise not only seriously curtails the validity of scores obtained under compulsory conditions, but is also apt to bring irate parents and members of conservatively oriented patriotic groups down hard upon the counselor!

Another form of voluntary measurement activity contains group knowledge and/or ability tests which are part of special projects.

These include the NEDT and PSAT for possibly college-bound pupils, the Air Force Qualification Test for those considering the military, and so on. Some schools give the GATB to seniors on an optional basis, aiming mainly at terminal youngsters. Still another type of voluntary testing is found in the various projects that occur elsewhere, but in which the school participates. The main example of these tests are the four nation-wide programs for those planning to go on to further education—CEEB, ACT, NLN, PCT (See Chapter Four).

How much testing and when to do it are often debated by counselors and others.

Looking at the six years of secondary education (or four in districts using the middle school plan), the question arises, "How much is enough?" This is a complex issue and the reader is referred to one of several excellent books on testing referenced at the back of this book for detailed discussion. Basically, most persons feel that two batteries per year is too heavy an incursion into instructional time and too costly, and to skip a year without any testing, while saving money, creates too many informational gaps to be practical. There is considerable debate over whether an ability measure is needed every year, or in some large city systems, ever on a compulsory basis. Some districts prefer to give their initial, junior high level ability measure late during sixth grade, while incoming students are still in elementary school. This has the advantage of making scores available during the summer for various planning purposes. However, in inner city and suburban areas, high pupil transfer rates may rule out, as many of the tested sixth graders leave the district during summer months, thus wasting the money expended on testing them. Moreover, a horde of incoming transfer students need to be tested in the fall, which has led many counselors to advocate testing everyone in the fall. This saves the trouble of make-ups.

Many authorities feel that an ability measure should be given every other year, that is, three of the six secondary school years. In a stable population, however, this approach centers around alternation of knowledge measures. Some schools prefer to use two different achievement/proficiency batteries, giving one battery in grades seven, nine, and eleven, and another in eight, ten, and twelve. The increasing tendency of test companies to "plug in" ability test scores statistically with knowledge ones for various comparison purposes thus necessitates either giving an ability measure every year or coding in the appropriate last year's score with current knowledge scores. This tends to tie or bind a school to one company's service, as many schools do not wish to pay the costs of yearly ability testing of all students.

Several large city school systems, of which New York City is the prime example, have made even group ability measures voluntary, because of complaints from black and Spanish-surnamed persons. The minority group spokesmen have pointed out that many standardized group ability measures are not wholly "culture-free," and thus discriminate against non-white and non-Anglo testees. This is a valid criticism, but it has been somewhat exaggerated for purposes of emphasis by some persons. Some districts have sought to find relatively culture-free tests as a result; interest in the Raven Progressive Matrices probably stems from this situation. In an area where this situation prevails, it's possibly best to reserve ability testing to special cases, using voluntary, individual measures. This could mean a WISC or WAIS given to black youngsters by a black psychometrist, and a Spanish language Stanford-Binet given to Mexican-American or Chicano and Puerto Rican youngsters by a Spanish-speaking psychometrist.

When (during the school year) to test is a lively debated issue. Fundamentally, there are three options from which to choose: near the start of the school year, in the middle, and near the end. There are no rules of thumb for deciding which time is best for which schools, but it's generally felt that high pupil turnover schools, mostly in inner-city ghettos and in affluent suburbs and near military installations, are wasting money by testing in the spring. Conversely, relatively stable student population schools—those in more static large city neighborhoods, in farming communities, and in many private schools—may be better off with spring testing, as this allows the leisurely, all-summer study of results by school personnel. An argument often raised against spring testing is that students must wait at least three and a half months (until they return in the fall) for score interpretations, and will have forgotten what the tests were like. An argument for spring testing is that teachers will have the best opportunity to assess instructional effectiveness for a given school year immediately at its conclusion. Some schools seek a compromise by testing earlier in the spring, rushing to interpret scores to students before they leave for vacation, then administratively studying scores over the summer. The advent of year-round school (quarter system,

15-45 plan, etc.) renders this debate obsolete, but poses some new test scheduling problems.

Fall testing has the advantage of assessing each youngster near the onset of the school year in question. It also gives pupils and teachers a chance to do something about things learned from test scores "right now," not next year. Mid-year testing probably came about as a compromise between early and late year evaluative philosophies. It lends itself nicely to calendars of schools that take a long Christmas vacation; i.e., answer sheets are away being scored while school is not in session anyway, thus no school time goes by while waiting for score reports.

When to test during the school day and week is also controversial. Some persons believe that testing should occur only in mornings, for physiological reasons. Schools employing this thinking often devote three half days or four one-third days to testing, running regular classes during the afternoons. While the physiological basis of this thinking is probably correct at the elementary school level, some persons question its applicability to adolescents. Other schools prefer to test one and three fourths or even two full days running, to get it over with quickly. Because truancy is always greatest on Fridays and Mondays, such testing is done in mid-week of a full five-day week, thus cutting down on the number of make-ups. A somewhat opposite philosophy, which also has many advocates, is the idea of using so-called two- or three-day "busted weeks" for testing—before state education association meetings, Thanksgiving, or Christmas vacations, between semesters, around Easter or Memorial Day, etc. The theory here is that since such shortened weeks are already imperfect for instructional activities, why not abandon them wholly and concentrate fully on appraisal? Each local situation is different, and quite possibly one approach is best for some schools, while a different one is best for others.

The counselor's publics must understand the "whys" of testing.

An interesting research study done on two groups of senior high pupils is worthy of mention here. Each group received the same nationally renowned, standardized scholastic aptitude battery. One group first went through a group guidance orientation process, during which members were carefully told the whys of testing, including what benefits they stood to gain. The other group received no orientation, other than being told that the school required them to take the test battery. The examiner found a statistically significant difference between the two groups, with the intensively oriented group receiving the higher scores. This finding should tell all counselors something! Namely, take time to tell the boys and girls *why*, and they'll get more out of testing. While no empirical evidence exists, a school superintendent who sought to explain measurement to high school students of a large middle-eastern district prior to testing has reported a considerable drop in absenteeism during testing over that reported in previous years. This should also tell us something!

The counselor's other three major publics, parents, teachers, and administrators, may also need some briefing regarding "what is in it for them." A great body of research evidence in the field of psychology points to the conclusion that people support and regard positively that which they fully understand. Conversely, they suspect and often oppose programs which they regard ambiguously.

A counselor must be prepared to interpret
individual scores to clients and parents,
and school-wide trends to teachers and administrators.

Some counseling programs make use of teacher-led group guidance sessions and/or explanatory literature furnished by test companies to facilitate score interpretation to youngsters and their parents. In most cases this is a wise move, as it saves counselors many hours of going over and over rudimentary measurement concepts. However, there's always a need for explanatory counseling interviews, individually with counselees, with small groups of teen-agers who wish to share their otherwise confidential scores, and with concerned pairs of parents. A whole book could be written on how to proceed with score interpretation; the following are but summary considerations: (1) Explain that a test has imperfections, and that a score is not wholly constant or final, reliability and validity being what they are. (2) Tell the difference between the two kinds of scores—ability and knowledge—yielded by compulsory programs, making sure that clients grasp the difference. (3) Rely heavily upon the percentile and norm group system of reporting scores: "John, according to this one test, you're at the 80th percentile in natural science. This means that among all the eleventh graders in the nation, you know more about science than four fifths of them, and less than one fifth of them." (4) Never, never, *never* be definitive: "John, this test proves you shouldn't go to college." Such a statement is never justified and is as out of place in a school as the statement "Heil, Hitler." Rather, say something like, "John, according to this one test, it appears that you might experience scholastic difficulty in college, especially in some universities."

While teachers and administrators may properly be expected to more fully grasp measurement principles than students and parents, counselors shouldn't take too much for granted. The basic tenet here is to caution colleagues that *correlation is not necessarily proof of causation.* For example, the fact that English achievement scores are lower among Miss Jones' students than among Mrs. Smith's doesn't mean Miss Jones is an inferior teacher, or even that Mrs. Smith is superior in ability to her. Even when ability test scores are lower in one school than in another, this may not mean that students in one school are "dumber" than those in the higher-scoring school. The basic job of the counselor as measurement consultant is to assist fellow faculty in spotting and analyzing trends. For instance, in one school district, a mysterious drop in verbal intelligence test scores and a rise in non-verbal scores over a ten-year period was traced to a change in student body composition. A large industry employing many engineers and other mathematically oriented persons had moved into the district; children of these parents tended to perform like their parents on ability measures, thus influencing test results.

Public relations values of aggregate test scores shouldn't be overlooked.

It's unethical, of course, to reveal individual pupil test scores to anyone other than the pupil in question and his parents, teachers, counselor, and principal. There's nothing wrong, however, with telling all the pupils and parents the overall school or class percentile scores. In fact, when these group scores happen to exceed national or regional norms, it might be wise to let the community-at-large in on the good news. Sometimes the best way to silence inaccurate, highly critical individuals who attack the school is to report school or district-wide knowledge test percentiles via area news media. A decision to resort to such means always rests with the superintendent. When the go-ahead to publish aggregate scores is received, the counselor, working closely with district public information officers, is called upon to help with the story. This assignment calls upon all the score interpretation skills a counselor has, as many newspaper readers, while not necessarily illiterate or "dumb," are very unfamiliar with measurement concepts. Basically, journalistic score interpretation centers around the nature of knowledge test batteries, and an explanation of percentile scores and norm groups. It goes without saying that ability test scores, even when group averages, must be very carefully handled when released, if they are used at all. Of course, interest test scores and those of affectively oriented instruments, even on a group basis, must *never* be published.

SUMMARY CONSIDERATIONS

Testing need not be a boring or dreaded obligation if this personnel service is approached in terms of what benefits it offers to each of the counselor's publics. The first task in building a utilitarian testing program is to see that pupils, parents, teachers, administrators, and most crucial of all, the counseling staff, appreciates what standardized measurement will do for them. The next task is to involve representatives of each of these publics in planning the program. A little teaching on the part of the counselor is in order here. It's his job to see that all concerned know what the different kinds of tests are, and have a rudimentary grasp of basic measurement concepts. Lastly, when scores are available, they must be put to work. Each public needs interpretive information, and it's the counselor's duty to furnish it.

SEVEN

Running the Testing Program Smoothly

A million and one little chores seem to confront the counselor as he seeks to run the testing program correctly, and neglect of any one minor detail threatens to ruin the whole operation. There are some ways for cutting down on the hecticness of these testing and score-distributing days. What are some procedures for insuring that the testing program operates smoothly?

COUNSELOR AS COMPULSORY TESTING DIRECTOR

The standardized appraisal instruments administered on a required basis in junior and senior high schools are quite differently given, scored, and interpreted than those taken voluntarily by students. For this reason, a counselor may be considered responsible for two testing programs, a compulsory one and a voluntary one. Sometimes tests administered in both types of programs are similar; sometimes even the same instruments are used. But, because of vastly different circumstances surrounding usage, compulsory and voluntary testing really are two distinct programs, and they are treated as such here.

Arrangements begin well in advance of test dates.

Once the selection committee has decided upon which tests to use, and when during the school year to give them, it is up to the counselor to see that proper orders are placed. While the test company salesman will take care of many details, it's the counselor's job, working through his secretary, to make sure that all orders are properly entered. When the various purchased supplies arrive, student aides should be ready to check quantities against orders, as well as to unpack, categorize and store the tests, answer sheets, manuals, and

119

other materials. Aides selected for this honor must be of demonstratedly honest reputations; if any question regarding this exists in the counselor's mind, it's better to have a secretary sort the testing supplies. By ordering far ahead of test dates, there's time to reorder in case supplies arrive short. The counselor must also plan classroom and time of school day utilizations carefully, using classroom or homeroom rosters, room capacity charts, and test manuals as references. He must know just how long each sub-test lasts, both in terms of reading directions and actual testing time. He must know any limitations of the school intercom system, if the building has one, both in terms of operational procedures and rooms not included. If short extensions or contractions of a school day are planned, the counselor must not forget to coordinate these with the bus contractor. If lunch periods are somewhat changed by sub-test length considerations, these changes must be ironed out with the head cook. Even the custodian gets into the act, as the counselor must learn how to turn the bell system on and off, so as to prevent a bell's ringing during a test and thus disturbing the pupils. Most test batteries are so constructed that sub-tests may be administered in any order. This flexibility helps a counselor hold dismissal, lunch, period-end, and other time changes to a minimum.

Thumb-rules for testing environment choice are as follows: (1) In very small schools (100 students and under), herd all students into an auditorium or some other large room, and test them together. the counselor reads test directions "live," while teachers serve as proctors. If two test batteries are used, for example, one for ninth and eleventh graders, and another for tenth and twelfth graders, two large rooms may be used. In this case, a verbally articulate teacher is chosen as a second directions-reader. (2) In larger small schools (100 to around 250 pupils), it's best to use the intercom to give directions, scheduling pupils into from four to eight of the better classrooms, according to class designations. Again, teachers serve as proctors, two to a room. Some authorities disagree with the contention that intercom directions are preferable to teacher-read ones; these counselors advocate having each teacher read instructions to his own homeroom group, regardless of school size. (3) In medium and large schools, intercom directions read by a counselor are best. Here, natural, homeroom testee groupings are the only way to go, in order to avoid confusion and scheduling chaos, with each teacher proctoring his or her respective homeroom. If a larger school wishes two grade-alternated test batteries, this is still possible if plans are carefully laid. When this is the case, the counselor-reader must follow a rigid time-schedule script, in which directions for one test are read to one series of homerooms, then intercom buttons are switched over, and the second series of homerooms receive instructions for their test. Careful planning is needed, so two sets of directions do not occur simultaneously. This procedure can be dangerous, however, and unless the counselor feels conversant with all aspects of such an operation, should not be attempted. Provision must also be made for use of testee waiting time of the group finishing their test battery first. Staggered lunch periods or short class meetings are two possibilities. When two sets of instructions are alternated via intercom, it's wise to color-code the room on-off levers, so no mistakes will be made. A school that does not have an intercom is faced with either grouping all testees into one very large room or relying upon several different direction-readers. Each alternative has serious drawbacks, except in very small schools.

If direction-readers other than counselors are used, it's imperative for a counselor to orient the readers to the whys and wherefores of test administration. Just giving them a test manual isn't enough! Test readers must never be placed in a room without some proctorial assistance—one proctor per 35 pupils is a bare minimum. Proctors should not be asked to serve more than one hour in a stretch, due to the monotonous nature of the duty. Sometimes it's best to ask the principal to issue proctorial assignments over his signature, as some counselors feel it contrary to their professional roles to direct fellow faculty. All of these arrangements must be taken care of well ahead of testing dates. Leaving any of these until the last minute is asking for trouble.

Student volunteers and school secretaries handle sub-professional tasks.

As soon as the selection committee has decided what tests to buy, a whole host of sequential tasks fall into the laps of pupils and clerical personnel. Some of these jobs are rather pedantic and dull, but others offer considerable intellectual stimulation. The counselor, as testing director, should take his secretary and volunteer aides into a sort of junior partnership as deputy and assistant directors. Only truly professional duties connected with measurement should be performed personally by the counselor; lower level tasks must be delegated. The diagram in Figure 7-1 traces secretarial and student volunteer assignments before, during, and after testing dates.

	SECRETARY		AIDES	
long before testing	type and mail materials orders		determine amounts of materials needed	
several months before testing	type pre-test student bulletin; check in-coming materials against copy of order		help orient peers to testing benefits; sort, stamp, and store materials	
day before or morning of testing	color-code intercom buttons; answer proctors' questions; disconnect or modify bell system		distribute test supplies to home rooms; count chairs; check out each room's intercom facility	
during testing	act as runner; take counselor's phone calls		none (they're being tested)	

	ANSWER SHEETS COMMERCIALLY SCORED	*ANSWER SHEETS HAND SCORED*	*ANSWER SHEETS COMMERCIALLY SCORED*	*ANSWER SHEETS HAND SCORED*
afternoon of and day after testing	alphabetize, package, and mail or deliver answer sheets to scoring service	supervise hand scoring	collect and store reusable materials	score answer sheets; collect and store reusable materials
about six weeks after testing	post gummed labels on records; make score rosters for teacher-advisors	post scores on records; make ditto rosters for teacher-advisors	distribute sealed envelopes containing leaflets, rosters, gummed labels to home room teachers	distribute sealed envelopes containing leaflets and dittoed rosters to home room teachers
up to three months after testing	assist in critique of program, helping improve next year's testing; type counselor's press release on results and mail same to local media		assist in critique of program; help explain significance of results to parents and friends (provided they have the intellectual capacities and testing knowledge)	

Figure 7-1

Students, not necessarily volunteer aides, should be used to help sell their peers and parents on the importance of testing. By passing the word that there's "something in it" for every teen-ager, these peer group public relations workers effectively lessen the chances of test day truancies by pupils who resent being forced to do something for which they see no reason. By communicating motives for testing to parents, these young message-bearers persuade adults to "cool it," and not to suspect group standardized measurement of being un-

American, racist, or immoral. A counselor, working through student leaders and using graphic aides such as a periodically-issued guidance newsletter, can do much to head off pupil and parent apathy and/or hostility toward testing. Later, after scores are available, the adolescent opinion-molders are again called upon, this time to urge peers and parents to come to see the counselor for score interpretation interviews.

Another post-testing student duty centers around possible mathematics enrichment activities for the gifted. Developing local norms is an excellent special project for interested students, working under the direction of mathematics teacher(s) and counselor(s). If the district has a central office data processing facility, or a leased telephone computer line, these may be incorporated into such a project. If the decision has been made to score test answer sheets locally by hand, rather than to subscribe to a machine scoring service, a local norms math operation becomes necessary. Another post-testing possibility for the gifted is for a student panel to present and interpret test results at a faculty, PTA, or school board meeting. This activity falls in the areas of audio-visual aids and forensics, as well as in the areas of math and guidance; therefore teachers from these areas should be involved in working with the pupil volunteers.

Teachers are briefed on their before-, during-, and after-testing duties.

Every teacher should have some responsibility in compulsory testing, as the program is a school-wide responsibility for all youngsters. (One possible exception to this principle concerns students in a self-contained educably mentally retarded (EMR) class. They should be tested, but they should receive tests specially aimed at their ability level, administered by their own classroom teacher. Ideally, EMR evaluation occurs simultaneously with general building appraisal. This way, EMR pupils will not feel different or "left out.") In order to avoid staff animosity, faculty assignments should be made and explained well in advance of the dates on which duties are to be performed. Basic teacher measurement program responsibilities are: (1) prior to testing—explaining reasons for testing to homeroom or other advisee-type groups; (2) during testing—proctoring; (3) post-testing—(a) conducting group score interpretations for homeroom or advisee gatherings, (b) participating in professional level score critiques with counselor and administrators. Other, specialized teacher assignments are occasionally made; for example, a teacher gifted in linguistic skills may read test instructions, or one mathematically endowed may help in statistical treatment of measurement data.

Some counselors, especially those in smaller schools, may wish to brief each teacher individually regarding his or her role in the testing program. If time permits, this personal approach is always preferable. In large schools, however, especially those with a small number of counselors, it's impossible to give each teacher a private run-down. The alternative is a general faculty meeting devoted to the forthcoming annual testing period. Each staff member's role in the testing program should be considered. To prepare the teachers for pre-test responsibilities, a counselor should review basic concepts to be discussed in the homeroom with the youngsters:

(1) *Why do we test?*—Basically, so students, teachers, parents, administrators, and counselors will receive data about what's being learned in school, and what abilities the student body has.

(2) *What good is this information to the average teen-ager?*—It tells you where you stand in relation to others your age in ability and knowledge, so you may better plan future high school courses (except seniors) and for job, further schooling, military, and/or matrimonial careers.

(3) *When will testing occur?*—It will be during *(periods)* on *(dates)*. Be specific!

(4) *Who will be told pupil scores?*—Each pupil will be told his or her own scores. Parents may request their own children's scores. School faculty may look up individual scores, but individual scores may not be released to others. Anyone who wishes to know will be told school average scores. Only pupils themselves may reveal their own scores to other pupils or to outsiders.

(5) *In what way are scores reported?*—Both individual and group results will be quoted as *percentiles*. This means that everyone will learn how high among all boys and girls in their grade, nation-wide, he or she stands in terms of ability and knowledge. For instance, if Johnny, a junior, is at the 80th percentile in natural science, this means that he knows more science information than about 4/5 of other eleventh graders all over the country. He knows less than about 1/5 of them, according to this test.

(6) *How soon will scores be available?*—Students should wait three weeks (if tests are locally scored) or six weeks (if tests are sent away for machine scoring), then they should see their counselor if they wish an individual interpretation interview. Homeroom group guidance sessions at which score reports are reported should be held. General questions should be answered as soon as possible after scores are made available.

When orienting teachers to test day responsibilities, a dittoed duty roster should be issued. The roster should list specific days and times for testing, as well as each teacher's room(s) and time(s) for proctorial assignment. What proctors may and may not do must be spelled out. For instance, testee questions regarding answering procedure may be entertained, but queries into correct factual responses may not. The principal may also use the counselor's testing roster to inform staff of test day administrative procedures, such as attendance-taking and disciplinary protocol. Teachers should be asked to caution students on the day prior to testing to be sure to eat a good breakfast the next morning. However, this admonition must be phrased carefully, to avoid the creation of a mother hen image.

When scores become available, several weeks after testing, home-room teachers should receive another bulletin. This missive contains notification to students that interpretive counseling interviews may now be scheduled. Also to be included are class- and/or school-wide average scores for announcement to students, as well as general comments suggested for use in explaining the percentile concept to students. Individual score reports should be passed out when this bulletin is read. Generally, test companies furnish pupil explanatory leaflets upon which scores may be copied from the print-outs supplied, or scores may be affixed to the leaflets by use of gummed-back labels. Each student should receive a personal document of some kind on which his score appears. These may be taken home to show parents, and brought with the student to counseling sessions.

During testing, the counselor is a busy person.

Shortly before the onset of testing, the counselor checks to make sure that test supplies are delivered to the appropriate rooms. Normally, test supplies include an ability test and answer sheet, a knowledge test battery and answer sheet, an electrolytic or a #2 pencil, and two sheets of scratch paper for each pupil. In high-turnover schools, an extra set of supplies for a possible new arrival is desirable. Each proctor may need a test manual. He certainly will need a copy of the duty sheet. A "Do not disturb" sign for each door is also included in the packet. A last-minute check of number of seats and the condition of the room's pencil sharpener should also be made. If armchairs are used instead of desks, care must be taken to see that there are a few left-handed chairs in each test room. The blackboard should have an eraser and chalk in its rail, so proctors can make needed blackboard announcements. Lastly, if desks or chairs are movable, they must be spaced far enough apart to prevent cheating. If alternate seating is used, a good system is to place a scratch paper on every other seat. Then, when students enter the room, they are told to sit only where paper is furnished. This avoids insinuations of dishonesty caused by having to ask pupils to change seats. If two age levels are tested together, such as ninth and eleventh graders, it's convenient to seat them in alternate rows, so answer sheets may be collected by grade (row). Two colors of scratch paper simplify this seating procedure: "All freshmen take a seat with a green paper on it, and all juniors sit where there's a white sheet of paper."

Immediately before testing begins, the counselor should check the intercom, his color coding of its controls, and his script and test manual. He should make sure his watch is on time and running, and that a pencil is handy for copying STOP! times from the watch onto the script. If directions are to be read live in a large auditorium, the counselor may want to have voice-helping supplies, such as cough drops and a water pitcher and glass handy on the desk from which he works. Lastly, the counselor may want to have a few non-test related pieces of work handy for short periods of inactivity just in case things go smoothly and boredom sets in.

When testing is ready to begin, the script calls for a preliminary announcement, used to settle testees down and to get everyone alerted to start. Having the principal read school announcements is often useful in this regard. Next, the preliminary remarks from the test manual are read, allowing lots of time for passing of materials and so on. This is followed by directions for the first sub-test. Later, when students take a break between sub-tests, a touch of humor on the reader's part is often good for relief of tension. If testing is to continue after lunch, pupils are told to leave materials face down on the desks, and the test room is locked. If the test room is to be used for classes prior to testing resumption, materials should be passed in order of seating. Thus, if everyone takes the seat he had before, materials can be redistributed simply.

Of course, things don't always go so smoothly, and occasionally proctors have a question or request more time before starting. At the beginning of testing, short delays may or even should be granted, but during testing, requests for delays should not be granted. The secretary must be on call to serve as a runner, in case some supplies are short. While pupils are working on a sub-test the counselor may wish to tour the building, making sure that no unnecessary noise or distractions occur.

Immediately after the conclusion of testing, a script announcement about delivery of materials is read. This message tells when and where to deliver test booklets (usually the counselor's office), where to throw away scratch paper (often in wastebaskets at the door), to whom to return pencils (generally to the proctor), and what to do with answer sheets. In small schools, where a proctor has all juniors, for example, in one room, it's best to have the proctor alphabetize the answer sheets prior to turn-in. In larger schools, where classes are split among several rooms, proctors should return each set of answer sheets to a receptacle marked for that particular class. The answer sheets are alphabetized by the secretary that afternoon or the next day. The last intercom announcement prior to dismissal should be a repeat of the promise to give each youngster a copy of his scores, and an interpretation interview if he wants one.

**Scoring tests, posting scores, and interpreting results
are important post-testing responsibilities.**

If tests are to be locally scored using overlay stencils, scoring should begin as soon as possible after testing. Fundamentally, such action is a cost-saving, time-saving move, but if it is done only for this reason, it is penny wise and pound foolish. That's because test companies, during machine scoring, program their equipment to yield all sorts of statistical scores. If the counselor lacks the statistical expertise and access to calculating or computing equipment needed to do similar comparisons, hand-scoring, despite the money and time it saves, is unwise. There used to be a third alternative, the state scoring services once operated by state education departments or universities. These have almost all disappeared from the scene, although in a few states they may still be of use.

If hand-scoring is deemed feasible, the appropriate overlay stencils must be purchased with other test supplies. In very small schools, the counselor and secretary can readily score all answer sheets. In larger schools, volunteer student or parent aides are used. But, when this is done, *all pupils must be assigned an alpha number, which is placed on answer sheets in lieu of names.* This must be done to insure confidentiality of score reports. Alpha numbers are best constructed with two components, an initial number for class year, followed by an alphabetical order number. So students will never be able to guess who's who, reverse alphabetical order should be used, as well as several dummy numbers at the start of each class list. For example, a senior girl named Mary Zueckendorff, the first twelfth grader in the reverse order for her class, would be 12-006, as the first five numbers, 001 through 005, are not given to anyone. The dummy numbers may be assigned to transfer students who arrive just before testing, if that is preferable to leaving them unused.

When raw scores are obtained via hand-scoring, these are plugged into previously created statistical formulae for construction of local norms and other calculations. Test manuals are used to determine national percentile scores of pupils. As stated previously, this local data processing endeavor makes an ideal mathematics enrichment project for gifted students, under supervision of the math teacher(s) and the counselor. Several sources cited in the bibliography are helpful in planning statistical analyses of the data. The next step is to copy computed national and local ability and knowledge test scores onto explanatory leaflets provided by the test companies. The drawing of "profiles" on these leaflets is generally left for each testee to do himself during a group guidance explanatory session. If student aides are used to transfer scores to leaflets, alpha numbers, rather than names, again must be used.

If a scoring service, either the test company itself or one of the few surviving state services, is being used, answer sheets are processed quite differently. After alphabetization, each class pack of sheets receives an identifying cover sheet and is bound with rubber bands or string. If the scoring service is located near the school, it's best to place the bound answer sheets in a box and deliver them in person, thus saving a few days of transit time. Score reports also may be picked up when they are ready, saving an additional few days. When scoring will be done far from the school, answer sheets, are packaged for mailing and sent out immediately. Postal regulations allow them to be sent Special Fourth Class—Educational Materials rate. If the counselor deems the expense justified, a few days might be saved by mailing them first class, or even air mail.

When the scores return, the counselor must be prepared for individual interpretive interviews with concerned clients and parents. He must also prepare homeroom teachers for group guidance sessions. Test scoring services provide class and schoolwide score rosters which contain individual pupil and composite score print-outs. These are helpful for this purpose. Generally, copies are retained by the counselor, principal, and superintendent, with teacher-advisors, if this system is used, receiving photo-copy or photo-copy ditto master copies of advisees' scores. Score report leaflets and gummed score labels are given to students by homeroom teachers, or in very small schools, by the counselor himself. Consultation interviews are scheduled with various members of the professional staff, in accord with previously perceived needs. Group average scores are released to news media, and printed in the guidance newsletter and staff bulletins, in accord with district policy.

The counselor's secretary should see that the set of gummed labels intended for school cumulative record folders is promptly affixed. Usually, one set of labels is purchased for school records, one for counselor's records, and one for individual pupil reports. When local hand scoring is used, scores must be entered on the labels by hand.

In all his interpretive comments, the counselor should seek to dispel the notion that test results prove or disprove things. No set of scores ever proved a teacher incompetent, proved one school to be better than another, or proved that a student is unable to attend college. Rather, test scores only indicate possible trends. They are analytic pieces of evidence rather than judgmental factors in themselves. The counselor should also stress the effects of standard error of measurement upon scores, making sure to dispel the erroneous "point" score notion held by many persons. Some tests, such as the SCAT and STEP, report in band scores, making this process easier.

Also, as stated previously, the percentile and norm group systems of reporting are no doubt best to follow if one wants to dispel the "point" score notion with pupils, parents, and the general public (for class averages). A counselor should develop numerous little anecdotes to use when explaining scores to his publics.

For example, when explaining percentile rank to a group: "Johnny is at the 60th percentile on the science knowledge test. This means that he knows more about science than about three out of every five juniors in schools like those in our norm group. He knows less about science than about two out of every five juniors in this same group." This leads to an explanation of what a norm group is: "A norm group means a large body of boys and girls who are very similar to yourselves. Our tests are based on public school, middle-western eleventh grade norms. This means that your percentile scores are comparing you to other juniors who attend public schools in the middle-western United States."

The counselor also needs to explain differences among and

between ability and knowledge tests repeatedly. Especially important is the need to caution clients and others that low scores do not necessarily brand an individual as "dumb" or "stupid."

COUNSELOR AS VOLUNTARY TEST PROGRAM DIRECTOR

There are two forms of voluntary measurement: that which moves about to fill a need uncovered during individual counseling, and group programs which are aimed at special categories of students. The former is a matter concerning the counselee and the counselor only. For this reason test scores obtained for this purpose must be treated just as confidentially as other counseling communications. This confidentiality extends even to the knowledge that a test was given, as well as to the score obtained. The latter type of volitional measurement is sub-divided into three categories: those programs conducted within the school at the counselor's instigation, those programs conducted elsewhere but participated in by the students, and those conducted within the school and given by the counselor but as part of larger programs elsewhere. The same ethics that apply to revelation of compulsory program scores apply to these tests, with one exception—pupils scoring high on certain achievement batteries, and therefore earning recognition or scholarships, are generally commended before their peers and in the local news media.

Voluntary appraisal demands a more personal touch.

Tests are made for counselors and clients, *not vice versa*. Therefore, use of appraisal instruments in counseling takes place only when both parties deem them helpful. Some philosophies of counseling encourage more test usage than others. For instance, the trait-factor branch of the Rational school of thought relies heavily upon testing; the various Non-Directive approaches rarely, if ever, call for them. Each counselor must look inward, deciding for himself just how much individualized standardized appraisal he wishes to use to supplement one-to-one counseling. He also must examine fairly his test administration and score interpreting competencies. No counselor should ever give an instrument for which he is not trained and experienced. For example, the WAIS and the Stanford-Binet are two highly valid individual ability measures; some counselors use them to give clients more meaningful appraisals than group measures can yield. However, if the tester is not extremely familiar with these tests and their scoring, she is likely to arrive at an erroneous IQ score, thereby defeating the very purpose for which the Binet or WAIS was given. Many affectively oriented measures require considerable counselor training other than that found in the normal counselor education masters degree program. For instance, the MMPI, a very reliable and valid instrument from a statistical standpoint, is deceptively easy to administer and score. But score interpretation calls for considerable facility in clinical psychology. Projective techniques like the Rorschach and the TAT are also comparatively easy to give, but their scoring and interpretation absolutely demand a psychological background possessed by only a handful of school counselors in the entire country! There is one exception to the rule of never giving a personality-type test one is not qualified to interpret; this is when a mental health referral agency has already accepted a student for therapy. If the counselor knows that this agency will want an MMPI profile on the client, for example, it is all right, with client permission, to administer him a test at school and to forward the score to the agency. This is a time-saving move. Analysis of the score will, of course, be done by agency personnel qualified to do so. Of course, certain affective measures are constructed with use by school personnel in mind; the Edwards, Bernreuter, Mooney, California, and MCI are examples. A counselor needs less clinical expertise to employ these, but even here, great discretion must be exercised. When dealing with personality-type tests of any kind in the school, voluntary, private usage during individual counseling is the only way to go.

A supply of optionally used tests should be at the disposal of each qualified counselor who wishes to use them. If the counselor has had a graduate course in individual IQ testing, a WAIS or a Binet kit is a wise investment. There will come times when a pupil, his parents, or the principal questions the accuracy of his group ability score, and wishes an individual measure. It usually falls on the counselor's shoulders to explain the situation to the youngster and to give the test. A counselor who uses a WAIS or Binet should administer a few tests each year to keep in practice. A specimen set of tests not otherwise used in the school, including scoring stencils and answer sheets, should be handy. These are used when someone disputes the accuracy of a student score obtained during regular achievement/proficiency testing.

If the counselor believes interest inventories to have value, reusable Kuder and Strong manuals, keys, and answer sheets are good to have. A set of one or two of their newer competitors, such as the

Minnesota or Flanagan, is also advisable. Several professional trade associations have also hired measurement consultants to produce specialized interest tests for their field only. (Accounting is the prime example.) These instruments are made readily available to counselors; their use with clients interested in these fields certainly cannot hurt as long as testing is made optional. Affectively oriented instruments are up to the counselor; only he knows his personal philosophy and his degree of competency in this area.

**Various nation-wide Saturday morning and other programs
will draw motivated students, if only the programs are sold to them.**

There are three types of group voluntary testing. First, there are the large operations held elsewhere under other auspices, in which the high school and its students merely participate. Major examples are the four programs concerned with admission to further educational institutions discussed at length in Chapter Five, the CEEB, ACT, NLN, and PCT. Second, there are the nationwide or regional programs in which the school cooperates on a more personalized basis. Examples are the PSAT-NMSQT and NEDT. These are aimed primarily at the college-bound student (see Chapter Five). Another type of operation in this category is the Air Force Qualification Test, which Air Force recruiting sergeants will administer, without obligation, to any interested high school senior. It goes without saying that the voluntary aspect of taking this instrument must be emphasized. Some optional in-school programs have traditionally been identified with fields other than guidance—the Betty Crocker Homemaker of Tomorrow competition being an example. This test is customarily given by home economics teachers. The third form of voluntary group tests are those given strictly by the school or district for local purposes only. Some common examples are use of advanced placement (ability plus knowledge) batteries with junior high pupils who wish to be in an honors program; making an algebra aptitude (special ability) measure available to seventh or eighth graders as a help in deciding between algebra and general math; giving the DAT to ninth or tenth graders to assist exploratory vocational thinking, or giving the GATB to twelfth graders to aid in career choice.

The success secret of all voluntary group testing programs lies in internal publicity. Too many times, a routine announcement is made to students over the intercom system: "Any ninth graders wishing to take the ... blah, blah, such and such ... *(by that time no one is listening)* . . . come to Room 110 after lunch next Tuesday." When next Tuesday rolls around, the counselor is dismayed to find a total of two youngsters waiting to take the blah, blah, such and such—the school brain who signs up for everything, and the #1 discipline problem, who came to see what disruption he might cause. Good internal publicity centers around warm, personal explanations aimed at the specific publics the test will benefit. The counselor should approach individual students who might, in his opinion, profit from taking a particular instrument. He should explain to these youngsters what the test is for, and why he feels they might profit from taking it. He must not, however, attempt to coerce pupils into taking the test. These are voluntary testing program components, and they must remain just that or the counselor is a hypocrite!

Individual invitations are supplemented with group and journalistic ones. These include external as well as internal efforts. The counselor should give explanatory talks to home rooms and to other student groups. He's wise to let parents and teachers in on the nature of the voluntary appraisal by speaking on it briefly at PTA and faculty meetings. Simply worded explanatory announcements about each voluntary appraisal effort should appear, well in advance of the test date, in each of the following: guidance newsletter (given to all publics of the counselor), student newspaper, principal's administrative bulletin, and community daily and/or weekly news paper(s). All informative efforts should stress the voluntary nature of the operation, give complete factual details regarding sign-up, dates, room, cost (if any), etc. They should also explain in simple terms what benefits devolve to students who take the tests. If such a sales approach is followed, students will make use of voluntary measurement opportunities afforded them.

EIGHT

Conducting Practical Research –
and Utilizing the Findings

If testing is a dreaded operation to some, then "research" is apt to be downright terrifying! This doesn't have to be the case, though, as some form of research is within the competencies of every certified school counselor. Let's see how Mr. or Mrs. Average Counselor may go about this often neglected personnel service, and what he or she stands to gain from so doing. Why should a counselor do research, and how does he go about it?

WHY RESEARCH?

Unlike college professors and counselors in university counseling centers, secondary level counselors are not required by their job roles to conduct research. It's highly unlikely that any junior or senior high or middle school counselor was ever fired from his job for failure to do research, and none probably ever will be. This, of course, removes the potential effect of extrinsic motivation from the situation; that is, counselors who do conduct research do so on their own volitions. There's no "publish or perish" syndrome at the secondary level. Therefore, any scientific investigations done there stem wholly from instrinsic motives.

Why, then, should a school counselor bother with research? Aside from the possibly semi-extrinsically motivated reason of attracting professional recognition, and thus ultimately achieving a pay raise, professional advancement or both, there are two reasons. Scholarly inquiry either takes place to satisfy man's intellectual curiosity, and thus add to his academic body of knowledge, or it may be conducted to solve a problem vexing his everyday existence, thereby ameliorating the life of man in society. The former variety is often called "pure" research, or "research for its own sake," while the latter is referred to as "practical" or "applied" research. At the university level, a distinction is often made between the pure research stressed in the natural sciences—chemistry, physics, and experimental psychology, and the applied research of applied sciences—engineering, medicine, agriculture, etc. Education, the field to which school counseling belongs, is an applied *social* science, in the same category as criminology, commerce, and librarianship. The more pure or traditional social sciences, on the other hand—history, philosophy, economics, etc., are more concerned with knowledge for its own sake, hence they emphasize pure research. Education, since its goal is improving society by better preparing the young for their place in it, naturally leans a bit toward the applied aspect of research.

While this dichotomy of research types is a valid concept, it's an exaggerated one. For instance, some of the purest research of all time has led to highly pragmatic applications, as witnessed in military and peaceful uses of nuclear energy. Conversely, practical attempts to utilize electro-magnetic waves for man's benefit has led to radio astronomy, a theoretical, pure scientific field, whose findings have as yet little social utility. Therefore, the school counselor interested in doing research shouldn't be too concerned about which kind of research he does. If the investigation is well done, chances are it will lead to both ultimate outcomes, namely, discovery of new facts for their own sakes, and benefits applicable to the lives of boys and girls.

HOW TO GO ABOUT DOING RESEARCH

A fundamental thumb rule for all research and researchers is to pick a topic in which one has interest. Be it pure or applied, the chosen topic must be one that intrigues the investigator and has stimulated his curiosity. A criticism of some research done in higher education has been that because it was a compulsory job-role component, some investigators did "any old thing" to hold their positions. Since their hearts weren't in these investigations, the finished products lacked quality. School counselors have no excuse; as there is no compulsion to do research in the first place, what they do produce had better be good!

Basic statistical and methodological concepts should be part of all counselors' repertoires.

Due to their involvement with testing, counselors are no strangers to fundamental statistical concepts. The mean and standard deviation and percentile systems of score reporting are both rooted in elementary statistics. In fact, statistics may be simply regarded as a systemized attempt to apply common sense to problem analysis. The common sense in this case is mathematical probability theory, which is merely a means of assessing the relative likelihood of the occurrence of something. All statistics does, to put it another way, is to provide tests for determining how likely it is that a given set of data did not result from chance. For example, many statistical tests report in *levels of significance,* which are stated as two- or three-digit decimal fractions. A significance level of .05 means that in the long run the difference found is in error only five times out of one hundred. An effect testing at that level would have resulted by chance only 5% of the time. The smaller the decimal fraction, the less likely a chance effect is occurring. For example, a .001 significance level means that in the long run, only one possibility in a thousand exists for chance to be the cause.

A fundamental concept common to all research is formulation of *hypotheses.* Hypotheses are statements which the investigator seeks to substantiate or overturn. They may be stated positively or negatively. An example of an hypothesis for a follow-up study of counseling effectiveness, stated positively, could be: "There will be a statistically significant difference between the counseled group and the control group." Stated negatively, the same hypothesis reads: "There will be no statistically significant difference between the counseled group and the control group." A negative hypothesis is frequently called "the null hypothesis." Statistically, it's the null hypothesis that's almost always being tested, but semantically, many researchers prefer to state their hypotheses positively. (See one of the many fine statistics books on the market for a detailed discussion of this topic.)

Every counselor is familiar with the so-called normal curve or distribution; in fact, the familiar bell-shaped chart, courtesy of some test-producing company, adorns many a guidance office wall. All bodies of data which are distributed normally, thus corresponding to this curve, are called *parametric*. Those whose data cannot be said to be normally distributed are *non-parametric*. There are certain statistical tests for use with parametric data and others for non-parametric data. Because parametric tests are more powerful, they should be used whenever a counselor is sure his data is normally distributed. If he cannot be sure, however, then a non-parametric test must be used.

Another fundamental statistical concept which must be observed during research is *randomization*. The major object of randomization is prevention of biased results. Specifically, it's a method of assigning persons studied to groups in such a way that each person has an equal chance of being assigned to any group studied. For example, if the principal has required all "problem" youngsters to receive counseling, a study comparing counseled to non-counseled students is impossible. As all the "problem" pupils would be in one group only, the two samples are thus not randomized. Several excellent research references are listed in the bibliography. An interesting series of books by Allen Edwards has helped many persons acquire statistical expertise, as they range sequentially from basic to advanced. The writings of Henry Kerlinger are regarded by many as helpful in learning research methodology; these also span a range from fundamental to highly theoretical.

Research may be done on processes, outcomes, and/or programs.

Counselors have three major areas to investigate. First of all, there are several important *processes* inherent to their work, the foremost of which is that of one-to-one counseling. Many counselors also engage in small-group counseling of one kind or another; here is another process that bears investigating. Activities within the realm of personnel services offer several possibilities. There is the vocational choice process, measurement process, articulation process, referral process, etc. Research into processes is concerned with identifying basic characteristics of what goes on during the activity in question. A high degree of present orientation characterizes this kind of study. Emphasis is on what's taking place now, not on what will probably happen in the future, or what genetic factors caused something in the past. Examples of process research are the famous studies of Fred Fiedler into the nature of the psychotherapeutic relationship. Fielder arranged for ethical observation of Freudian, Adlerian, and Rogerian therapists by various kinds of raters. The raters, who did not know which kind of clinician they were watching, were instructed to group them into categories. Fiedler found that his raters easily grouped beginning practitioners into each of the three categories. They failed, however, to group experienced therapists correctly. This led Fiedler to conclude that there is an ideal therapeutic relationship toward which all successful clinicians gravitate as they gain experience. An example of process research by a school counselor would be the analysis of tapes of several counselors' interviews. A hypothesis is being tested that the amount of reflection of client affective statements will correlate positively with professional success, as determined by salary. The researcher is trying to ascertain whether the frequency with which a counselor reflects has anything to do with his measureable professional success, and/or vice versa.

Outcomes research basically involves looking for differences over time. It takes three forms: the causative, predictive, and follow-up. Causative research delves into the past to answer the question *why*. Examples are various studies sociologists have made of delinquent boys in which childhood experiences were probed for possible commonalities which might have caused later social alienation. An example of causative outcomes research by a counselor is objectively tracing parental childhood recollection of a group of senior girls choosing cosmetology as a career. Here, the counselor is seeking to ascertain whether certain early childhood experiences might predispose girls toward this career field.

Predictive outcomes research is very closely dependent on probability theory. It seeks present indicators of future performance, and the statistical significance levels for these. Many research studies of the CEEB and ACT professional staffs are good predictive research examples. One of the better known of these determined that high school grade point is the best single predictor of future college success. CEEB freshman class profile charts are an attempt to apply pragmatically the findings of predictive studies (see Chapter Five). A counselor might do an interesting predictive study by comparing eighth graders' algebra aptitude test scores to their grades later earned in ninth grade algebra or general math.

Follow-up studies assess outcomes of counseling by comparing counseled to non-counseled clients at later chronologic intervals during their lives. Some studies have sought more subtle differences within a counseled group, seeking to relate these to possible differences when counseling occurred. The many published studies of John Rothney serve as references for counselors thinking of doing follow-up investigations. An interesting study by David Campbell compared a counseled to a non-counseled group after 25 years. He found that the counseled (while in college) group was definitely ahead of the non-counseled in many factual and emotional areas during college, but after 25 years, the non-counseled had caught up in all but two areas. Other researchers also report a similar "catching up" phenomenon, which has led to speculation that perhaps counseling does help, but the uncounseled merely get help somewhere else, or resolve their own problems. A follow-up study of interest to school counselors would be keeping track of counseled and non-counseled junior high pupils during each of their senior high years. Grade point averages of each group would be compared, as well as number of activities engaged in, amount of disciplinary problems, etc.

Research into *programs,* the third major type, is a little less exciting, perhaps, than that into either processes or outcomes. This is because a great many programs' findings yield data descriptive of things other than human relationships or activities. For example, study of number of clients seen per day, average interview lengths, relative usages of informational materials types, etc., have a dry connotation. Programs research is needed, however, if counselors are to support their budgetary requests for increased guidance services. A case in point is using such research to quash the view that one counselor is adequate for a high school of 1,000 students. By citing actual numbers of clients seen over a year's time, and the number of serious cases in which he was unable to become involved due to schedule conflicts, a counselor objectively backs his contention that a second counselor is needed. Examples of good programs research are the various studies made by state education departments of how funds were spent under the National Defense Education Act of 1958 and its extensions. Ralph Berdie has published some interesting investigations of how counselor *time* was being spent, another important program dimension. An interesting piece of programs research would be for a counselor to determine the number of pupils who availed themselves of the various personnel services during a given school year.

**Experimental research is best from a
mathematical standpoint, but descriptive, correlational, and
archival studies have their place, too.**

There are four different approaches to research; which one is used in a given study depends on the nature of the problem at hand. The most accurate research approach from a statistical standpoint is the *experimental* or *empirical* method. In this approach, all variables are held constant for two randomly selected groups, an experimental group and a control group. An experimental variable, or research treatment, is manipulated for the experimental group but not for the control group. A before and after objective measure is given both groups. Therefore, any differences observed between experimental and control groups on this measure must be due to manipulation of the experimental variable, as all other differences were held constant through randomization. This technique is borrowed from the natural sciences, where it is used much more than other approaches.

There are two forms of experimental research: that planned before the fact, and that done after the fact. The former is a study that is first planned, then an experimental treatment is administered. The latter involves finding two identical groups, save for one past difference in their lives, and measuring them at the present to see if there are any differences. A good example of the former type of experimental research in the guidance area was that already described in Chapter Seven. A counselor randomized two groups of tenth graders, using ninth-grade ability and knowledge test scores (the *before* measure) to guarantee that there were no intelligence or achievement differences between experimental and control groups. The experimental group received extensive group guidance sessions (the experimental treatment) devoted to why testing is important. The control group received none. Then, both groups took the DAT. The investigator found the experimental group had significantly higher scores than the control group. The conclusion was drawn that a testing orientation program can raise tenth graders' DAT scores.

An example of the latter form of empirical study is taking two groups of incoming college freshmen—the experimental group, which received counseling in high school, and a control group, which did not. Various attitudes about counseling are investigated; statistical treatments are used to determine whether there are significant differences between the two groups. This type of experimental research is not quite as reliable as the former type, as giving of a true *before* measure is impossible.

The second most effective research approach is the so-called descriptive or *case study* method. This approach is based upon systematic, observational data collection. Whereas the experimental approach utilized one or at most two observations of many individuals, the descriptive method uses many observations of one or a few individuals. It frequently seeks to get at the genetic or causal factors of a phenomenon by studying many aspects of that phenomenon closely and scientifically. An illustration of this approach is the problem of a youngster who cannot learn well. At first, IQ is suspect, but a Binet rules this out. Inability to read due to defective vision as a cause is eliminated by an eye check. Emotional problems appear unlikely after extensive counseling interviews and personality testing. Finally, perusal of teachers' anecdotal comments seems to indicate a mysterious inability to pay attention *at times*. The counselor, suspecting a problem centered around periodic or coming-and-going hearing loss, sends the client to his family doctor for an ear examination. The doctor finds a condition of the inner ear bones to be causing the student's problem. Surgery clears up the condition, and the subject's school performance improves.

An example of a famous descriptive study is the late Lewis Terman's investigation of genius. Terman studied boys and girls descriptively, seeking to identify common factors in their lives that could be related to the fact that their Binet IQ's were in the genius range. By so doing he hoped to gain genetic insights into the nature of intelligence, as well as predictive data regarding adult performances of youngsters of this type.

The third most effective research approach is the *correlational* method. This is the most mathematically oriented of the four approaches, and in many ways the easiest research to do, from a time and effort standpoint. Fundamentally, correlational studies seek to discover mathematical similarity or "fit" between two sets of data. This fit, or coincidence, as it's sometimes called, may be positive or negative. In positive correlation, the high scores of one variable occur together with the high scores of another, and low with low, such as in a comparison of ability and knowledge. In negative correlation, the higher one set of scores, the lower the other, in an inverse relationship. This form of correlation is demonstrated by comparing job satisfaction to employee absenteeism—the higher the satisfaction, the lower the absenteeism, and vice versa.

The reason correlational research is not as methodologically strong as either the experimental or descriptive approaches is that *correlation does not prove causation*. The fact that two things "go together" doesn't mean they have a cause and effect relationship. For example, if A correlates well with B, there are three causal possibilities left to be explored: (1) A might be causing B; (2) B might be causing A; (3)

Both A and B might be caused by C, a yet unisolated factor. Of course, establishing causation isn't always the goal of research, although it frequently is. Sometimes establishing correlation is an end in itself. Also, correlational investigation sometimes reveals areas for further exploration via the descriptive or experimental method.

There are two principal families of statistical treatments used in correlational type research. These are the analyses of variance (ANOVA), and the correlation coefficients (r). The former are more statistically powerful than the latter, but more rigid assumptions ·must be met before ANOVA may be used. While normally thought of as a parametric statistic, there's even one form of ANOVA suitable for non-parametric data. There are several *r*'s a researcher should know about, one for comparing two sets of data representing just about every combination of the four numeric scales—nominal, ordinal, interval, and ratio. They carry such intriguing names as Pearson's product-moment, Spearman's rho, Kendall's tau, rank correlation, and Kendall's coeffecient of concordance, to list a few.

Some of the more famous correlational studies are those under-taken by standardized test manufacturers and developers. Beginning with the pioneering work of the late Arthur Otis in 1917, attempts have been made to compare scores of new group ability measures to Binet, WISC, and WAIS scores. Because individual IQ measures are more accurate than group ones, creators of new group instruments are understandably anxious to see how closely scores on their tests correspond to the same testees' individual test scores. An example of a correlational research study of interest to counselors is the comparison of verbal ability test sub-scores to English knowledge test scores, and non-verbal ability scores to mathematics knowledge scores. There's a difference of opinion among experts regarding the true nature of factors comprising intelligence, and such a correlational study might yield additional insights.

The fourth approach to research is the most difficult to substantiate statistically. This is the so-called *archival* method, a research technique used mainly by historians, theologians, and journalists, who must often delve into recorded events of the past. Whereas experimental, descriptive, and correlational studies almost always investigate present-day phenomena, which for education means events in the lives of living boys and girls, archival studies probe the past. Because many past records are sketchy and unscientifically written, archival studies are usually, but not always, less reliable than those of the other three approaches. They also are often the most tedious to undertake, as long hours in dusty library stacks and over microfilm readers are frequently needed to dig out needed data.

A certain amount of statistical methodology is applicable to archival research. Often, sampling techniques employed in descriptive studies may be adapted to archival work, so a true random sample of data is obtained. Also, primary sources should always be taken over secondary ones, to lessen chances of reporter bias in the historical dimension. Certain rudimentary mathematical summaries may be used in justifying conclusions, but nothing like the elaborate statistical tests used in other approaches are normally possible. Percentages of occurrence of reported events are often as far as a researcher may go. For instance, one group of philosophers might be reported as making 40% more allusions to the basic goodness of man in their sampled writings than another group. Well-known archival-type studies of relevance to counseling are some of the earlier works of the late A. H. Maslow. Maslow investigated the lives of successful historical figures, searching for common personality qualities. This work led to the formulation of his hierarchical theory of self-actualization. A possible archival study for a counselor at the local level is to delve historically into the guidance function. School records and senior citizens' recollections are probed to discern how counseling and personnel services were performed prior to the existence of the position of counselor in that school. Some interesting work has been done at the college level along these lines by Eugenie Leonard and by Barry and Wolf.

Students, teachers, administrators, and maybe even the general public frequently ought to become involved.

Good research is like a high school basketball game. Lots of thought, hard work, and preparation go into getting the team ready and into their game performance, yet the contest is top enjoyment, not work, for the spectators. And, if the score is close late in the second half, suspenseful feelings about the outcome mount as the final buzzer nears. The counselor's publics are the "spectators" of the research effort. Because he's almost always the only school-connected person doing research, he's somewhat like the basketball team, a small group of boys also representing their entire academic community in an endeavor. Just as everyone in town respects a highly motivated effort on the basketball court, so will they respect one in research, even if the researcher doesn't "win" (come up with positive findings). Someday, the counselor will proudly announce that a report of one of his research studies is being published in a nationally circulated professional journal. This is analogous to the basketball team's going to the state tournament; excellence has been achieved in each area of scholastic endeavor.

The counselor's various publics frequently learn of his research by being asked to participate in it as subjects, to help with data collection, or to give their ideas about what topics to investigate. (After all, the basketball team has the advantage here; its games are a little more publicized than the counselor's activities, especially research ones!) There are many potential studies centering on each of the counselor's publics—effects of counseling on students, success in group guidance by teachers, differences of opinion between administrators and counselors, parental counseling expectations, community counselor role concepts, to name a few. Progress reports should be printed in the guidance newsletter and local newspapers, as long as research still going on isn't influenced. The findings are most important of all to disseminate; months of speculation now culminate in learning what the researcher really did find. No one would deny to basketball fans the knowledge of who won the big game; neither should the counselor keep his "fans" guessing. Counselors could do much more research to benefit students than they're currently undertaking; a follow-up study of graduates to discern what occupation they've entered is an example.

There are many more professional reasons for involving local publics in research. Sooner or later, the one most likely to assert itself is the financial. The school board will want to know the economic implications of findings, local businessmen will be very interested in potential savings to them resulting from new vocational choice insights, and so on. This is not to disparage the most applied aspect of the ultimately applied—money. Saving money is not a crime, nor is it even necessarily a neurosis. Conducting research for the primary reason of finding ways to economize is probably not wise, however. It's usually best to pick a more intellectual rationale for applied research, or maybe even to attempt pure research. The counselor shouldn't worry; the money-saving angle will come about as a by-product. Almost every research finding there ever was has been adapted by someone to make (or save) a few bucks.

Another reason for involving local publics in research is to help people. After all, counselors are supposed to be doing this. Let's consider a hypothetical case: A drug usage problem is disrupting many student lives, and those of their family members. The counselor, without revealing confidences, is able to do a descriptive study of several teen-aged addicts and their families. He discovers that lack of father-son and mother-daughter social activities, caused by overtime-working fathers and working mothers, appears to be a causal factor in adolescent drug use. In consulting with concerned parents who come to him for help with drug problems, he discusses his research findings. He also uses them in dealing with clients, and shares these findings, in a professional manner, with other counselors through publication.

Area key punch, programming, and data processing facilities are often available through previous guidance contacts.

One deterrent factor for many counselors wishing to do research is the lack of supportive facilities in the average secondary school setting. The typical university graduate department in which the counselor earned his masters degree literally abounded in research-concerned men and machines. Near at hand was a friendly major professor who discussed Bayesian statistics every morning with his wife over breakfast; just down the hall was a room filled with calculating machines and numerous reference books. Not much farther away was a university computing center with the latest in mechanical brains and all sorts of supporting hardware. Down the street was a modern library with innumerable references for use in building reviews of literature or pursuing archival investigations. And somewhere near was a bulletin board where sundry helping hands—key punchers, programmers, and typists—huckstered their services for a fee.

This is a far cry from the high school, although the facilitative climate for research is much better now in larger schools than it was 20 years ago. For example, business education departments are starting to buy key punch machines and train students in their use. Mathematics departments sometimes offer statistics as a senior elective, thus bringing teachers versed in this sub-field onto the secondary scene. Many large districts now have their own computers, or at least off-hours lease arrangements with banks or other computer owners. And some faculty lounges now feature professional libraries. It's even possible in some schools, although almost heresy to suggest it, that a few very gifted senior pupils might assist the counselor as research aides. Perhaps the university level system of research assistants for professors may be copied, in simplified form, for high school use. This is a very radical suggestion, to say the least, as many schools will not allow students to open non-personal mail or answer the telephone, let alone play a research role! At the risk of being called a communist, however, this author dares to suggest it.

The climate for research in smaller senior highs, junior highs, and middle schools is as yet grim. These institutions either just aren't big enough to afford or need specialized hardware like key punches or calculators, to say nothing of computers, or else their younger student ages tend to rule out the presence of research-oriented persons and machines. Counselors in these schools must look extramurally for research help. One possibility is to utilize contracts made during practice of other personnel services. For instance, personnel managers of business firms with which the counselor has done job placements may allow after-hours usage of key punches, calculators, and even a little computer time. Psychologists at mental health referral agencies with which the counselor has dealt may give statistical, methodological, and/or programming help if properly asked. Admissions counselors at nearby colleges and universities where the counselor has helped clients enroll may "pull strings," if asked in the right way, to enable him to use library and other facilities. If the counselor has built his contacts and treated them courteously, they'll come through in his hour of need. Another possibility is parents. Here again, if goodwill bridges have been built, parents will return the favor when the counselor needs one. Almost every parent body contains a myriad of skills, including those for research facilitation. Here's a mother who key-punches; there's a mathematician father who programs. Here's a mother who types; there's a father, executive of a firm, who'll sneak the counselor's cards in on the company computer. All in all, if a counselor knows his parents, and interacts with them as he should, he won't be at a loss when a little research assistance is needed.

WHAT HAPPENS WHEN IT'S DONE?

Research done elsewhere is sometimes open to criticism for lack of dissemination or follow-up of its findings. If it's pure research, it often is not properly publicized, thus preventing the new information learned from taking its rightful place in the appropriate body of knowledge. Some applied research results are only used to deal with the specific narrow local problem at hand, with no attempt made to apply them to similar situations elsewhere. Any counselor doing research has the obligation to see that its results have some impact— on the scholarly field of knowledge, and upon humanity.

Local publics benefit from research findings.

It has already been stated how findings might be used to improve the lives of some local residents. As soon as a study is finished, not only an applied study completely geared toward helping some particular group, but any study, the counselor should look around for local relevancies. For some pure research, this is restricted to merely sharing findings with community members intellectually able to appreciate them. With some kinds of applied studies, a certain narrow class of individuals that are afflicted with the problem investigated are the only local beneficiaries. The example of the drug addiction investigation illustrates findings of this type. When this is the case, the counselor must see that as much as possible is done to apply what he has learned to helping all community persons in the category studied. Sometimes a general benefit appears likely through the application of findings; for example, the saving of tax money brought about by learning how to cut school costs without curtailing any services. Here the researcher is obligated to bring this poten- tiality to the attention of administrators and school board. Perhaps he may wish to suggest that some of the funds his research has saved be used to finance an increased level of guidance services!

The counseling profession everywhere profits from the dissemination and presentation of results.

There are two "official" ways to share research findings—by publishing journal articles and by giving papers at conventions. In both cases, the study is written up in similar format, the only difference being that in one case the article is presented graphically, and in the other, orally. A research report should not be lengthy as both readers and listeners tend to saturate easily. Between ten and 20 double-spaced pages, typed on one side of the paper only, is generally about right. Longer research reports are known as mono- graphs, and are normally reproduced for distribution alone, rather than printed in journals or delivered verbally. Often, shorter synopses of monographs are disseminated in the same ways that articles are.

Research articles normally contain eight parts. These, in order, are:

1. *Title, author's name and abstract.* The abstract is a short resume of what the article is about. It very seldom is more than four sentences long.

2. *Statement of the problem.* Several paragraphs explain what it is the researcher seeks to learn, and why he believes the topic to be fruitful for study.

3. *Review of literature.* Here, the researcher briefly discusses relevant writings of others pertinent to his topic. Usual sources are journal articles, books, monographs, unpublished doctoral dissertations, and ERIC documents. This isn't a general review of all literature in the area, but annotated reports of writings that bear directly on the specific, narrowly defined topic under consideration.

4. *Description of the sample.* This section, often very short, tells what kind of situation is under study. For example: "All eleventh graders in three large (over 2,000 enrollment) middle-western public high schools were subjects of this study." Often, little more is needed, although all general information about the place, persons, and time in history being studied that is relevant must be included. No individuals, school, or local community may be mentioned by name, or described so readers (listeners) can figure out actual identities. Two exceptions to this rule are archival studies in which all persons mentioned are long dead, and studies restricted to non-human data, such as usage frequencies of guidance filmstrips, etc.

5. *Methodology.* This section outlines investigative strategy. It tells what approach (experimental, descriptive, correlational, archival) is used, and what the specific study design is. All statistical tests used are listed; and instruments administered to subjects are either reproduced in the article, or clearly referenced so others may look them up.

6. *Findings.* In this section are reported whatever the researcher discovered, and at what statistical significance levels, including negative as well as positive results. Frequently, tables, charts, or graphs are used to make data clearer to the reader. No interpretive or speculative comments are allowed in this section; only the bare facts.

7. *Discussion.* Here's where the counselor tells the world what his findings mean. Relevancy of what was learned is speculated upon; in pure research, the place where newly discovered facts fit into the overall scholarly field is demarcated. In applied research, the discus-

sion contains definite recommendations for pragmatic usage of findings.

8. *References.* This section is always done in strict bibliographical format, with no text at all. The form used in journals of the American Psychological Association is a good one to follow. All sources cited in the literature review must be referenced, as well as statistical tests and instrumentation obtained elsewhere. Any writers cited elsewhere in the article are included, too. *Footnotes* are not a regular article component, only ancillary to it. Modern tendency is to use them only to give credit. This normally means listing the author's institutional affiliation and possibly the university from which his graduate degree was earned; recognizing any agency which supported the research, either financially or with released job time; and acknowledging anyone who helped with some phase of the study, such as a student assistant or research design consultant.

Articles are customarily typed on bond paper and submitted flat, in triplicate, by first class mail to journal editors as listed in their respective publications. Cover letters are desirable, but only to identify the situation, not to "sell" the manuscript, which must stand or fall on its own merits. How to choose publications for submission is discussed in Chapter Fourteen. When a paper is being presented at a conference, a copy must be sent to the appropriate program chairman prior to a pre-convention deadline. This is so it may be reproduced for distribution to persons in attendance, and later published as part of the convention proceedings.

The counselor advances professionally because of his endeavors.

The community and profession both benefit from research, but what about the counselor-investigator himself? Basically, there are two types of gains. One is the aesthetic, intangible personal feeling of achievement that comes from discovering a heretofore unknown piece of knowledge. This feeling becomes even more enjoyable when this new information is employed to benefit humanity. The second gain is the tangible one of earning professional advancement and thus enhanced remuneration as a result of being a seasoned educational researcher. It was stated at the beginning of this chapter that no secondary counselor was ever fired for failing to do research. While this is true, the opposite side of the coin is not. Counselors are promoted for doing research; superintendents, especially those committed to merit pay and differentiated staffing, do take note of these voluntary, extra-professional activities. School boards especially like to hear of studies which save the district money, a frequent research by-product, and will reward investigators accordingly. Counselors who wish to apply for more prestigious positions with other school districts likewise gain from having done research. Since so few secondary educators engage in scholarly investigation, a superintendent is bound to be impressed by the one applicant he has who does.

Another form of professional advancement consists of being chosen for elective office in one of the several counselor's organizations listed in Chapter Fourteen. Counselors who wish to be tapped as candidates by the various nominating committees should carefully consider doing research. It looks pretty impressive to one's peers when one is a successful, publishing researcher, and this fact might just make the difference.

NINE

Getting Results from
Professional Referrals

One of the most complex personnel services of all is the referral function. Not only are the factual knowledges that counselors need involved and complex, but the emotional aspects of this task are often complicated and intense. There are certain strategies and procedures that counselors may call upon to make their referral operations go a little smoother. What are some of these procedures for the referral service?

BOTTLENECK FOR THE HELPING PROFESSIONS

The referral personnel service, in which school counselors bring together clients and various professionals qualified to deal with special needs, is an important one. Frequently, a counselor identifies a student problem requiring help from a specialist more suited to deal with it than is the counselor. This generally occurs in the area of emotional disturbance, when the counselor determines that a given high school boy or girl would profit from therapy with a psychiatrist or clinical psychologist. Less frequently, counselors find themselves cooperating on behalf of youngsters with such assorted fellow professionals as speech clinicians, welfare workers, rehabilitation counselors, parole and probation officers, private agency social workers, employment counselors, marriage counselors, and family physicians, attorneys, and clergymen. Many referral types exist, some aspects of which are touched upon in other chapters of this book. This chapter focuses upon cooperation with other members of the so-called "helping professions," i.e., psychiatrists, clinical psychologists, and those social workers with which these persons are sometimes associated. The emphasis here is on referral of pupils for emotional and related reasons. Of course, many principles expediting referral for personality problems readily adapt to referral for other reasons.

The major problem in referral is not identification of disturbed youngsters by counselors, nor is it any lack of quality in services rendered by psychologists and psychiatrists. Instead, it's school-referral agency articulation gaps, both during intake prior to therapy, and implementation of recommendations following it. One of the saddest incongruities of modern society is that while we have succeeded in upgrading the professional quality of school counselors, psychiatrists, and psychologists, we have lowered the effectiveness of their services! The villain responsible for this crime against children is the red tape, bureaucracy, and impersonality that has seemingly grown along with social complexity. Perhaps school counselors need to develop skill in a new pupil service, namely, lateral articulation, or colloquially speaking, bottleneck smashing. If services rendered adolescents by all members of the helping professions are to be optimally effective, someone must break down the barriers to efficient interaction among these persons. The school counselor, that catalytic enabler, is the logical red-tape cutter, bottleneck smasher, what-have-you, for the helping professions.

REFERRAL—AN ORDERLY, THOUGHT-OUT PROCESS

The effective counselor knows and interacts with his community's referral agencies.

Let's suppose that a counselor's house caught fire one night, and his wife hurriedly telephoned the fire department. "We'll be right over," the dispatcher assured her, "as soon as the driver finds his road map, so he can figure out the best way to your house." As silly as this little analogy seems, it's a perfect parallel to the way some counselors go about referral of crisis cases to various professional agencies. These counselors wait, like the firehouse driver, until an emergency arises. Then they scurry for the Yellow Pages, seeking to learn where a referral may be made. Finally, they expect speedy service from agencies with whom they have never before had contact. Little wonder these same counselors complain about waiting lists and time-consuming intake procedures. The tragedy of such a situation is that it's the emotionally disturbed or socially deprived counselee who suffers. Just as the house in the story will burn down before the firemen arrive, so will the child's personality or familial condition deteriorate, perhaps irreparably so.

The best time to choose appropriate referral agencies and shorten waiting periods is before crises arise. The effective counselor knows, visits, and interacts with his community mental health and social agencies regularly, as a matter of professional policy. His cooperation with fellow helping professionals should have nothing to do with whether he's referred anyone to them or not. Not only does this open line of communication facilitate handling of the crisis case when it occurs, but it also provides opportunity for continuous dialogue and feedback, which serves to make both referral agency and counselor more effective. A good practice is to visit referral agencies during various public and professional events that almost all of them sponsor. These include open houses, conferences for school personnel, and various fund-raising events—chili suppers and the like. Another good practice is to drop in early in the school year to discuss referral for the months ahead with agency intake officials.

Basically, mental health referral agencies fall into six basic categories, namely, public, quasi-public, private, university-affiliated, mental hospital-affiliated, and commercial:

1. *A public agency* is one created by state or local governmental statute to serve a certain political entity, such as a city or county. This agency is responsible to either a public official or an elected board of trustees, and draws its financial support from tax monies. A county mental health clinic is typical of this category.

2. *A quasi-public agency* is privately organized and controlled, but receives a portion of its support either directly from local government, or from public charitable effort, usually the United Fund. This type of agency also serves a geographical area, and is generally governed by a privately chosen board. An example is Family and Children's Service.

3. *A private agency* is one owned by some group within society, such as a fraternal organization, church, or non-profit foundation. This group also "pays the freight," and for this reason may elect to restrict agency intake to members' children, or to certain categories of children.

4. *A university-affiliated agency* is set up and governed by a medical school or psychology department of a university. Its purpose is to procure patients needed for the education of psychiatrists and/or clinical psychologists. It draws its support from the university, and is subject to academic governance.

5. *A mental hospital-affiliated agency* is an outpatient facility operated for less seriously disturbed clients by a residential institution also serving psychotic inpatients. This referral possibility came into existence when mental hospitals created it for the purpose of easing their own cured

patients back into society via a "half-way" situation. The hospitals soon found it advantageous to admit others to this service, for preventive rather than rehabilitative treatment.

6. *A commercial agency* is a private practitioner, either a psychiatrist or a clinical psychologist. Frequently, several of these professionals organize a medical or psychological clinic, rent facilities, and set up a practice in the manner of other medical or dental professionals. Sometimes, when this is done, a psychiatric social worker is hired by the clinic for intake and liaison assignments. Because it's necessary for the practitioner(s) to make a living directly from client fees, this type of referral agency is normally most expensive for teen-agers and their parents.

Referral institutions may also be categorized by type and intensity of therapy offered. In somewhat simplified format, treatment may be lumped under one of five headings, namely, inpatient, outpatient, educational, specialized, or a combination of elements of the other four.

1. *Inpatient therapy* involves the youngster's leaving both school and family situation, and taking up residence at the referral agency for the purpose of receiving psychotherapy.

2. *Outpatient therapy* consists of the client's remaining in school and home, while visiting the referral agency for psychotherapy on a regularly scheduled basis.

3. *Educational therapy* means the transfer of the student from the regular public school to a class attuned to the needs of the disturbed. Sometimes this only entails movement to a different building within the same school system or locality, while at other times it means taking up residence in an inpatient facility operating a school as part of its total program.

4. *Specialized therapy* is aimed at a specific personality-related adolescent problem, such as drug use. These programs, both inpatient and out-patient, admit only those individuals afflicted with the problem in question.

5. *A combination program* merely means that a client receives two or more of the preceeding types of therapy, either simultaneously or one following the other. Combination therapy could mean receiving two kinds of help from the same referral agency, or participating in the programs of two or more different helping institutions.

It's frequently beneficial to a counselor to build a list of his area referral possibilities, categorizing them by such variables as type of administrative control, programs available, costs, location, etc. Then when an emergency arises, the cogent facts are right there, summarized in black and white. Figure 9-1 shows a sample list.

ANYTOWN AND SURROUNDING AREA MENTAL HEALTH REFERRAL AGENCIES

AGENCY	ADDRESS	TYPE	PROGRAM(S)	CONTACT PERSON	COSTS	REMARKS
State Univ. Child Psychiatric Clinic	618 3rd St. 4th floor Anytown	university-affiliated	outpatient psychotherapy	Phil Smith, Psy., Social Worker 645-8230, x 45	ability to pay	very short waiting period
Coal County Mental Health Clinic	Route 3, Box 18 Eastchester	public	outpatient family therapy	Maxine Stern, PhD, Psychologist 688-2991	ability to pay	will not see child without parents
Family & Children's Svc.	1313 4th St. Anytown	quasi-public (United Fund)	outpatient	Stan Miller, Social Worker 645-2200	$4.00 min., ability to pay	under-staffed; may have to wait
Recovery, Ltd.	218 12th Av. Eastchester	private	inpatient, drug recovery; outpatient addict groups	Rev. Jack Bowles, Director 688-3344	patients "work for their keep"	drug problem cases only
County School District disturbed class	Route 3, Box 99 Eastchester	public	day school for emotionally disturbed	Frieda North, Principal 688-2159	free	need psychiatric diagnosis to get in
Our Lady of Good Counsel Child Ctr.	Route 1 Anytown	private	in & out patient therapy, school for disturbed	Sr. Mary Celia, Director 645-3681, x 7	in = $1500 per sem. out = $10 per hour	take all faiths; prefer to go through family pastor
Anytown State Hosp. crisis intervention center	38 2nd St. basement entr. Anytown	mental hospital affiliated	short-term intensive in-patient care	Dr. Wm. O'Shea, Resident Dir. 645-2380, x 218	free	family M.D. or law enforcement officer must refer
Dr. Sam Silverstein, psychiatrist	212 7th Av. Eastchester	commercial	outpatient psychotherapy	doctors' answering svc., 688-2999	$25 per hour	will reduce fee in school consulting cases

Figure 9-1

Counselor and client jointly decide on a course of action.

If a boy or girl is to profit from referral for emotional or related difficulties, he or she must have confidence in the chosen course of action, and, ideally, share in its planning. This could mean giving the counselee a voice in referral agency selection. The only time this principle should be neglected is in a crisis situation, where the student's mental health state has deteriorated to possible psychosis, or if suicide has been attempted. In these cases, no time may be wasted attempting to "sell" a client on referral, or in seeking to elicit his cooperation in a selection process. (Such a client would probably lack the lucidity needed for decision-making, anyway.) But in cases where the child is not an immediate threat to himself or others, the *whys, wheres,* and *hows* of referral are a must topic for one-to-one counseling.

Frequently the school principal, the youngster's parents, or both, have already decided that the disturbed student must either be removed from school due to problem severity, or see a referral agency as a condition of remaining in school. If either situation exists, the counselor should inform the pupil forthwith. An administrative dictum such as this is a "given" of the counseling situation, a fact of life with which the client must cope. The worst thing a counselor can do is seek to sugarcoat the pill or soften the blow. The sooner the student faces up to the consequences of his problem, the sooner he will be motivated to receive help for it. Emotional illness, of course, is not the fault of the counselee, and he should not be led into feeling guilty for his past behavior. This is not good mental health, nor is it what "accepting consequences" means. However, it's possible to demonstrate to a pupil that his personal and social behavior is inadequate for dealing with a normal life situation, without inducing guilt feelings over past actions. Once the client accepts his inadequacy, he'll be motivated to modify his behaviors. It's very doubtful that a pupil who is dragged to a referral agency against his wishes gets any benefit from it, no matter how qualified its therapists. Therefore, it behooves a counselor to first sell his client on the desirability of referral whenever humanly possible. In addition, if counselor and client discuss and plan referral strategy together, it's much more likely that the young person will cooperate with efforts to help him, and gain more from the experience.

A different sort of "sales problem" occurs when the counselee confides a problem in the counselor that is not readily noticeable to others. Examples include habitual drug use, sexual promiscuity, kleptomania, etc. Because no authority figure in the adolescent's life is aware of the situation, there is no compulsion or persuasion being exerted to seek help. This type of referral circumstance underscores the importance of client participation in the choice process. If the youngster isn't sold on referral (assuming the counselor feels the problem to be beyond his competencies), there isn't going to be any.

Teachers and administrators sometimes become involved in the referral process.

Many referrals made by counselors never come to the attention of other school faculty. This is as it should be. A client discusses a personal problem privately with his counselor; the two of them agree on need for referral and work out a plan of action.

In cases where the counselor is making or assisting in a referral, parental consent must be obtained. In some cases, this will mean convincing the counselee to break the news at home, before the counselor calls to broach the referral topic. Only in cases where the client is too troubled to attempt this, or is estranged from the home, should the counselor break the news. Of course, if a counselee flatly refuses to discuss a referral recommendation with his parents, the counselor, after giving the client a reasonable time to relent, may call. Parental consent is required in all cases where the counselor is acting in an official capacity in referring. Of course, if a counselee discusses a problem in counseling, then refers himself, say to his pastor, a drug-user's helping person, or a draft advisor, this is a different matter. Parents need not be informed in this type of "referral," because no school action is being taken to implement it.

The youngster visits the referral agency, often with his parents; the agency shares information with the counselor, again with client permission. Together, agency, parents, and counselor pool their efforts to help the troubled counselee. No one else knows of the problem; in fact, no one else may know, as the confidentiality ethic is operating.

This example illustrates one type of referral case. Another pattern occurs when the troubled pupil has been disruptive in school, or discovered participating in bizarre or abnormal behavior there. The overt manifestations of the child's problem are anything but confidential; every teacher and student in the building is aware of them. The disturbed youngster invariably has been ejected from a class and sent to the principal for discipline. Many times this is a proper initial response, as many emotional problems induce outward manifestations unavoidably disciplinary in character. For example, theft, sexual misconduct, or fighting in the school building may stem from emotional disturbance. These behaviors must be subject to immediate disciplinary action if a school is to function normally.

The counselor becomes involved in cases of this type when the principal or a teacher, or, in rare cases, a group of students, dumps the problem in his lap. The persons bringing the matter to the counselor's attention recognize their inadequacy for dealing with the emotional aspects of the situation. They have administered whatever discipline the case appeared to warrant, and concluded that further remedial steps are needed. In fact, a principal may make matters pretty clear, especially after conferring with a distraught teacher who cannot control the deviant youngster. "Get that boy professional help, or out he goes," the administrator informs the counselor.

As a fellow professional educator, the counselor owes it to his colleagues to assist them in their hour of need. He also must make it clear, however, that referral in these cases has to be a cooperative effort. Faculty interaction in handling this kind of problem is a two-way street; while the counselor takes a leadership role in pushing a referral (if in his professional judgment one is needed), the principal and teachers have roles to play, also. Fundamentally, other staff members have three types of referral-expediting tasks to perform, namely, observational, persuasive, and supportive.

Observational duties involve making systematic, objective observations of student behavior, much in the manner of an elementary school teacher's anecdotal record. Specific behaviors, without any moral or evaluative judgments, are recorded. Witnesses are listed, and each behavior is described as accurately as possible. Places and dates pertinent to the various incidents are noted. One purpose of observational duties is to provide tangible proofs that referral help is needed, in case the client, parents, higher school authorities, or referral agency questions the need for professional help. Another purpose is to provide meaningful diagnostic and background data for the referral agency.

Persuasive duties are efforts made to convince various parties to a case that referral is needed, and after referral has occurred, that agency recommendations must be followed. The disturbed student, parents, district administrators, referral agency, other teachers, etc., may need convincing that a problem is serious. In addition, some parents, teachers, and other students need persuasion that certain of their actions are making matters worse. The principal, teachers, and counselor recommending referral frequently have a sales job to do on other parties to the case, if referral is to first become a reality, and then do any good.

Supportive duties mean presenting a united front to the powers that be. Once a principal, teacher, and counselor have determined, for example, that an adolescent should attend a class for the disturbed, rather than remain in regular high school, the decision must be treated as a collective, unanimous one. "The three of us have decided . . .," not, "Mr. Jones thinks that. . . ." Professional educators involved in a case must, once a clear course is charted, back each other at all times. The counselor, for instance, should never be forced to "go it alone," especially when the important and touchy matter of someone's mental health is at issue.

The counselor must often sell parents on the need for specialized professional help.

Some referral cases never come to parental attention. A teen-ager discusses a private issue with a school counselor, and a referral decision is made. The counselor discusses the matter with the client, who then makes his own arrangements, and the entire case remains a confidential counseling matter. As stated previously, the referral itself isn't school business, thus the normal requirement for mandatory parental permission doesn't apply. Sometimes this is the way to go; adolescents are little kiddies no more, and it's occasionally wise to exclude parents from a case entirely. Another set of referral circumstances may arise, in which it's the parents who bring a student's emotional problem to the counselor's attention. Many distraught couples have turned to their child's school counselor for help; some of these cases lead to eventual professional referral, others are dealt with by joint counselor-parental effort. In either of these two types of referral situations, where parents are never aware, or where they instigate the request for help, there's no need for a counselor's sales pitch. Either they should not be told anything, or they are so sold on the need for help already that they actively seek it.

When parents must be told because either a counselee's mental health status appears in jeopardy, or his school conduct has degenerated to serious levels, then the counselor has a ticklish job indeed. No one likes to hear that his beloved child is deficient in any way, even if he strongly suspects so himself. The fact that one's offspring may be afflicted with mental illness is the hardest pill of all to swallow. Although we live in an enlightened age, and emotional problems are no longer regarded as Divine punishment for familial sin, a proposed trip to the "head shrinker" for junior is still a rough, rough concept for most parents to accept. While no hard and fast set of rules applies to dealing with this difficult counselor duty, certain general principles may be identified for use in helping parents accept and cooperate with referral necessity. Each counseling case is unique, and must be "played by ear." The following guidelines should be considered from this flexible frame of reference only.

1. *Seek to quash parental guilt feelings.* Many parents may become emotional when confronted with a counselor's referral suggestion. They may express sorrow, indifference, or non-committal shock, or they may defensively vent hostility upon the purveyor of bad news. The counselor must not display irritation at these parental emotional displays; after all, it's their own flesh and blood youngster who's in trouble, a highly disturbing happenstance. Above all, in order to dispel the emotional reaction and get to the cognitive aspects of the case, the counselor must exhibit acceptance of the expressed parental feelings. He must let the parents vent their reactions, be they sad, passive, or angry, for emotion may only be dissipated by allowing its free expression, and factual matters may only be taken up as such after emotional displays have run their course. Once this has occurred, the counselor must build the parents' self-confidence by minimizing the idea, if mentioned, that they are responsible for the present state of affairs. The reason that personality problems of children are so threatening to parents is because of guilt feelings: "What did we do to make her turn out like that?" is a question counselors often hear. Even mental retardation is less hard to accept, because, as parents see it, retards are "born that way," whereas disturbed children "get that way" (that is, "get that way in their home environments"). One line of reasoning that a counselor may take is to point out that no one knows what causes mental illness, although it is known that numerous factors are involved. Therefore, no single thing parents did could possibly be to blame. Also, since the parents love their child, and tried to do their best by him, they should not feel guilty. Guilt is a proper emotional response only

when the guilt-producing behavior results from actions considered wrong or "bad" at the time of commission.

2. *Explain the school's position.* As school liaison person, the counselor has the job of interpreting school decisions to parents and communicating parental feed-back to the school. In referral matters, the counselor must clarify for parents what has already officially transpired in their child's school problem. For example, the principal may already have suspended the disturbed youngster, or recommended to the superintendent that the teen-ager attend a special school. The child, ashamed, has not told his parents, and the principal's letter, if indeed it has arrived, is unclear to them. Whatever has or has not happened at school must be told to the parents, who have every right to know all the facts in their offspring's case, except for confidential counseling information. Moreover, as they may not be familiar with school procedures and educational jargon, the counselor must be prepared to explain these in laymen's terms. Most important of all, reasons for various school moves must be explained to the parents, who will be far more apt to concur if given why's and wherefore's. As liaison person, a counselor helps parents see the situation from the principal's and teachers' positions. For example, if the disturbed child has repeatedly disrupted an English class, the counselor describes the teacher's frustration at being unable to fulfill her contractural obligation due to one pupil's conduct.

3. *Turn the old stigma argument around.* Often parents raise a sincere argument against their child's being either taken to a psychiatrist or placed in a school for the emotionally impaired. They use the old stigma argument; that is, getting the adolescent special help will brand him as different, single him out for ridicule, and actually worsen his problem. When faced with this reasoning, a counselor may point out that it's the current situation that is stigmatizing the child; it's his present conduct that marks him as different and causes referral necessity. Psychotherapy is aimed at making the troubled adolescent less different, so stigmatization will cease. Placing the teen-ager in a special class likewise diminishes his feelings of being different. This is because the students in the present school environment have already dubbed their disturbed peer with the colloquial stereotype for persons having mental health problems. Among cruel and heartless students who might tease a peer with an emotional problem, there's little likelihood that *their* appraisal of his

condition will ever change, no matter how much improvement subsequent therapy brings. On the other hand, transfer to a new educative environment gives him a fresh start. His new classmates have no weird or queer stereotype, and thus afford him a chance to play a more normal social role, free from peer group expectations of abnormal behavior.

4. *Stress the reversibility of the mental health situation.* If a parent makes a comment like, "Our little girl didn't use to be this way," the stage is set for the counselor's contention that referral can restore her to good mental health. The fact that emotional difficulties are curable if prompt steps are taken, while handicaps such as mental retardation and cerebral palsy are not, is a powerful argument for selling parents on referral need. The analogy may be made that if the child fell on the stairs and broke her arm, the parents would indeed rush her to a physician, so if she is found to have a personality disorder, she should immediately be taken to the appropriate specialist for healing that problem. The counselor may have to calm parents' fears that the child is "going crazy," pointing out in simple terms the difference between neuroses and psychoses. Yet, he must also call a spade a spade, and explain that neurotic behavior sometimes progresses toward a psychotic state if not checked. Of course, most neurotic conditions do not progress toward psychosis; instead, they remain constant, appearing to get neither better nor worse. It is still important that a youngster with this form of condition receive help, because "look how much happier he'll be if we can clear this up." Some counselors may not wish to use the terms "neurotic" and "psychotic" at all, substituting the terms "mildly disturbed" and "seriously disturbed."

5. *Include parents in referral agency selection, reviewing administrative details carefully and pedantically.* Parents should have a say in referral agency choice, not only because this psychologically predisposes them to implement its recommendations, but also because some agencies require their being interviewed along with their child. They have a right to know what they're getting into, and it's the counselor's job to see they understand this in practical terms. The counselor has an obligation to explain all referral options open to parents, covering costs, frequency and duration of visits, types of therapy, etc. He should also be prepared to offer his own referral recommendations, and to defend his choice(s) if called upon to do so. He must remember that if the parents decide to take their teen-ager to a bona fide commercial referral agency at their expense,

rather than go through the channels he suggested, they have every right to do so. A good tip for reviewing referral possibilities is to endeavor to see things from parental perspective. A counselor who is sensitive to the emotional and factual needs of others should have little trouble. Always keep in mind family cognitive dimensions, including educational level, economic capacity, and religious affiliation, in addition to conative factors that the parent-child relationship creates.

6. *Keep in touch.* Some counselors do an excellent job of observing the first five parent referral liaison guidelines, but neglect #Six, probably because of the threat of mutual embarrassment. The counselor, feeling that he knows certain highly confidential facts about a couple's offspring, and realizing that they know he knows, avoids face-to-face meetings. Perhaps discretion is the better part of valor, and if either parents or counselor cannot avoid embarrassment, this may be advisable. This should only occur in very rare cases, however. The counselor who perceives this situation coming up frequently perhaps needs to cast himself more fully in the role of family friend and confidante. Even in these few rare cases, any feelings of touchiness must not be allowed to interfere with follow-up and implementation of agency post-therapy period recommendations. Telephone, mail, and verbal messages borne home by the referred client, if he has remained in counseling with the counselor, are potential indirect communication channels. These means are handy if it has been decided to send home periodic counselee school progress reports. Almost always, therefore, it's not emotionally or practically wise for parents and counselor to physically avoid one another. For example, some parents who received psychotherapy or consultation as part of their child's referral process, look to the counselor as a symbol or reminder to persevere in new behavior patterns. Just as a reformed alcoholic might rely upon a religious artifact as an inspiration to stay sober, they seek a reassuring smile from their son's counselor as a help in sticking to newly adopted child-rearing practices. If the counselor avoids parent contact in this instance, he actually hurts his client's cause. Furthermore, in smaller communities it's difficult for a counselor to avoid anyone, and to remain aloof from certain persons is not only highly inconvenient but also downright rude. A good thumb rule for eliminating embarrassment during meetings is always to have a conversational topic ready that's far removed from sensitive areas. If the parents wish to inquire about referral-related matters, let them broach the topic. And

if they do have the courage to bring up their personal problem, a counselor worth his salt will discuss it with them, embarrassed or not.

A counselor never allows red tape to damage a student's mental health.

Social complexity and impersonality have brought about abuse of a one-time legitimate institutional administrative procedure, the so called "waiting list." Originally, maybe, waiting lists served a bona fide fairness function, in guaranteeing observance of the democratic "first come, first served" principle. The author suspects that this waiting list function has waned, and they now serve largely as cover-ups of bureaucratic ineptitude. This cynical view may, of course, be challenged, but having seen what "pull" and knowing the proper individuals can do to waiting lists, he doubts there is much need for their continued existence. A school counselor cannot tolerate delays during the referral process. Picture a disturbed high school boy or girl undergoing a psychotic breakdown or committing suicide while marking time prior to the onset of therapy—this is enough said! A counselor faced with referral hold-ups may call upon several formidable allies to apply pressure where needed. If either parents or the referral agency are dragging their feet, the school principal, client's teachers, and in some cases, superintendent of schools might lend a hand. If the disturbed adolescent's conduct has led to involvement with the law, welfare and/or probation work- ers, perhaps even the juvenile judge might be induced to pick up the telephone. If parents are cooperative but referral agency is slow to move, a counselor can frequently get them to make inquiries. The two most powerful allies of all, provided that the parents want them to become involved, are the family clergyman and physician. The counselor, most knowledgeable person of all regarding referral agency infrastructures, must advise his allies regarding whom to call. One soft-voiced but insistent plea to the proper agency executive is worth 100 harrangues at the switchboard girl. Of course, this hardnosed counselor response to delays must not be an insensitive one. If there is something he may do to speed the intake process, he must do it—even if it means going beyond duty's call—or be a hypocrite. For example, he might drive the client to a referral appointment if parents are unable to do so, or help the agency with intake paper work, if their own clerical forces are overloaded.

Follow-up effort insures that referral agency recommendations are implemented. If the referral decision is to remove the counselee from the present school environment and place her in a more therapeutic educative situation, the referring counselor has only *passive* follow-up responsibility. The counselor, social worker, or other pupil personnel officer at the new institution has the job of *active* follow-up. Active follow-up means obtaining recommendations for dealing with the disturbed client from referral therapists, communicating these to teachers and parents, and seeing that they're followed. Passive follow-up also means obtaining recommendations, but filing them away under lock and key, in case the youngster ever returns to the counselor's jurisdiction (many do). In cases where the referred teen-ager remains in the counselor's school, active follow-up becomes his baby. The success of home and school recommendation implementation during the post-therapy period is often more important than the therapy itself. The following are points in achieving good active follow-up:

1. *Obtain a release from client or parents and seek prompt interaction.* Referral agencies will not give confidential information to anyone without client permission, or, for younger clients, parental permission. This is proper practice, and must be observed by the counselor as well as anyone else. The counselor must seek this release as soon as feasible, and initiate immediate agency liaison, so there will be no delay in putting new ideas into effect.

2. *Work understandingly with school faculty to effect changes.* Usually, the referral agency social worker tackles the ticklish job of communicating recommendations to parents, leaving briefing the school staff to the counselor. In so doing, the counselor must not seek to impose foreign administrative or teaching behaviors upon his colleagues. Rather, he should explore ways in which existing building and classroom methods may be bent to achieve a more therapeutic environment for the counselee. It's not good mental health to excuse a disturbed student from complying with certain rules; a far better procedure is to stress rules that all can obey. Neither is it good personnel procedure to expect a principal and teachers to completely revise their ways of doing things just to accommodate one pupil—and the counselor. If, instead, the counselor stresses flexibility of existing practices rather than a whole set of new ones, he's far more likely to effect changes beneficial to his client.

3. *Enlist student aid whenever ethically permissible.* If the trou-

bled pupil's problem is unknown to his peers, then he's the only one who may inform them. Frequently, however, the fact that Billy or Susie has been in a special school, or to see a psychologist, is common student body knowledge. When this latter situation prevails, a counselor is sometimes able to therapeutically modify counselee environment by appealing to mature, trustworthy students to help. In so doing, he must not reveal any confidential information or data, but only the fact that certain things will "help Johnnie." He should only involve pupils who already know their friend "has a problem." For example, another high schooler may be privately urged to talk his troubled peer into coming out for a sport, asking a girl to a dance, helping build a home-coming float, etc. Such manipulative steps may be taken only if (a) they are consistent with referral agency recommendations, and (b) the peer group change agent can be trusted not to reveal his suggestion's origin.

4. *Continue the counseling relationship, blending agency insights with your own.* The client who has been through a referral process is probably not "cured," but only helped. It's the counselor's task to take up counseling where the therapist left off; this may only be achieved by conferring with the therapist. However, a counselor must remember that his personality and professional training differ from the therapist's, thus precluding blind continuation of the perceived referral agency approach. Rather, the counselor should work with the student as he sees fit, using agency recommendations to perfect his own technique. Above all, level with the counselee, discuss the referral experience with him as an equal, ascertaining what *he* thinks the agency wants him to do to improve, etc. After all, client perception of reality *is* reality for all practical purposes, and this must be the starting point for post-referral counseling.

TEN

Consulting with the School Staff –
the Guidance Team in Action

The "personnel services team" is not just a theoretical nicety encountered only in doctoral-level counselor education classes; it must become a working process in every American secondary school. But how? Everyone agrees that consultation is an important counselor duty, but little concensus exists regarding its optimally effective implementation. Just how may a counselor go about working with his fellow educators in ways that really pay off?

WHO'S THE OPPONENT IN THIS GAME?

Chapter Ten of this book is not the first attempt in the literature of the counseling-personnel services field to use an athletic analogy to illustrate operations of a so-called personnel services or guidance "team." The consultant-to-faculty counselor function and joint counselor-staff projects on behalf of clients do indeed bear certain resemblances to the smooth, cooperative efforts of football players seeking to defeat an opponent. The problem with analogies is that authors sometimes either become "cute," carrying them too far, assuming similarities between parallel situations where none exist, or overlook initial, basic relationships. First of all, if there's to be a personnel services team, let's know whom we're playing against, and what our opponent's capabilities are! Just as a football team scouts its future foes and plans game strategy accordingly, so must the guidance team accurately comprehend its rival.

Fundamentally, joint counselor-staff projects and consultation are aimed at a multi-faceted enemy. These "players on the other team," to state things analogously, are *all factors that interfere with optimum emotional and academic development of high school boys and girls.* They include conative foes, such as various adolescent personality and social inadequacies, and cognitive ones, like college and job admissions requirements. As modern society becomes more complex, it seems that the opposing "bench" has more players seated on it, ready to enter the game! For example, such foes of youth as effects of hallucinogenic drugs and urban core deterioration were largely immaterial to counselors until the mid-1960's. The personnel services team can only win its contest, like a real football team, in relative terms—that is, by out-scoring the other side. Absolute victory, or completely eliminating all derogatory influences and situations from teen-agers' lives, is out of the question. The realistic goal of the guidance team is to make lives of students (the "fans" of this game analogy) a little more nearly perfect, a little closer to some optimal, utopian ideal.

NOT A COACH, BUT THE QUARTERBACK

Analogizing further, what is the counselor's role, or "what position does he play?" Because the counselor is a fellow educator of administrators, teachers, and educational specialists, he is *not* the team's coach. Here's where the analogy breaks down; this team has no coach—or at least, no individual has this type of designation on the guidance team. (The principal is in some ways like a coach, but "team captain" better analogizes his role, as he is an active "player.") If there's any coach at all, he's not a person, but a symbol or concept, namely, the ideal American society, or optimally beneficial environment—whatever that means. This is the mentor for whom the "players" all work so hard! Since the counselor must function as professional equal to his fellow personnel services team members, he cannot play a coach's role, since this connotes being an authority figure, a "boss" of the other players. Such a counselor image is not conducive to the accepting, dialogue-among-equals philosophy essential to good counseling and consulting relationships.

The counselor is a two-way player on the guidance team. He's the "quarterback" on "offense"; that is, he calls the shots in operating various personnel programs aimed at helping students. These are the team's "plays." He's the "defensive signal-caller" on "defense"; that is, he advises teammates on tactics to use in thwarting "opponent plays," i.e., student problems. The exercise of the consultative function by the counselor are the team's "defenses." Just as football offensive plays are pre-conceived, carefully executed manuevers to advance the ball, so are the counselor's school programs designed to further pupil maturational development. Just as football defenses are systematic, thoughtfully planned strategems for frustrating opponent plays, so are the counselor's consultative efforts designed to stop various deleterious influences on counselee lives.

RESPECT THEIR PERSPECTIVES, UTILIZE THEIR TALENTS

Just as different members of a football team have differentiated assignments and responsibilities, depending on position played, so do various guidance team members exercise specialized functions. This differentiation occurs in two ways, namely, in perspectives and in talents. *Perspective* differences among school staff members are based upon professional positions held. Analogously, these compare to guard, tackle, half back, and other football positions. Just as a quarterback does not throw forward passes to his center, neither should a counselor ask a principal or teacher to perform a task inconsistent with his professional role. *Talent* differences among school staff are based upon differential abilities, interests, and aptitudes. These are analogous to the speed, size, experience, and other variables contributing to a football player's make-up and ability. A quarterback would not expect a 140-pound guard to repeatedly keep an opposing 260-pound tackle away from the passer. Neither, for example, should a counselor ask a young teacher relatively inexperienced in human relations skills to explain a certain program to an unusually difficult parent.

Use of perspectives and talents has a positive side, too. A quarterback certainly calls upon his most powerful ball-carrier to grind out those last two difficult yards to pay dirt. So does a counselor ask his principal, the faculty member cast in a leadership role, to help expedite a recalcitrant referral situation. The quarterback, in calling a pass pattern, seeks to isolate his speediest receiver alone against a reputedly slow defender. So might the counselor request that a teacher, possessor of a masters degree from a certain prestigious university, assist a graduating high school senior, wishing to matriculate there, in gaining admission. All in all, the counselor, as a human relations specialist, appreciates and respects both the frame of reference and the constellations of traits of each staff colleague. Just as appreciation of individual differences by a quarterback leads to optimal performances on a football field, so does proper personnel utilization by a counselor engender maximally effective pupil personnel services.

Each teacher has a rich background of training and experience upon which to draw.

No two classroom teachers are alike in the professional backgrounds or personalities they bring with them to the school faculty. However, every teacher is exactly the same in occupational frame of reference, namely, a contractual obligation to convey a specified body of facts, skills, and concepts to the young. This dichotomous situation has certain implications for the counselor, as leader of the personnel services team. First of all, it behooves him to learn what each teacher's unique strengths and characteristics are, so these may be tapped as a student guidance activity resource. Sometimes these teacher traits are obvious, as they're connected with the teaching field. An industrial arts teacher, for instance, may be assumed to have considerable expertise in handling machine tools. This, in turn, makes him a natural resource person for advising several boys who seek summer jobs of a mechanical nature, provided, of course, that he's willing to do so. Not all teacher characteristics are this obvious, however. For example, a foreign language teacher might have as her hobby collecting rare coins or stamps. She might be more than willing to advise similarly interested high schoolers, but unless the counselor takes the trouble to become acquainted, he's never going to learn this. One good idea for counselors is to make a list of important non-confidential faculty data, such as avocational interests, colleges attended, vacation and travel plans, etc. Many staff abilities go untapped because no counselor or administrator bothers to discover them.

Second, the specific professional perspective common to all teachers must be respected by counselors during consultation on client classroom difficulties. Occasionally a counselor loses sight of the fact that teachers have a job to do, and becomes irritated over their reluctance to bend teaching procedures to fit client needs. A counselor confronted with this situation must endeavor to see things from the teacher's point of view. This does not mean surrendering counselee considerations in favor of teacher considerations. Instead, it means acceptance of varying viewpoints, followed by dialogue in which counselor and teacher work out a plan of action beneficial to both problem student and instructor.

What are some personnel activities in which teachers may facilitate pupil development, without dilution or contradiction of their basic instructional mission? Basically, teacher personnel contributions fall into four categories: (1) homeroom guidance and quasi-counseling activities, (2) observational data collection, (3) joint guidance-teaching field (interdepartmental) projects, (4) serving as resource specialists.

1. *Homeroom guidance and quasi-counseling activities* are regular teacher duties in many secondary schools. In others, similar teacher actions have sprung up on a less formal, unstructured basis. A system of homeroom teacher-advisors for secondary pupils is based upon the psychological need each normal child appears to have to identify more closely with a particular teacher than with all teachers equally. This factor has long been recognized at both grade school and college levels, but only in recent years has its importance been established for high schools. Apparently, every student, regardless of age, likes to have a teacher to call his very own. A system of teacher-advisors helps fill this pupil need. Homeroom guidance and quasi-counseling activities are of three types:

a. Teachers may use the homeroom period to perform various cognitive level personnel functions. Examples are achievement test score interpretation, Social Security card application, ACT and SAT signup, showing vocational films, filling out class schedules, etc. The counselor informs teachers which activities are current, providing essential materials and procedural orientation.

b. The period may also be used for group guidance sessions, in which an affective or emotion-related topic is presented and discussed at the cognitive level. Examples include teaching human relations principles, discussing problems of getting jobs, viewing films on dating etiquette, conducting study-skills workshops, etc. Once again, the counselor provides teachers with necessary materials and briefing, but more leeway is allowed, due to differing staff interests and competencies. A warning is in order here against forcing homeroom groups to participate compulsorily in group counseling or sensitivity sessions. Because homeroom membership is involuntary, commonalities necessary for successful group counseling may not exist. If persons are asked to join in conative level activity against their will, only trouble results.

c. Teacher-advisors should have some time available for individual conferences with advisees who wish to discuss minor problems or school matters. Such quasi-counseling is not a substitute for the counselor's regular counseling program, but a complement to it. Teachers are quite qualified to lend an understanding ear to normal teen-agers' day-to-day concerns, and to advise them on various cognitive aspects pertinent to school careers or vocational development. This teacher function relieves the counselor of numerous minor problem involvements. The counselor assists teachers who feel they are capable of entering into quasi-counseling relationships, explaining to them the nurture of therapeutic, one-to-one, helping interview behaviors.

2. *Observational data collection* (anecdotal record-keeping) by teachers gives counselors vital facts for helping clients with emotional disturbances or serious learning disabilities. Frequently, a counselor or referral agency is at a loss to decide what's troubling a youngster. Each teacher with whom the pupil has contact is asked by the counselor to systematically note behavioral manifestations. These observations are factual and objective; no interpretive or judgmental material is logged. (Teacher opinion is welcome, of course, during consultation, but the anecdotal record isn't the place for it.) Many counselors have a regular observational data form or school log for teacher use in recording behaviors. Since this procedure is an imposition upon teacher time, adding to daily work load, its use should be confined to serious cases, and then for a reasonable length of time only.

3. *Joint guidance-teaching field projects* become possible whenever a counselor's personnel activity overlaps an enrichment area for student learning in a particular school subject field. Some examples are: community occupations survey (social studies), work-study programs (industrial arts, business education), group guidance on social behaviors (home economics), science scholarship test preparation (science), publishing a guidance newsletter (English, graphic arts), group guidance on aesthetic appreciation (art, music), building local achievement test norms (mathematics), etc. Learning, whether about one's personality or about a field of formal knowledge, is never compartmentalized. Counselors and teachers may help their students gain in many ways by cooperation on joint endeavors. In addition, a faculty that works together becomes more efficient; as staff members become more responsive to colleagues' needs, their own performances improve. Counselors should take the lead in breaking open those compartmentalized, departmental boxes that often impede relevant, life-oriented student learning.

4. *Serving as resource specialists* allows teachers to contribute to pupil growth more individually than does either teaching or partici-

pating in structured personnel programs. Each teacher is an individual, with interests, talents, and personality all her own. To tap a particular constellation of traits for a specialized pupil personnel need is highly flattering to a given teacher, but properly so. A resource specialist program functions thus: During individual counseling, counselor and client mutually decide that certain specialized information or advice is needed. Because the counselor has been "on the ball," he knows that a certain teacher is well versed in the area under discussion. He therefore suggests to the counselee that he approach the teacher in question, requesting the needed information. A counselor might wish to semi-formalize the resource specialist program by asking teachers in advance if they'll be on call as consultants upon appropriate topics. Either way, this program makes for optimum staff utilization within a psychologically sound framework.

The principal has a unique contribution to make.

As individual cast in a managerial, leadership school faculty role, the principal has a viewpoint unlike any other staff member. Resurrecting our guidance team—football team analogy, the principal is likened to team captain. Since he's not a counselor, he's not a team leader or quarterback in the sense of running the student personnel program. But because he's the official authority-figure within the school, it's often the principal who implements a counselor-proposed personnel activity via executive edict. Here's a major reason why counselor and principal must have close working relationship. The counselor, as school guidance specialist, suggests a certain personnel program; the principal, as overall head of the school, orders it put into effect.

An administrator has a perspective all his own. Since he's top man, or boss, of an entire school facility, he's ultimately responsible for its continued success. He therefore seeks optimal performance in *all* school areas, of which personnel services is but one. The administrator hopes to increase instructional quality and learning, and to decrease student emotional and disciplinary problems in his school. Pupil personnel programs and consultation are vital to achieving this administrator's goal, as they serve to both enhance academic learnings and diminish behavioral difficulties. A good principal realizes this, and therefore supports a broad, active counseling and guidance program. After all, there's "something in it for him," in that running a more successful school enhances his own reputation and chances for professional advancement. The other side of this coin, obviously, is that when things go wrong, it's the top man who's ultimately blamed. A counselor must appreciate that fact, and not become impatient when his principal wishes to weigh carefully all variables before approving a new personnel activity.

The counselor consultation function is often important to a principal. Frequently an administrator seeks greater comprehension of psychological factors underlying various student actions. He may wish to ascertain the possible emotional effects of alternative possibilities in pupil discipline. In such matters, the counselor is the logical resource person upon whom the principal calls. Sometimes it's the counselor who needs advice, and he taps his principal's leadership perspective. For example, a counselor may ask his administrator how a certain guidance activity might "go over" with the board of education, community, or a teacher group. Or he might seek the principal's support in promoting an activity already in existence. Occasionally, in personnel programs where the counselor must of necessity direct or supervise teachers, he may deem it wise to request the principal to inform them of this fact. However, if a counselor expects his principal's backing and support, he must be ready to reciprocate. It also helps an administrator to receive staff backing, and a counselor must remember that supportiveness is a two-way street.

A joint guidance-administration personnel project offers a rare maturational opportunity to participating students, and at the same time strengthens mutual counselor-principal understanding. These projects also pose an inherent danger in that inadequate ground work or improper pupil orientation may lead to alienation of participating youngsters from their peers. One project that has been tried by some schools is turning absentee-checking responsibility over to students. Another possibility is to allow student volunteers to spend free school hours on quasi-administrative assignments, such as textbook ordering, receiving, and/or processing. If handled properly, these activities can return great benefits to everyone involved.

The school nurse is a team member with special, often overlooked abilities.

The school nurse's mission is to enhance the healthfulness of student's lives, and to a lesser extent, improve health conditions within their home and school environments. There are many potential overlaps between guidance and school nursing, including joint action in mental health referral cases, identification and remedying of learning disabilities such as defective vision, and cooperative group counseling on pupil problems of mutual interest, obesity being an example. Most counselors do an excellent job of including school nurses in these and other mutual concern areas, and vice versa. Yet despite this fact, the nurse is seldom looked upon by educators as a full-fledged personnel services team member. This probably stems from the fact that school nurses are members of the health service family of professions, while counselors, teachers, and administrators belong to the educational profession. Most schools had nurses before they had counselors, which has led to certain nurse-connected duties being delimited without consideration for counselor involvement.

Actually, the nurse has a striking commonality with the counselor in that both roles are fundamentally pupil-centered. Each worker is primarily concerned with helping individual students overcome various personal problems, and secondarily concerned with environmental modification of school and home in the pupil interest. The guidance team functions more smoothly when the counselor includes the school nurse actively in a wide variety of personnel activities. Four major types of participation should be stressed: (a) Mutual consultation and interaction between counselor and nurse should occur whenever a client problem falls in both jurisdictions. This activity may be broadened when necessary into case conferences in which principal and teachers also participate. (b) The nurse's professional opinion and observational data should be solicited in all mental health and learning disability referral cases, except those where total confidentiality exists. Her medical knowledge adds a new perspective in many instances. (c) All guidance programs should probably contain at least one joint counselor-nurse project. Project nature varies with individual and situational specifics. A typical joint operation example is a weight-watchers or complexion-improvers group counseling process. (d) The nurse's interaction with boys and girls should be broadened far beyond a vision-testing, Band-Aid applying, temperature-taking routine. For instance, as a resource specialist in the health careers area, the nurse may advise students who feel vocationally inclined in this direction. Counselor and nurse might even jointly chaperone a nursing school visitation by interested graduating seniors as further activity along these lines.

When outsiders need persuasion to respect a school student personnel decision, the nurse's public image is a vital asset. Apparently, the aura or status surrounding members of the health service professions is greater than the charisma of public school educators. The nurse is a key resource person whenever a difficult personnel action, such as removal of a pupil from school for mental health reasons, must be explained to others.

The librarian is so a first-stringer!

The school librarian's perspective, at first glance, doesn't seem to have much to do with pupil personnel services. Her mission is to direct acquisition, cataloging, and housing of cogent books, periodicals, and audio-visual aids, and to supervise student usage of same. However, a little ingenuity on the counselor's part can bring the librarian right into the mainstream of guidance activity in three major areas.

1. Building a library collection of occupational, educational, and social reference materials may in some schools fall in the librarian's as well as the counselor's jurisdiction. Chapter One covers in great detail the performance of this duty by a counselor. In some cases, however, due to budgetary, office-space, or tradition factors, the librarian shares this responsibility. Moreover, some librarians take an interest in this area, and wish to build such a collection, regardless of what the counselor is doing. It behooves both these professionals to get their heads together, regardless of situation, on behalf of improving the school collection of guidance-related literature. Each stands to gain immeasurably from exposure to and interaction with the other's perspective.

2. Most librarians sponsor a club or group of student helpers who work voluntarily in the library during free periods. This club is, of course, under the librarian's jurisdiction, and the counselor should not horn in. In many schools, library club is one of the most successful pupil personnel activities in operation. In two different schools with which this author was familiar, library club was exceeded in popularity as an extra-curricular activity only by interscholastic athletics. What's advocated here is not counselor take-over of this group, but his working with the librarian to capitalize on its tremendous latent client benefits. For example, certain counselees experiencing social problems may gain therapeutic encounters by participating in library club. Counselor-librarian cooperation brings this about.

3. The librarian is a valuable resource specialist in at least two areas. As resident school reference material expert, she knows a lot about knowledge acquisition, both in finding material, and in using it effectively. The librarian is the "how to study authority" on many a high school faculty. Thus, a counselor may wish to refer a client having study-skills difficulties to the librarian for remediation. The second, more obvious, resource specialty is that of career consultant to teen-agers contemplating librarianship vocations.

Various remediative specialists join the attack on student problems.

Almost every school has either on its staff or on call various specialists who teach or do therapy with adolescents who have different behavioral disabilities. These helpers include speech clinician, remedial reading consultant, and teachers of special rooms for the mentally retarded, physically handicapped, or emotionally disturbed. Each of these professionals has a primary mission of working directly with individuals or small groups of students, assisting them to either overcome their disability or learn to cope with it. They have a secondary mission of working with other school staff and parents, explaining to them ways to help variously afflicted youngsters. Each remediative specialist is a pupil personnel worker of sorts, in that he engages in a certain program designed to help a particular category of pupils.

Counselors have numerous opportunities to mutually consult and undertake joint projects with remediative specialists. This is due to the fact that almost all student problems are multiple. Many of the vocational, learning, and emotional problems of counseling clients have speech, reading, retardation, or other factors present. For instance, emotional insecurity sometimes includes stuttering as an overt manifestation; a physical handicap might preclude certain jobs after graduation; retardation could well be the root of school hatred or inability to read. This general multiplicity often leads to simultaneous client involvement with the counselor and one or more specialists. It follows that each professional, attacking a pupil problem from a specific frame of reference, could profit from conferring with like-minded colleagues. Of course, in so doing, the counselor must not reveal client confidences, but still there's plenty of potential benefit in these meetings of minds.

Many times, all school staff working with a certain student hold a case conference. Frequently, parents, social workers, referral agency case workers, rehabilitation counselors, and other properly concerned parties also participate. The counselor, as guidance team leader, sets up these conferences, sees that they progress amicably, notes proceedings, and insures that recommendations are implemented. Each professional person working with a given pupil contributes to this collective decision-making process from his or her perspective This multi-faceted attack upon an adolescent's problem marshals all possible resources, and is an example of an effective personnel services team in action.

A major project in which counselors and remedial specialists often cooperate is intake screening of students to determine those eligible for remedial programs. At the high school level, this includes vertical liaison with counselors and remediative specialists of feeder schools, so counseling and remediation efforts will articulate. If a counselor is charged with horizontal liaison, that is, responsibility for requesting records of incoming transfer students, it's a good idea to inquire of previous counselors regarding possible remediative needs. This way, a pupil's former program may immediately be continued without psychologically and educationally damaging interruption. It's usually a wise practice for the counselor to send a memo to all teachers and administrators shortly after school begins every fall. This memo is an attempt to locate any previously undetected remedial cases. A sample is shown in Figure 10-1.

After possible remediative cases are identified, the counselor sees that each case is evaluated by the appropriate professional. Teachers and administrators don't always guess correctly; for example, a student who fails to turn in completed assignments might be tabbed "retarded," while in actuality he is "unmotivated." Speech and reading referrals are evaluated by the speech clinician or remedial reading consultant; possible retards are given a WAIS or Stanford-Binet by the district psychometrist or psychologist; suspected handicapped and disturbed teen-agers are seen by the counselor, who may then consult with parents, family physician, rehabilitation counselor, and/or school psychologist, as appropriate. This generalized procedure points up the need for smooth staff teamwork; if one guidance team member "drops the ball," a pupil in need may fail to receive vitally required remedial services.

School social worker, psychometrist, and psychologist perform their special jobs when called upon.

Just as a football team brings a kicking specialist off the bench to boot a field goal or extra point, so does the counselor call in a school

MEMO

TO: all staff   DATE: 9-30-73
FROM: John Jones,   SUBJECT: identification of students
        counselor   with special needs

Do you know of any student(s) who you feel would profit from one or more of the specific programs listed below? If so, please write their names, and check the appropriate program(s) needed. Feel free to make any explanatory comments you wish on the back of this form. Your remarks will be held in confidence; please return this form to the counselor in a confidential manner. If you later find you have omitted anyone from this form, please stop in the counseling office and give me his or her name. Thank you for your cooperation.

POSSIBLE SPECIAL PROGRAM NEEDED

STUDENT NAME & GRADE	counseling	speech therapy	remedial reading	slow learners' room	handicapped class	emotionally dist. room	study-skills workshop	assistance for disadvantaged
. . . .	( )	( )	( )	( )	( )	( )	( )	( )
. . . .	( )	( )	( )	( )	( )	( )	( )	( )
. . . .	( )	( )	( )	( )	( )	( )	( )	( )

Figure 10-1

social worker, psychometrist, or psychologist to perform a spot role. These professionals are the substitutes of the personnel services team; players who aren't regulars, but are there waiting on the bench when need for them arises.

The school social worker is a trouble shooter of sorts, a visitor of homes, and like the counselor, a liaison person who deals with outside-of-school agencies and persons. The social worker's mission varies from district to district, but basically he's the staff member who investigates non-school events and places that are influencing student lives. Some districts saddle their social worker with attendance-enforcement duties; when this is the case, he's less valuable as a personnel services team member. That's because (a) his public image, especially among pupils and parents, becomes more nearly that of law enforcement officer than professional educator, and (b) he's usually so busy tracking down truants that there's little time left for anything else. But when the social worker is used properly by the district administration, he's a valuable asset to the guidance team indeed.

For instance, school social workers are involved in assisting student families afflicted with poverty and related problems. A counselor, working closely with a poor client, usually finds it psychologically detrimental to the counseling relationship to seek assistance for the family himself. (Getting the youngster or his father a job doesn't damage counseling, but putting them in a relief or charity role usually does.) Therefore, the counselor, with client permission, calls in the social worker, who helps the family. Sometimes, counselor, nurse, and/or principal discover that a serious health problem exists in a home. To intervene themselves can cause rapport problems with those children at school, and give rise to parent charges of interference. Here again, the social worker is called in.

The psychometrist is a giver of individual tests and other highly specialized appraisal instruments. Usually his major role is intelligence testing, although many psychometrists administer diagnostic tests like the Illinois Test of Psycholinguistic Abilities and Purdue Pegboard, and projective techniques like the T.A.T. and Rorschach. A psychometrist's value lies in his perspective as detached, purely objective measurement specialist. While many counselors are as qualified to give all tests that most psychometrists give, doing so has two disadvantages: (1) Time spent administering individual appraisal instruments could be better spent in counseling or practicing personnel services. (2) The counselor is too emotionally close to clients, and too professionally close to school faculty and parents. An IQ score computed by a counselor might reflect subconscious emotional influence, or its validity could be challenged by someone suspecting ulterior motives. He might be accused of cheating, so a counselee could make (or not make) a state cut-off score for special class membership, to cite one possibility.

So, call in the psychometrist, let him do the testing; that's what he's being paid for. Psychometrists should attend all case conferences at which their appraisal is being used in decision-making. Also, a counselor must always establish whether the psychometrist will interpret his findings to the client. Some do, some don't. If the psychometrist doesn't wish to engage in student explanations, the counselor should obtain the test results and do so himself.

The school psychologist, in some school districts, is more helpful to counselors than in others, depending upon assigned duties. For example, some systems combine the psychologist and psychometrist roles, which severely curtails time available for pupil psychotherapy and staff consultation. (Tests take a certain time to give and score; inter-personal relationships may always be shortened.) Other systems, equally penurious, combine the position with that of research director. That school psychologist is usually too bound up in attendance projections and salary cost analyses to do the guidance team much good. The proper mission of a school psychologist is primarily to engage in diagnosis, therapy, and referral of youngsters having apparent serious personality or learning disorders. Second, he consults with faculty and parents on the remediation and handling of these children. Third, he does experimental and statistical studies directly related to various aspects of his primary and secondary roles.

In severe cases of emotional disturbance and behavioral disability, the counselor calls in the school psychologist. In essence, the counselor is acknowledging his own lack of competence in a given situation and "going higher," just as a teacher refers a less serious problem to the counselor. Whenever the psychologist is involved on a case, he should attend case conferences and play a role in needed parent and teacher explanations. The counselor must make note of the psychologist's recommendations and see that they're implemented.

TEAMWORK GETS THE JOB DONE

Just as each of eleven football players must properly execute a different assignment if a play is to succeed, so must each personnel services team member perform his mission well if a student is to be lastingly helped. One missed block ruins a football play; one indifferent school performance cancels out guidance efforts of several other professionals. Each helping attempt from every staff member, those discussed previously in this chapter, adds up to a sum total of considerable magnitude. The counselor must see that a coordinated assault is made on each pupil problem, seeking to focus all efforts directly upon eliminating it.

Analogizing once more, guidance work, like football, is a game of cooperation and teamwork. On the field, blockers clear the way for ball-carriers, passers throw to receivers, holders spot the ball for kickers, and so on. This same basic helping concept applies to the personnel services team. Teachers refer to counselors, principals support librarians, psychologists consult with speech clinicians, etc. Counseling as a process is predicated upon give-and-take, two-way dialogue among equals who care, or, colloquially speaking, on "getting along." Personnel services, to function efficiently, must reflect this counseling philosophy. The counselor, as team quarter-back, and his principal, as captain, set that kind of example in their own staff relationships, and politely insist upon its prevalence in all school personnel service activities.

ELEVEN

Consulting with Parents –
Someone Who Cares

Dealing with parents is a necessary component of every school counselor's job. There are certain do's and dont's that may be spelled out, but it's impossible to pedantically set forth a cook-book recipe for parent relationships. This is because changing situations and circumstances make each case unique. A better approach is to have an overall strategy that may be modified when necessary. How does the counselor go about fostering amicable and productive liaison with parents?

MAN (WOMAN) IN THE MIDDLE

Because they fall naturally into a liaison position between various school-connected publics, counselors are often cast in a mediator or arbitrator role. Most counselors don't mind such a duty when it involves an outside group and the school—for example, the Welfare Department and the school administration. When two school-connected groups or individuals from two such groups fail to have a meeting of the minds, however, most counselors are less eager to cast oil upon the waters. Obviously, a purely natural reluctance to get into it or to take sides sets in, as counselors become rightfully concerned over potential damage to their rapport if an individual or group perceives them as biased. This syndrome puts a counselor in a difficult spot, as many members of all four major school-connected publics—students, teachers, administration, and parents—expect him to take a positive stance in clearing up inter-group and inter-personal disputes. In other words, the counselor is damned if he does, and damned if he doesn't! Intervention in internal school controversy may stamp him as partisan, but failure to do so may label him deliquent in fulfilling the duties of his professional position. This situation frequently becomes critical where parents are concerned. For instance, a parent might become engaged in bitter controversy with a teacher over a course grade given a child, with the principal over an allegedly too-harsh punishment meted out to the boy for truancy, or with the youngster himself over interpretations of the school's dress code. To further complicate matters, what if this hypothetical parent, or, for that matter, group of parents, had earlier sought out the counselor, to express satisfaction with the way in which he operated the testing program? Now they're back, under less-pleasant circumstances, seeking counselor involvement. To refuse alienates them, to jump in may alienate others. Just what does the counselor do?

STRATEGY FOR PARENT RELATIONSHIPS

While indeed there is no magic formula for intervening in disputes, yet always emerging from the fray with unspotted professional image, there is a conceptual framework for intermediary operations that holds unpleasantness to a minimum. Before describing this approach, however, it's vital to spell out when a counselor *does* keep hands off and refuses to become involved. A rule of thumb may be stated that a counselor should not assume the liaison role in internal school disputes unless (a) the controversy is obviously over a guidance-related matter; (b) one or both parties in the matter request his intervention; (c) his principal or other superiors request it; (d) through use of his introspective human relations skills, he perceives both parties wishing his involvement; or (e) a grave moral injustice may result if he does not. All other times, a wise counselor keeps his olfactory organ clear of controversy!

Before spelling out a conceptual liaison framework, a final point must be made—not all counselor-parent dealings represent counselor efforts to ameliorate controversy between parents and someone else. Many times, the relationship is a consultancy one, in which the counselor explains college admissions procedure, adolescent psychology, school grading policy, or some other guidance-related topic to a concerned father and mother. Such conferences are two- rather than three-sided. The counselor's job here is not to adjudicate a disagreement, although one may have indeed precipitated the parents' informational need. Instead, as authority on teen-aged behavior and institutional student personnel procedures, the counselor helps parents by passing along needed facts. Even in these less controversial situations, however, there's need of a standard operating procedure, one based on good inter-personal relationships. Tact, psychology, and plain old common sense form the basis for all parent-counselor dealings, whether they be of the mediational or consultative variety.

The groundwork for good parent relationships is laid prior to need.

Consistent with his own interests, personality, and obligations a counselor should strive to establish numerous parent acquaintance-ships throughout the school attendance area. These contacts will be informal, semiformal, and formal. Those of the former variety are made through practice, at all times, of good old-fashioned cheerful-ness and gentlemanly (or ladylike) behavior. A "Good morning" here, "How are you?" there, and "Is your father feeling better?" someplace else pays off later in rapport benefits. A good thumb rule for informal contacts is to memorize something that is important to each parent (business, family, hobby, etc.) and inquire pleasantly about it upon casual meeting. Semiformal contacts take place at various mutual membership organizations—religious, political, hobby, and social—or during routine business and commercial transactions. Formal contacts occur at school functions where the counselor is acting in his professional capacity, and when paths cross during the more serious social proceedings—weddings, funerals, legal dealings, and the like. While semiformal and formal contacts are not appro-priate for small talk, as are informal ones, there's always room for a kindly exchange of pleasantries. Moreover, all three forms of parent-counselor interaction afford the counselor opportunity to become known to parents and other community residents. The value of familiarity in dispelling ignorance of the counselor is a recurring theme throughout this book. If the counselor is not well known, the chances of ambiguous perceptions of him and his school role are greatly increased. These in turn easily lead to suspicion and hostility toward him on the part of parents.

While numerous parental contacts are desirable, there are two pitfalls which counselors must avoid: (1) Never push oneself onto a community to the extent of over-eagerness or even hypocrisy. Joining organizations is great, provided that they are consistent with an individual's traits and feelings. Insincere, hypocritical conduct eventually becomes known, and boomerangs against an individual. In short, "belonging" is wonderful, but "catering" is abhorrent! (2) A counselor, by being on good terms with numerous parents, always runs the risk of appearing too "establishment-oriented" to clients. There's always the possibility that a teen-ager, seeing his counselor talking cheerfully with his father, will cease to confide in the counselor. Some persons, in fact, have gone so far as to suggest that counselors, in order to retain student rapport, must disdain all contact with parents and other authority figures of society. Counselors are even advised by these persons to dress and wear their hair in such ways as to clearly identify themselves as being on the side of students. While it's certainly true that over-familiarity with parents, police officers, the school principal, and others damages rapport, it's also true that artificial catering to pupils damages it. Nothing offends a teen-ager more than a phony, and the counselor who dresses like a student may receive contempt and ridicule, rather than rapport, as a reward. On the other hand, some counselors sincerely believe in effecting certain commonalities with their clients. These counselors should indeed dress, wear their hair, etc., as they feel they should; for them to effect an establishmentarian appearance is just as phony. The key to building and keeping rapport with parents, pupils, or anyone else, is sincerity and being one's self. A counselor who is insincere, regardless of what camp he claims he's in, will be rejected by all. This is why a counselor can practice good human relationships with everyone, and not alienate any one segment of his personal world. Having a friendly word for everybody, regardless of race, age, status, or religion, is neither "establishment" nor "mod" behavior; it is human behavior. If such a policy is followed, it's very unlikely that client rapport will suffer from exchanging pleasantries with parents. After all, sincerity is an essential counselor quality, and as every high schooler knows, sincere people don't "rat" on their friends—even student friends!

When parents confer with the counselor,
his official mission must be clarified at the onset.

Most parents do not have a clear-cut concept of what a counselor does, and thus enter into conferences with one while under great ambiguous stress. Frequently, they equate being summoned or invited to school by a counselor with a similar request from the principal. "What has my child done wrong now?" is apt to be their frame of mind as they enter the guidance office. Other parents harbor a different type of counselor-role misinformation. Having heard or read somewhere that counselors help students, they make appointments with the counselor to request all sorts of help. For example, they may want the counselor to assist their daughter to be chosen a beauty contest winner or their son to be named starter on the basketball team. Other parents may bring a more reasonable attitude with them to a conference, but are nevertheless ill at ease because of ambiguity or misconceptions. The first thing a counselor must do, therefore, at any parent conference, regardless of why it is held, is to clarify his professional role. Such an explanation must be kept simple, and at times has to deal with the negative, i.e., what counselor is *not,* as well as positive role components. For instance, a counselor is not a disciplinarian, nor does he have authority to compel teachers to extend preferential treatment to students. These are two negative role characteristics that unfortunately must frequently be tactfully explained to parents.

Of course, the positive role elements—what a counselor is—are the most important aspect for parental clarification. First, a counselor must stress the fact that his primary obligation is to pupils. The counselor is the faculty member hired expressly to help boys and girls, to listen to their problems, discuss their schedules and future plans, interpret their test scores to them, etc. Thus, the counselor's primary allegiance is to his clients, rather than to the other, adult publics of the school. This leads directly to the second step of the explanatory process. While counselors indeed help clients, this help is rendered in such a manner as to decrease immaturity and dependency. For example, a counselor does not fill out a class schedule for a student or find him an after-school job. Instead, by discussing schedules or job-seeking behaviors with the youngster, the counselor makes it possible for the counselee to complete his own schedule or obtain the job himself. Third, a counselor must explain that even though his foremost duty is to the students, he's completely willing to assist parents. The rationale for such assistance is this: parents love their children; want to see them happier and more successful, both in school and in life in general. Counselors also develop empathy and concern for pupils, likewise wishing them to be happier and more successful. Therefore, parents and counselors have a common interest in bettering children's lives. They're on the same side, where interest in adolescent well-being is concerned. It thus becomes logical for counselors to give helpful suggestions, as appropriate, to parents, because such help ultimately benefits those parents' children. Since counselors are hired to help students, they may do so directly through counseling and personnel services, and indirectly, by assisting parents in doing a better job of rearing their offspring. Fourth, a few brief words on specific counselor job-duties often help parents to more fully comprehend what guidance is all about. A brief description of the counseling process, how it takes place and why it is beneficial, as well as nutshell descriptions of the several personnel services, go a long way toward dispelling ambiguousness in parental minds.

Who requested a parent conference
is a factor in shaping counselor strategy.

There are three kinds of counselor-parent conferences: those requested by the counselor, those requested by the parent, and those requested by the third party, generally teacher, principal, or student. The basic strategy followed by a counselor in parental dealings will vary somewhat, depending on who initiated contact. The basic counseling philosophy employed by the counselor will not change, however. Let's consider the three types of conferences in turn:

1. *Counselor-initiated parent contacts should, with two rare exceptions, be made through the client or at least with his knowledge.* To call in a parent without first informing the child in question is unwise, and is likely to damage rapport and create an image of two-facedness. The two exceptions to this policy are as follows:

(a) If a counselor fears that a client is likely to do injury to himself or others, the ethics of the profession allow revealing of confidences. A counselor faced with such a situation generally summons parents and school administrator to an emergency meeting. To inform a disturbed client of such a conference in advance might only worsen his homicidal or suicidal tendencies. (b) Occasionally, a counselor receives secret information that his client has won a great honor, such as a scholarship, which cannot be told the student prior to a certain date. Sometimes the counselor in these circumstances wishes to share the information with parents, so they may better prepare for the happy event. Perhaps they wish to hold a reception in their child's honor; prior knowledge would be useful. A counselor may contact parents secretly in this instance, using good judgment as his guide.

Most counselor requests to visit with parents are not as dramatic as the two exceptions to the no-secret-meetings rule. Usually, they stem from two sources, either a counselor-presumed parent informational need, such as college financial aid explanation, or a client-revealed home problem. The latter case, of course, may never be discussed with parents without client permission. The former case, as it is strictly cognitive and a general need of all parents, may, but even here, it's best to communicate with parents through their child. When a counselor and his client, or group of clients, have decided that counselor-parent dialogue is desirable, the student(s) extend(s) the invitation homeward. In a cognitive, information-giving context, this is more likely to mean a group conference, with several pairs of parents seeing the counselor at once. A good way to initiate this type of conference is to send factual preliminary information, for example CEEB or ACT financial aid statements, home with pupils. A scribbled message from the counselor, coupled with a student verbal reminder, invites all those wishing further clarification to a meeting at school. Test score interpretation and class schedules of incoming pupils may be handled in a similar manner; parents hear general information from the counselor in a group, while examining individually prepared score reports or schedules of their own youngsters.

When a proposed parent contact involves a problem situation in the home, the first thing a counselor must do is ascertain the practical feasibility of his intervention. Will it help the situation? Will he be labeled a busybody? Will the client only get into worse trouble if the counselor requests a conference? The best way to answer these and other questions that arise is to consult the counselee. After all, he is closest to the situation, and best able to forecast how his parents will react. Only if the client agrees it would be helpful to all concerned should the counselor request a parent conference. The question naturally arises as to what to do if the conference really is desirable, but the client, out of embarrassment, indicates it is not. The answer to this paradox lies in the major goal of counseling, namely, the fostering of maturity. One hopes that the client in question would ultimately perceive the need for parental inclusion, and finally come around to consenting to it, as the counseling relationship progressed. It's very doubtful that any good would result if the counselor contacted the parents against client wishes, because of client resentment. Moreover, in these cases the parent or another school staff member often eventually requests a counselor-parent conference, making the need for pupil consent moot. Sometimes, when consent is granted by the counselee, the counselor may elect to send a written note home with the client or call the parents on the telephone himself in lieu of a verbal message borne by the youngster. When either of these alternative invitation modes are observed, (1) the contents of the note or call should be shown or told the client; (2) parents should be informed that their child and the counselor both deem a counselor-parent conference advisable.

When parents arrive for a counselor-requested conference (both parents should be present whenever possible), special provisions must be made to make them feel at ease. Often overlooked, pedantic details, such as the availability of coat racks and ash trays, are frequently important in establishing an optimally favorable psychological climate. The counselor's office is normally the best place for the meeting. Whether the child is also present cannot be predetermined in any book, or by using any set of guidelines. Sometimes it's best for the client to be present, other times not. Still other situations dictate two conferences, the first with parents and counselor alone, a second including the client as well. The counselor must exercise professional judgment regarding which course to follow, after surveying the specific circumstances at hand.

Sometimes parent or counselor work schedules make it very difficult for a father, mother, and counselor to get together without severe inconvenience to someone. When this problem threatens, ingenuity is often the key to its solution. Sometimes unconventional times and places are best for a conference, for instance before work in the morning, or over a school lunch. Sometimes evening is the answer, but usually evening conferences are best only if all parties are going to be present in the area anyway. (For example, this writer once met a boy's parents between halves of a school basketball game.) Late afternoon is another possibility; this lends itself well to catching parents on the way home from work. (Again, this writer once met parents while the football team he coached was showering in the locker room.) In short, three concerned people can always find a mutually agreeable meeting time and place if they try hard enough. However, a good rule of thumb for counselors and other school faculty as well is not to visit homes for conferences unless parents or their children request it, or places of employment unless parents request it.

2. *Parent requests to see the counselor are made in many ways, and for numerous reasons.* Sometimes students bring in oral or written conference requests; at other times a letter or phone call to the school office is made; still other communications come directly to the counselor via mail or telephone; and, occasionally, a parent

. appears at the office door unannounced. Reasons for wanting a conference are legion; most requests probably stem from parental perception, either accurate or exaggerated, that their offspring is having an academic, disciplinary, emotional, or moral problem. Probably the second greatest cause of parent-requested conferences is the desire to obtain further information about a school or guidance program of which they've heard, such as achievement testing, college visitation, or work-study. A third common reason parents seek the counselor is because their youngster has become involved in a serious conflict with a teacher, the principal, or another student. On rare occasions, a couple seeks out their son's or daughter's counselor for help with their own marital or vocational problems. Having heard favorably of the counselor from their child, they turn to him themselves. This situation is the greatest compliment a school counselor can possibly receive, although a left-handed one. How deeply a counselor wishes to become involved in helping parents with their own personal difficulties is a professional question each counselor must answer for himself. Factors include counselor training and personality, the nature of the problem, the school situation, and availability of community referral sources.

Regardless of the reason parents wish to see him, a counselor should oblige as soon as possible. There are two exceptions to this rule, however: (1) A client interview should never be abruptly terminated in the middle just because V.I.P.'s arrive at the office. Neither should a scheduled interview be postponed for this reason, unless it can still be held later in the same school day. After all, the counselor's primary obligation is to the students. (2) Sometimes it's best to let a few days pass before seeing parents known to be irate, or a few minutes elapse if parents arrive at school in such a state. The reason for this is to afford the upset parents a chance to cool off, so they will not make statements of which they'll later be ashamed. The delay is *not* to cater to counselor cowardice or afford him a chance to concoct a story. When dealing with irate parents, or, for that matter, with any angry visitors to the counselor's office, a good thumb rule is to dispel hostility by accepting it. Don't argue back or defend; instead, let the upset individual state his true feelings. Show a quiet understanding of the hostility even though it may appear to be quite irrationally based. Statements like, "You've every right to be angry," or "There's lots of justification for your anger," are good, but the counselor must allow his irate visitor to do most of the talking.

The most delicate situation of all during parent-requested conferences arises when parents ask that their visit be kept secret from their
offspring. Many counselors seek to avoid this in advance by making
openness with the pupil a prerequisite for seeing the parents. This
policy may be the way to go, although some persons might argue
that it could scare off a couple urgently in need of help. Each case is
unique, and a counselor must exercise professional judgment when
such a request is made. Normally, it's wise to dissuade parents from
trying to keep the conference itself secret. The counselor may point
out that more than likely the student or one of his friends either saw
the parents in the school building or observed their automobile
parked outside. If the youngster learns of the visit in this manner,
while his parents and counselor remain silent, he will experience
serious ambiguity-stress, and his imagination will blow the problem
up much bigger than it really is. Moreover, the child will cease to
trust both parents and counselor, whom he now perceives as being in
league behind his back. When confronted with these facts, most
parents will agree to tell their youngster that a conference took
place, or ask the counselor to do so. This doesn't mean that the boy
or girl must be told all that was said; for example, certain highly
private matters, marital infidelities and so forth, are best treated with
confidentiality. After all, the counselor respects the client's private
confidences, and it's only fair play to respect those of the parents as
well. Generally, if parents meet with a counselor on a matter bearing
upon their child, the child should be told that the conference took
place and what it was about. Private parent matters that came up
during this conference should not be told. A counselor must exercise
good judgment in deciding where to draw the line.

3. *Frequently a third party deems a conference necessary, and
requests the counselor to arrange it, and to participate.* So-called
"case conferences" fall into this category; here an administrator,
appropriate teachers, both parents, and the counselor join forces to
work out improvements in the school and home environment that
will benefit the pupil in question. Because the counselor has a
legitimate liaison function to perform, requests from an administrator to set up such a conference are a proper delegation of authority,
and not buck-passing. Consequently, the counselor should assume
the responsibility for finding a mutually acceptable date, time, and
location for the multi-sided conference, and see that all participants
are notified. He should also act as recording secretary during the
conference, and be responsible for follow-up afterward, checking to

see that conference recommendations are implemented. In arranging such a meeting, the counselor should tell parents on whose authority their presence is requested. "Our principal, Mr. Jones, feels that we should all get together to discuss your son's school progress," is a typical inviting statement. If the counselor fails to indicate that the principal or a teacher requested the meeting, parents may conclude that the counselor acted independently on the basis of interview information. This can be dangerous, as it leads to parents demanding to know of their offspring what on earth it was she told the counselor that upset him so much he's convening a confab. When a case type of conference is to take place, the counselor should check the physical facilities beforehand, making sure that adequate seating, coat racks, note paper, etc., are available. During the conference, he may wish to keep a record of proceedings on a form designed for this purpose. Upon conclusion, all parties present sign the form, a copy of which is then given to each participant. Photo-copy, multiple carbons, or chemo-carbon procedures make this an easy task. There are two advantages in giving all participants a signed, written record of a case conference: (1) It prevents anyone from later misrepresenting or distorting what actually was said. (2) It provides handy follow-up reference for implementation of recommendations. A sample of a typical conference record form is presented in Figure 11-1.

Occasionally, a third party recommends to a counselor that he meet a given pair of parents in a two-sided conference. While such requests are no doubt well-meant, entering into such an arrangement may cause problems. A counselor faced with this request should express willingness to do so to his suggesting colleague, but should also make it clear that when the parent is contacted, the referrer's identity will be revealed. This protects the counselor from accusations of being a busybody when other persons learn of his involvement. This policy is also in accord with the themes of frankness and ambiguity-diminution, upon which much of this book is based.

Another form of parent conference occurs when a student asks his counselor to confer with his parents. Here again, a counselor should consent to do so, but only if the client himself will invite his parents to participate. This course of action is in keeping with the premises that maturity results from doing things for oneself, and that a person wishing something must have the courage to seek it. However, after a client has asked his parents to visit the counselor, the counselor may then also call them to urge a meeting, if this action appears wise.

ANYTOWN HIGH SCHOOL GUIDANCE DEPT.

RECORD OF CASE CONFERENCE

Pupil_____ Class_____ Homeroom_____ Date_____

Reason for Conference:_____

_____

_____

_____

Summary of matters discussed:_____

_____

_____

_____

_____

_____

_____

_____

_____

_____

_____

Suggestions adopted for helping pupil:_____

_____

_____

_____

_____

_____

_____

Those present for conference: (Each participant please sign name, and indicate role or title (principal, teacher, parent, nurse, psychologist, counselor, etc.) after name. Each person present is to receive a completed signed copy of this form. One copy is also filed in pupil's guidance folder.

_____   _____

_____   _____

_____   _____

_____   _____

Figure 11-1

Sometimes telephoning them from the office while the counselee is present, or jointly writing them a note, is a good practice. Another benefit of requiring the client to make the initial overture is that it lessens the chances of the counselor being drawn into petty family quarrels. A pupil, upset for the moment over some trivia, has a chance to think twice about the advisability of formally bothering parents and counselor with it.

Still another form of parent conference in which counselors are sometimes asked to participate is the "hearing" type. Here, school authorities require a student to confer with properly interested staff and his parents, generally over a disciplinary or academic problem. Actually, this form of meeting is merely a case conference with the youngster present. The counselor's role in "hearing" type meetings differs little from that during regular case conferences, with one important exception—he must make sure that his client understands what's being discussed, and has an opportunity to state his side of the story. This latter type of instance is where the two forms of conference, the consultative and the mediational, merge into one. Here, the counselor both advises parents and faculty and seeks to ameliorate a dispute or conflict between a teen-ager and the adults who impinge upon his life.

**Counselors must guard against embarrassment
as the aftermath of parent conferences.**

Some counselors have a problem when they later meet parents with whom serious, confidential matters have been discussed. Apparently, recollections of what transpired cause embarrassment, and the counselor, reluctant to speak, hurries on past the parent, or avoids a meeting in some way. This is a purely normal reaction for many persons, and nothing of which to be ashamed. The problem is most acute when the earlier conference included discussion of sexual matters. The danger of letting embarrassment lead one to avoid a particular parent is that avoidance may be misconstrued as hostility or disinterest. Once more, the ugly spectre of ambiguity rears its head, as the ignored parent wonders why his former helping friend refuses to speak. However, if the counselor forces himself to acknowledge the parent in question, he may blush or show other signs of uneasiness that only serve to embarrass both parties. What, then, may a counselor do? Basically, the answer lies in the mental file of personal interests that all good counselors have compiled. As the counselor sees a parent approaching on the street, perhaps a father with whom his son's homosexual problem was once discussed, he prepares to introduce a topic that has neutral emotional connotation. "How's that home workshop of yours these days, Bill?" quickly throws both men's minds far away from unpleasant memories of their prior meeting. (Use of first names must be natural, however. A counselor should never force parents onto a first-name basis unless he's sure they wish it. Of course, as a counselor cultivates parent rapport, first-name basis friendships will arise.) No one emotes while reflecting upon a cognitive interest area, and verbally interacting about it. A good counselor must be prepared to skillfully introduce topics of conversation that avoid emotional problems, just as he sometimes must probe into these touchy areas when counseling or conferencing. This approach is far superior, in almost all cases, to simply avoiding someone with whom a traumatic topic was once discussed. Sometimes parents wish to discuss further the formerly traumatic matter, rather than avoid its mention. A skilled counselor has to be alert to pick up affective cues that this is so; as ability in human relationships develops, this talent comes naturally. And when this is the case, a counselor must be willing to review past problems and talk about their present implications, regardless of embarrassment or touchiness. After all, the counselor is a family friend and confidante, and must never shirk responsibility in this area.

SOMEONE WHO CARES

This chapter has divided parent conferences into two general categories, mediational and consultative. It also has compartmentalized them three ways, depending upon who sought the meeting—parents, counselor, or a third party. Four common causal topics of parent conferences were also suggested. Regardless of what type of conference occurs, who proposed it, or why it's held, however, basic counselor philosophic approach remains constant. This rationale pervades all counselor-parent dealings, even though specific strategies employed during various conference situations might vary. The basic approach is actually no different from that employed during counseling relationships, or in conferences with members of other adult publics. It therefore is closely related to the rationale a counselor employs in his counseling with boys and girls (analytic, Rogerian, neo-behavioral, positive thinking, etc.).

There are, however, certain human relations-oriented commonalities among all counseling approaches. These are very important in setting the tone for parent conferences, and both precede and then influence the specific topical considerations taken up during the meeting. Simply, they may be summarized as creation of the feeling that "someone cares." This includes dispelling ambiguity through clarification of the counselor role, establishment of rapport, and making all parties present feel at ease. Normally, these tone-setting goals are achieved by allowing the parents to do most of the talking. They must have an opportunity to explain why they feel as they do, what their opinions are, what questions they have, etc. Getting things off one's chest at the onset causes a person to be more receptive to cognitive inputs that result later in the meeting. The one important exception to letting parents do the initial talking is the need for counselor role definition, and, if the conference is school-requested, a statement of reason for the get-together. Sometimes, at the very beginning, it's best for the counselor to clarify these things in order to both dispel ambiguity emotionally, and inform everyone of key basic information factually. If the counselor or another school person has requested the conference, this preliminary statement is more lengthy than if parents requested it. Once this is accomplished, though, a wise counselor "shuts up" and allows parents to "speak their piece." While this is occurring, the counselor must display positive regard toward parent feelings, even though he might secretly disagree. After all, these perceptions do have meaning to those verbalizing them. This approach is consistent with promulgation of the "someone cares" tone and pays dividends for all concerned.

A possible exception to the policy of letting parents talk so freely at the onset occurs when the parents are shy, due to lack of education or verbal fluency. To urge such parents to verbalize extensively only turns them off more, and heightens their embarrassment or inferiority feelings. When faced with this situation, the counselor may wish to resort to the tactics of low-key leading questions, drawing the parents out in a friendly, non-threatening manner. It may be necessary to avoid using large words and technical educational jargon, which only serves to "rub into" less educated persons the fact that they are so. Questions that get to the point, yet do not require extensive answers, such as "Do you and your son get along well?" or "What kind of job do you think he should seek?" are frequently good. These give less fluent parents a chance to speak their feelings and give their views. This is really no different psychologically from letting the more verbal parents completely dominate the opening stages of conference dialogue. No different, that is, if the counselor has done the probing in such a manner that the less verbal or shy parents feel at ease and unthreatened.

In order to develop a genuine concern for the problems and feelings of others it's necessary for a counselor to vicariously get into their shoes, or see things from their viewpoint. This doesn't mean a surrender of his opinions to those of parents; rather, it means enhancement of mutual understanding and sensitivity. All humans are basically selfish, and tend to expect others to react to a given situation as they would react themselves. Counselors must be on guard against this tendency, as it is fatal to achieving good parent conferences. Being able to appreciate the viewpoints of all is what makes conferences go. The counselor, as catalyst and enabler of these meetings, has the prime responsibility for insuring that this atmosphere pervades all parental interactions, both with himself and with other school-connected persons.

TWELVE

Involving the Community—
No Stone Unturned

There are so many ways in which counselors may
include townspeople in some professional guidance activities, if only they'd try! Perhaps the reason more
counselors do not is that they aren't sure how to
proceed. The irony of this situation is that since the
counselor's role in many schools is so ambiguously
perceived, it's the counselor who has most to gain from
interacting with the community. What are some of the
ways for doing this?

LIP SERVICE MUST CEASE

Every graduate student studying to be a counselor (and every
other education student, too, for that matter) continually hears and
reads that "a professional educator must become involved with the
community." Few tenets of ivory tower educationists receive wider
dissemination or greater emphasis than this plea for local public
interaction by school faculty members. Somewhere, however,
between college class and professional practice, the universally
proclaimed axiom is usually lost in the shuffle. Far too frequently,
misunderstandings arise between townspeople and school staff that
could have been averted, had simple grass roots human relationships
been nurtured by the educators. It's highly ironic that counselors,
those people who are supposed to understand sensitivity, group
dynamics, and similar affective processes, are sometimes the worst
offenders. From both philosophic and practical standpoints, a counselor must build bridges of good will and understanding between his

program and the community it influences. To do so not only is consistent with fundamental principles underlying good counseling relationships, but also enhances the success of various pupil personnel services, which of necessity impinge upon the local, at-large community.

GETTING OFF ON THE RIGHT FOOT

The counselor's role is often ambiguous.

Most persons within a community, even some of those connected with the school, are not sure what counselors do in their work. Many people, especially those middle-aged and older, did not have a counselor in the high schools they themselves attended. Therefore, they lack familiarity with the guidance function, and often form inaccurate counselor role concepts based on fragmentary information and stereotypes. Even persons who had a counselor during their high school years may not have an accurate picture of what counselors do. This is due to wide diversity among guidance programs and the fact that a goodly portion of a counselor's work is treated as confidential. Also, many students go through high school without ever seeing a counselor, or encounter him for only one aspect of his duties, such as testing or scheduling. Consequently, they acquire either no counselor role concept, or an inaccurate one, based solely upon their involvement with him. Several recent research studies have supported this contention that counselor role is generally not well understood. These investigations seem to indicate that various population subgroups tend to expect counselor assistance in their own specific role fulfillment.

The tragedy of an ambiguous role perception lies in the suspicious feelings, which eventually become hostile ones, that it engenders. Persons tend to fear what they fail to comprehend, regarding it a threat. While counselors cannot, of course, reveal confidential information, they can and should explain the general nature of their work to school district patrons whenever possible. Even if a person doesn't allow his ignorance of a school counselor's work to lead to hostility, this is still dangerous. That's because every community member is, in some way or other, a potential contributor to the guidance program. Each person who doesn't know what guidance is all about is one less possible collaborator for the counselor. The loss of even one likely community resource person—someone who might otherwise contribute to more effective personnel services from his own unique frame of reference—makes the guidance program a little less good than it might be. In this age of automation, social change, and increased specialization, counselors need all the extra help they can get!

Groundwork is laid via countless informal contacts.

The cornerstone of good counseling practice is universal acceptance of fellow human beings. Every single individual on earth is a worthy person—just because *he is a person*. This basis tenet is an essential prerequisite for a school counselor's optimum success. That is, the most effective counselor is one able to display interest in *any* student, as well as in *all* teachers, *all* parents, etc. The secret of good community interaction lies merely in applying this same basic universal acceptance policy to extramural relationships as well as school ones. This doesn't mean the counselor is obligated to counsel with everyone on earth who so requests. Instead, it merely means he should strive to display acceptance and positive regard toward all people he encounters, not just those directly connected with the school.

By fostering a positive attitude toward all persons he meets, the counselor takes a necessary first step toward building community goodwill and cooperation with his program. The second step is entering into appropriate local events in keeping with his interests, abilities, and values. A counselor who participates in community affairs, whether social, religious, political, or recreational in nature, builds bridges for future reciprocal support for his school and guidance program. Such a counselor not only destroys the negative influences of ambiguous counselor role perceptions, but also creates the positive benefit of numerous personal contacts. These bonds of good will eventually result in improved personnel services. For example, a grocer whom the counselor patronizes might give a student a part-time job; a corporate executive with whom the counselor bowls might donate a piece of used office furniture to the information service; a politician whom the counselor supported might intercede with a college on behalf of a graduating senior desiring admission.

A community resource inventory must be built prior to need.

Chapters One and Two have already made the point that assessment of available employment opportunities must precede a counselor's job placement efforts. Also, Chapter Nine has admonished counselors to survey area referral resources before serious student personal problems arise. Therefore, this chapter contains only cursory reference to the role of community interaction in part-time and career job placement, and in referral of pupils with grave emotional difficulties to appropriate agencies. There are several other purposes for building a resource inventory, as subsequent paragraphs illustrate. Methods of collecting and filing resource information vary from counselor to counselor. Basically, however, any such collection must stem from the numerous formal and informal contacts that every counselor makes during professional and social interactions. Building a reference file merely involves standardizing and codifying what's "between the ears" of anyone genuinely interested in others. One procedure is to create a cross-referenced set of topically filed 5 x 7 inch cards. These list basic data of each resource person, and summarize the type(s) of contribution he wishes to make. On the reverse side is kept a chronological log of actual school assistance efforts. Figure 12-1 shows a typical reference card.

LOCAL RESIDENTS HELP IN MANY WAYS

Resource specialists show and tell clients what careers are really like.

Resource specialists constitute a sort of live information service; here are occupational monographs that talk back! These are people who "tell it like it is," much to the appreciation of students, teachers, and parents. The advantages of using an owner or employee of a local business to describe the work done there to pupils, instead of assigning them reading matter on the job in question, are several. First, credibility always increases with positive audience familiarity with message source. Thus pupils are more apt to pay attention to a local barber, for instance, as he describes the pros and cons of a career in his trade, than they are to either a barber from a distant city, or a monograph or film or barbering. Second, the resource specialist, alive and present in the school building, is able to engage in dialogue with students, provided the group is small and informal. Third, a resource specialist, active practitioner in his field, can cite the latest developments and current conditions, whereas printed and A-V material rapidly becomes obsolete. Fourth, having access to the tools and other materials of his trade, the resource specialist is able to add realism to his presentation by bringing some of these to show students. Also, valuable vocational learnings may result from tactile sensory inputs. (For example, what's it like operating hair clippers?)

LISTING(S): career consultant, chaperone, JV officiating
NAME: Anderson, Harry B.   PHONE: 733 - 8191
ADDRESS: 613 Elm, Anytown   07826
OCCUPATION: machinist, J. B. Martin Company
BUSN. ADDRESS: 211 4th Ave., Anytown   BUSN. PHONE: 898 - 2100
AVAILABILITY: can get off during day with prior notice, keeps
Fri. nights open to ref. JV basketball games, enjoys
accompanying 1 or 2 college visits per year.
FAMILY: wife, Grace, has helped counselor score tests,
son, Daniel, graduated AHS, '63, lives in California,
daughter, Susan, graduated AHS, '69, married, lives locally
HOBBY: active in Republican Party at county level.

(Face of card)

CHRONOLOGY OF SCHOOL INVOLVEMENT:

1. April, 1965, - talked to seniors about machinist careers
2. Winter 65-66 - officiated 7 home JV basketball games
3.   "   66-67 - officiated all 12 home JV games
4. Feb. '67 - talked to seniors on machinist trade
5. April '68 - went overnight with counselor & 4 seniors to Yale U.
6. Feb. '69 - went with bus load of seniors to Penn St. U. visitation day
7. Winter '69-'70 - officiated 10 JV games (no longer on night shift)
8.   "   '70-'71 - officiated all 12 JV games
9. May '71 - went with science tchr., counselor & 6 seniors overnight to Harvard U.
10. Winter '71-'72 - worked 11 of 12 JV games and JHS tournament
11. Oct. '72 - appeared on panel in senior problems class, rep. local G.O.P.
12. Winter '72-'73 - worked all 12 home JV games
13. April '73 - talked to senior group on machinist work
14. May '73 - went w/ counselor & 5 seniors to visit Kutztown State Coll.
15. _____
16. _____
17. _____
18. _____
19. _____
20. _____

(Back of card)

Figure 12-1

Fifth, boys and girls, when meeting the resource specialist, may make valuable contacts for possible future permanent or part-time employment.

Of course, there are a few inherent drawbacks to the use of resource specialists. First, just because someone is, for example, a successful machinist, don't automatically assume that he is facile in group speaking. Resource specialists must be chosen for their ability to convey information as well as for success in their field of work. Second, a counselor calling upon certain local career representatives and not others runs the risk of implying school endorsement of one professional or tradesman over another. When there are several physicians practicing in a community or neighborhood, for instance, this problem is hard to avoid, as the number of teen-agers in a senior class who aspire to become doctors is often small. One way out of such a dilemma is to invite all the local M.D.'s to appear on a resource specialist panel discussion on medical careers. Third, a resource specialist may expect a reciprocal favor or two from the counselor. There's nothing wrong with that, unless the desired recompense involves breaching ethics. An example is a merchant asking to receive all the school business in his product line in return for speaking to youngsters about retail sales work.

Parents act as volunteer aides and trip chaperones.

Provided that certain cautions spelled out in Chapter Thirteen are observed, parents may be used to help out in the guidance program. Many times, parents are grateful for what the school has done for their offspring, and wish to return the favor. The most obvious ways this may occur are through donating a few hours a week doing office work or tutoring, and accompanying college or job field trips to assist with supervision. It almost goes without saying that various ethical and legal safeguards must be observed when parents do these things. Parents must not see confidential school records, nor attempt (unless they are psychiatrists, psychologists, or counselors) to do counseling. They may not completely replace certified staff in assuming responsibility for students, but must only complement them. They may not, unless fully state licensed and district insured to do so, drive school buses, or in some cases, even private cars containing pupils.

Some persons object to using parents as aides and chaperones on the grounds that their presence alienates boys and girls, who object to their being around. This is a very real danger, but in this writer's opinion, one that doesn't have to happen if certain safeguards are observed. The following guidelines should prevail whenever parents serve as aides or chaperones, so as to prevent teen-agers from being turned off. *First,* parents who possess an emotional need to "boss" or overly direct students shouldn't be recruited as aides or chaperones. Nothing spoils a job field trip more for a teen-ager than being deluged with unwanted vocational advice from an overbearing adult, to cite one example. If parents with a high need for authoritarian behaviors volunteer to help the counselor, they should be assigned to academic tutoring, where greater directiveness is justified. *Second,* parent-chaperones should either be given a largely passive role when the campus or employment site is reached, or sent to carry out some assignment apart from pupils. The boys and girls should transact their business upon arrival, without chaperones close by to see that they do it right. Youngsters need this opportunity to demonstrate their maturity; having adults around deprives them of the chance and causes their justifiable annoyance. Any student who cannot be trusted when given such freedom should not be taken on the field trip in the first place. *Third,* it's sometimes best to avoid having a parent's own child present in the office when the parent is aiding, or on a trip which he or she is chaperoning. Individual cases must be judged as they arise. *Fourth,* low-key, informal contact between parents and adolescents must be possible, but not pushed. Waiting in the guidance office to see the counselor or riding in a car to and from a college visitation are two good opportunities for students to interact with an aiding or chaperoning parent. This contact makes for dialogue among persons of different viewpoints, and can do much to bridge the so-called generation gap, provided it remains spontaneous and natural. No matter what barriers age and social status may erect, good accepting, spontaneous human relations techniques will surmount them, if but for a little while.

Youth groups and activities become reinforcers of counseling gains.

Counselors are occasionally heard grumbling about requests for favors made by various youth-serving programs and institutions. Groups like the Y.M.C.A., Boy Scouts, Babe Ruth Baseball League, Junior Achievement Club, model airplane clubs, etc., are forever requesting things like class lists, permission to make announcements, or names of likely parent volunteers from counselors. Counselors should not look upon such requests as impositions upon their time, but rather as golden opportunities for professional reciprocity.

First of all, these and similar groups have one vital commonality with the counseling profession—they're all in the business of helping teen-agers. Thus, it behooves these allies to coordinate their efforts and compare notes. Second, showing consideration to worthy outsiders' requests is just good plain human relations—something counselors must always be practicing. Third and most important of all, counselors often become able to place clients in various youth programs, the possible benefits of which have become obvious during counseling. By way of elaboration, the following examples are postulated; obviously, these procedures lean toward a behavioral modification counseling approach, and for this reason will appeal to some counselors more than others.

> A junior high counselor, asked by the operator of a local Young America football program to help publicize this endeavor at school, obliges him. Later, to augment his counseling with a seventh grader beset with hostility feelings, the counselor recommends to the youngster that he participate in combative sports, working out his hostility in a socially approved manner. Because a sign-up deadline has already passed, the counselor utilizes his rapport with the football program director to secure the client's inclusion.

> A senior high counselor honors a request by the head of the neighborhood Campfire Girls organization to furnish an address list of tenth graders. He later uses this contact to obtain membership for a counselee. It seems that counselor and client arrived at a mutual decision that more low-pressure social interactions were the key to overcoming the girl's shyness problem. The Campfire Girls hold promise of providing the means to this end.

> A graduating senior tells his counselor of two vocational problems troubling him. The young man has reservations concerning his tentative career choice of physical education teacher, and is also worried about his financial readiness for college. Thinking quickly, the counselor recalls that during the past year he helped his community YMCA physical director find teachers who wanted summer youth work. The counselor now gets his counselee a summer job teaching swimming at the YMCA, so he can obtain both vocational (conative) insights and financial (cognitive) remuneration. Having been helped by the counselor, the Y executive is anxious to reciprocate.

Various allied professionals "set students straight."

With one major exception, members of the so-called "helping professions" bear a relationship to counselors similar to that of youth-serving organizations and institutions. Before delimiting the ethical relationships between school counselors and these persons and explaining the exception, however, it's necessary to identify them. Allied professionals are divided into two general categories, depending on who employs them—the counselor's school district or someone else. The latter, outside-employed category is again subdivided; these extramurally salaried helpers may be grouped according to the nature of economic endeavor hiring them, namely, public agency, non-profit organization, or profit-making affiliation, such as a private medical practice. Finally, all helpers may be delimited in terms of closeness or similarity of duties performed by each to those done by school counselors. For example, state employment service counselors perform duties very similar to school counselors, clinical psychologists do some things similar to the work of counselors, and probation officers have only a minimal commonality with counselors. The chart illustrated in Figure 12-2 lists the various helping professions and outlines their relationship to school counselors. A broad definition of the term "helping profession" is employed, and many jobs listed are somewhat peripheral to the usually accepted "helper" concept. Each job, however, contains some aspect of a societal role of rendering assistance to the young.

The principle which places more stringent ethical limits upon counselor utilization of allied professionals than upon use of various volunteers is this: A fellow member of the helping professions may only be called upon to assist clients in keeping with his or her occupational role. For instance, a welfare worker may only be asked to talk with a given client if a bona fide welfare problem exists, not just because this particular helper is adept at "shaping kids up." Nor may a psychiatrist in private practice be imposed upon to speak with a certain counselee, unless the possiblity for a normal physician-patient relationship, including remunerative aspects, exists. Neither may a personnel manager of a local business be asked to dole out all sorts of free vocational advice to students, except if a reasonable chance he might hire at least one of them prevails. Of course,

	Helpers Employed by School District or School Service Agency	Helpers Employed Elsewhere		
		public employees	non-profit organization employees	profit-making organization employees, or those in private practice
DUTIES NORMALLY CLOSELY RESEMBLING THOSE OF HIGH SCHOOL COUNSELORS	elementary & middle school counselors community college counselors	employment svc. counselors rehabilitation counselors personnel mgrs. of governmental agencies	college admissions workers & counselors vocational school couns. college financial aid officers private school counselors	personnel mgrs. of business & industry clinical psychologists & psychiatrists specializing in adolescent clients admissions personnel of private vocational schools
DUTIES NORMALLY SOMEWHAT RESEMBLING THOSE OF H.S. COUNSELORS	school social wrkr. psychometrist school psychiatrist behavioral disabilities diagnostician speech therapist school nurse	welfare & social workers—public military recruiters	welfare & social workers—private drug rehabilitation center workers draft advisors clergy in youth svc. work	employment agency operators clinical psychologists & psychiatrists—gen. practice marriage counselors
DUTIES NORMALLY ONLY SLIGHTLY RESEMBLING THOSE OF HIGH SCHOOL COUNSELORS	attendance officer principal vice principals teachers librarian audio-visual coord. curriculum specialist	police officers juvenile judges probation & parole officers public defenders administrators of orphanages & juvenile corrective institutions	clergy in pastoral work YMCA, Scouts, Boys' Club, etc. executives administrators of private orphanages & juvenile service homes & agencies	attorneys tax consultants M.D.'s other than psychiatrists travel agents specializing in youth tours & programs

Figure 12-2

counselors must keep communication channels open with all fellow helpers in their school attendance area, as plenty of opportunities for proper involvement of these people will arise. This often calls for a good deal of tact and discretion, as over-association with certain helpers, such as those in law enforcement work, may cause pupils to suspect their counselor of betraying confidences. However, when allied professionals come forward to volunteer extra, off-the-job time to assist the guidance program, the ethical situation changes. Then the friendly social worker, psychiatrist, or personnel manager could be called upon to talk with students, regardless of relevancy of specific pupil problems to these professionals' normal work roles. A prudent counselor learns to recognize this latter case and regulates his professional dealings accordingly.

THE COUNSELOR EXERCISES LEADERSHIP

Joint school-community projects benefit the young.

Not all counselor cooperations with the community should begin with after-the-fact responses to overtures from outsiders or students. While counselors indeed must be attuned to ideas from prospective volunteer aides, youth program directors, parents, clergymen, and others, they should initiate some projects, too. Many more effective school-community operations could take place if only counselors would assume the initiative in organizing them. As school faculty member ex-officio charged with helping youngsters for their own sakes, the counselor is a natural to exercise leadership in this area. Additionally, in most schools he is also designated liaison person for dealing with sundry outsiders. Some typical joint projects with strong guidance connotations are: an annual vocations fair, a certified baby-sitter placement bureau, establishment of a summer teen activity center, a marathon gap-bridging (generation, racial, economic) rap session, a regional conference on children and youth, and so forth. Figure 12-3 shows an outline of an attempt at the latter activity; note the many community involvement aspects.

Civic organizations will lend a hand if asked.

Many community service and social groups are offically charged by their society's rules with the duty of helping the young. Consequently, these associations contribute money and/or labor to various worthy efforts—scholarship programs, glasses for the needy,

ANYTOWN HIGH SCHOOL GUIDANCE DEPARTMENT
ANNUAL CONFERENCE ON CHILDREN AND YOUTH—Feb. 12, 1972

8:00 to 9:00 a.m.—registration, senior high gym foyer—coffee & doughnuts courtesy of senior home economics students & PTA mothers

9:00 to 10:00 a.m.—keynote address, "Bridging the Generation Gap," by Rabbi Samuel Perlman, pastor, Beth Israel Temple (auditorium)

10:00 to 11:30 a.m.—rap sessions

Session A—Room 101, chmn: Stan Smith, JHS counselor
Session B—Room 103, chmn: Mrs. Shirley Greene, state welfare department
Session C—Room 104, chmn: Sister Mary Elaine, counselor, Maryville Catholic H.S.
Session D—Room 204, chmn: Anytown police chief Phillip B. Costigan
Session E—Room 206, chmn: John Bronsen, M.D., psychiatrist

11:45 to 1:15 p.m.—luncheon, school cafeteria, courtesy Anytown Board of Education & school lunch staff
Grace: Rev. Robert McIntyre, Pastor, First Baptist Church
Remarks: Dr. Seagram White, chairman of counselor education, University of West Virginia

1:30 to 3:00 p.m.— Panel discussion, auditorium, "Can We Involve Youth?" Rabbi Perlman, Dr. White, Anytown Supt. of Schools James Jirik, & Student Council President Josephine Palermo

3:00 to 3:30 p.m.— coffee break, gym foyer, courtesy of Anytown Association of classroom teachers

3:30 to 5:00 p.m.— return to rap session groups to discuss panel's presentation
5:15 to 7:15 p.m.— dinner, school cafeteria, cost: $2.50 (includes ticket to basketball game following dinner program)
Grace: Father Hans Mueller, Pastor, Our Lady Catholic Church
Program: Remarks by Alex Spyropoulos, Director, Pennsylvania State Employment Security Department, including showing of movie, "Is College for Everyone?"

7:30 to 9:30 p.m.— basketball game, gymnasium, Anytown vs. Sinclair City, conference participants present dinner tickets at door for free admission.

All conference participants will receive text of Rabbi Perlman's talk, the panel discussion, and summary of points discussed in each rap session in mail following the conference, courtesy of Anytown business education students.

Figure 12-3

playgrounds, summer baseball leagues, recognition awards, and the like. When a service group already has a well-established youth service project, the counselor's role is a liaison one, in which he brings it to the attention of eligible students. Often, organization officers approach the counselor or other school authorities, formally involving them in pupil selection and other phases of their service activity. When this occurs, counselor role is restricted largely to liaison, as the program's nature is already well established and functioning. Many fraternal-type groups, however, although their by-laws pledge them to youth service, have no set program for fulfilling that obligation. Thus it follows that the counselor may assume a far more active role than liaison and coordination when dealing with these organizations—namely, the counselor takes a leadership role in soliciting their support for some aspect of his program, or endeavor of one or more of his clients. If the counselor has made a study of his community's resources, he'll know what groups might be amenable to such a proposal. And, if a counselor has cultivated community rapport, there will be members of each approached organization ready to vouch for the merit of his request. Maintenance of an up-to-date community resources inventory is a must, if a counselor is to take advantage of all potential youth-serving projects of his local area. Figure 12-4 presents a hypothetical resources list, containing both formal and nebulous youth-serving commitments of various groups.

PROFESSIONAL RECIPROCITY—KEY TO SUCCESSFUL COMMUNITY PARTICIPATION

A counselor cannot and should not seek to be all things to all people. After all, his primary commitment is to the students, and he has no time to attend to every request or problem originating within the general community. However, there are many times when a counselor should attend to non-school matters—namely, whenever these promise to benefit pupils, guidance program, and/or school. Too many counselors interpret their work roles too narrowly, disdaining all duties but one-to-one counseling in their offices with clients. While this should be the major thrust of counselor effort, community interaction must also take place as it promises many benefits for youngsters, guidance program, and educational institution. A hypothetical episode best illustrates this point.

ORGANIZATIONAL RESOURCES INVENTORY

A. Formally Established Programs

Group	Activity	Persons Officially Involved	Dates	Remarks
Anytown Amer. Legion Post	Govt. Day	designated legionnaire, JHS counselor & JHS soc. stu. teacher	each Oct.	9th graders visit courthouse & lunch
Legion Post	Senior Award	Post Commander, SHS Principal Guidance Director select winner	March 1	$100 scholarship to college of choice
Anytown Lions Club	Sight-Saving Program	Lion-Elem. School Fac. Comm. selects pupils for free glasses	any time	although a grade schl. project, will continue with child until 16
Anytown Kiwanis Club	Summer Teen Center	Kiwanis-SHS Fac. Comm. meets to plan yearly effort	each Feb.	$200 & "work day" by members donated

B. Informal Youth-Service Commitment

Group	Commitment	Likely Contact Persons	Meeting Data	Remarks
Anytown Civic Club	"assist young persons"	Phil Schmidt, Bob Anderson (several other fathers are also members)	1st Mon. night of month, at school	have given $ to youth projects in the past
Anytown Rotary	service organization	Jim Conners, Mike Riley	every other Wed. noon for lunch—area restaurants	never been approached
Coal County Women's Club	several teachers are members— have pushed school assistance	Maxine Goldberg, Susan Brown, Anne Ericsen	monthly at member homes	in 1970 gave $100 to buy a vocational film
"The Mouthpieces" (area lawyers & wives)	"help youth avoid going astray" (by-law quote)	Roger Maataala (schl. dist. attorney is member)	monthly dinner meetings—area restaurants	have given free counsel to indigent juvenile court cases

Figure 12-4

Once a week, the counselor shops in a grocery store near his home. Because he's a congenial person, he always has a kind word for the store owner. The counselor's attitude toward the grocer might be termed 20th Century non-directive acceptance, First Century emulation of Jesus, or just plain human decency. One day, the counselor emerges from a client interview to find the grocer waiting in his outer office. It seems he's having a mathematical problem regarding fruit and vegetable prices. The grocer, having heard boys and girls discussing percentile test scores while in his shop, suspects his counselor friend to be mathematically conversant. Now, there's 15 minutes before the next counselee is due for an interview. (The counselor was going to sneak a cup of coffee in the faculty lounge during this time, but now realizes that a fellow human being with a problem comes first.) So the counselor goes over the arithmetic finer points of percentage rise of cabbage prices with his friend, setting him straight and ending his confusion. They finish just in time for the next counseling interview, with a young man seeking part-time work so he may save money for college. Interestingly, the counselor is able to place this motivated teen-ager in an after-school job at his friend's grocery. Later, the grocer, remodeling his store, donates an old shelf rack to the information service for housing occupational books. Still later, the grocer is elected to the school board. Because of his association with the counselor, he's more knowledgeable of educational matters than he otherwise might be. And, because of one long-ago act of kindness, he's now influenced to vote for continued high level of guidance services.

The illustration points up the relationship between true professionalism and human consideration. The counselor did not act unprofessionally; there was no undue catering to the grocer to curry favor. Basic acceptance, a counseling attribute and affective quality, combined with statistical expertise, a cognitive skill needed by counselors, to further the lot of human beings. The grocer reciprocated from his frame of reference (the boy's job, shelf rack, community leadership) because he, too, was an accepting person. It's this type of community relationships that counselors must nurture, if they, their programs, and the schools they represent are to be optimally successful.

THIRTEEN

Delegating Clerical Chores
to Sub-Professionals and Aides

Many, many counselors have complained about the gradually mounting swell of secretarial-like duties that are inundating them. There is a way to turn these into a positive benefit for clients and others. The solution involves an orderly system of aides and guidance forms. Just how may such an operation be implemented?

WHY BUSY-WORK PILES UP ON COUNSELORS

At first thought, one might conclude that in this modern era of computer technology, data processing, and all sorts of fantastic business machines, a counselor's work would become easier, not more complex. So what if the counselor is in charge of scheduling, and the entire testing program? Can't he sit back and concern himself with intellectual decision-making, and let the machines take care of the mountains of clerical work that these two personnel services require? Theoretically, of course, this is the way things should be, but of course, as every counselor knows, such a work situation is far from reality! The reason that the advent of modern office procedures and equipment onto the school scene has served to increase rather than diminish counselor work-load is a simple one. Counselors have found themselves put in charge of data processing in many instances, due to the obvious relationship of computer technology to several traditional counselor duties: measurement, scheduling, research, aiding student college selection, etc. Many superintendents have reasoned that the counselor, being conversant with statistics, testing, and personnel management, is the most qualified staff member to assume control of the new educational technology which so vitally relates to these areas. And indeed, in most cases, these administrators are 100% correct. The problem arises from two factors relating to these new educational responsibilities: (1) A computer facilitates many non-guidance operations within a school system, for example, payroll preparation, school lunch accounting, attendance-reporting, teacher load equalization, curriculum research, etc. The hapless counselor, placed in charge of data processing, thus finds himself responsible for many tasks totally unrelated to the counseling and guidance field. (2) Often, "being in charge" does not carry with it the same connotation this term implies in business or the military. The counselor is not only "in charge" in the professional, managerial connotation of, let us say, a data-processing payroll system, but he's in charge of feeding the IBM cards into the sorting machine, too—at best a semi-skilled, clerical chore. In other words, while a counselor's masters degree education might properly be utilized by asking him to write a computer program, it's also wasted when he must oil the machine or lick shut the envelopes that contain computer output. Counselors perhaps should lend their expertise to implementing computer technology within a school district, possibly even to the point of helping with a few non-guidance duties. But, if so assigned, they must have available both trained career secretarial help in adequate amounts, and student volunteer aide assistance for tasks beneath the competency level of secretaries.

THE WAY OUT FROM UNDER

Being in charge of scheduling, testing, pupil records, and even room utilization is not necessarily bad.

Such an assignment becomes easier to demarcate by constructing a list of school operations that have been adapted to data processing or other automated office procedures. This list may be built in the form of a continuum, at one end of which are activities obviously within the guidance realm—testing, scheduling, student college selection, and the like. At the other end of the continuum are tasks which have no direct connection with guidance whatsoever—lunch program accounting, payrolls, state aid formulae, etc. In the middle of the line, a gray area exists; here are listed counselor duties somewhat peripheral, but still relevant to guidance to some degree. These include pupil records, class grade reports, teacher and room loads, and so forth. Counselors must select a point on this continuum

where, in their professional judgments, guidance stops and administration begins. It makes sense to a superintendent that testing has
more to do with helping adolescents than does the custodian's
payroll. Superintendents are reasonable men, and more often than
not will agree to a demarcation of duties that places, for instance,
pupil scheduling under the counselor, and school lunch bookkeeping
under a deputy superintendent for finance. Of course, the mid-
continuum gray area is where negotiation enters in; perhaps counselors should give a little, and consider helping with data processing
for some peripheral duties. Pupil record keeping, to cite an example,
is not wholly guidance related. A youngster's attendance record is
definitely not a counselor concern, while the same student's course
grades and recorded test scores are. Possibly, the counselor might
bend and accept supervisory responsibility in this area, as long as it is
understood that this does not extend to enforcement of attendance
regulations. Another gray area matter, this one not as much subject
to data processing, is the matter of obtaining and sending records of
transfer pupils. Here again, maybe a counselor might bend some, too,
as one can argue that expediting transfers is certainly "helping" boys
and girls. The question of teacher and room load supervision
concerns an area a little farther afield from the mainstream of
guidance work than either pupil accounting or record transfers. Even
here, however, some persons might argue that a counselor should be
involved, in order to better manipulate the school environment on
behalf of students and fellow educators. Such a viewpoint, for
example, is consistent with the "Social Engineering" counselor role
philosophy.

Regardless of where a counselor and his administration draw the
line, however, one important point must be established—namely,
whether the responsibility in question is to be executed using
modern data processing or more old-fashioned clerical procedures,
adequate sub-professional technical level support must be placed at
counselor disposal. In larger school districts, this means receiving
whatever assistance is needed from the data processing technician
generally located at district administrative headquarters, and having a
full-time secretary available to each school's counseling staff. A
suggested ratio is one full-time secretary to four full-time counselors,
but, for schools having less than four counselors, a minimum of one
half-time secretary should always be maintained. This is because
certain clerical chores connected with guidance exist, no matter how
small the junior or senior high school or how few its counselors.
Smaller public school districts, and almost all private and parochial

schools, cannot afford the luxury of a data processing specialist per se on their staffs. Some have utilized the services of a business or mathematics teacher, who handles this duty along with a reduced teaching load. This is a good arrangement, far superior to loading the duty upon a counselor, but in addition, it is wise for at least one counselor and one administrator to familiarize themselves with various aspects of the data processing operation. Thus, while the half-teacher/half-specialist works directly with all data processing endeavors, a counselor explains guidance program needs to him, while an administrator does likewise for payrolls and other non-guidance activities. The counselor's role in data processing might be said to be that of a consultant or helper, but never a workhorse.

It's difficult to obtain a secretary, so treat her properly when you do.

A good way to sell a superintendent upon the counselor's need for a secretary is to present him with an accurate record of how a counseling day is spent. When he questions the large amounts of time spent typing letters, preparing input for data processing, and posting test scores on cumulative records, the counselor may then ask who else is to do these things. He may next relate the many pupil contacts lost by having to spend so much time on mundane chores. The argument is finally clinched by pointing out that the counselor is more highly paid by his district because of his graduate education than are most teachers, yet, because of these many sub-professional tasks, he's unable to spend his working hours doing what he is educated and paid to do. Denying the counselor secretarial support is in effect denying the school district a portion of the professional level counseling services for which it's paying.

Let's suppose that the hypothetical superintendent has relented, and assigned the counselor of a one-counselor school a secretary for four periods of a seven-period day. The next problem for Mr. Hypothetical Counselor is to handle his secretary's work load in such a way that she is not treated the same way the counselor was. Specifically, this entails not insulting her intelligence and training by delegating to her tasks of an essentially menial nature. But how can this be avoided? Certainly, no superintendent would allow hiring a secretary to the secretary!

The answer lies, in this writer's opinion, in student, parent, and senior citizen volunteer aides. In order to most fully utilize a trained secretary's talents, tasks beneath her competency level must be delegated, just as those beneath the counselor's level are delegated to the secretary. In fact, a three-stage hierarchy of duty-levels may be delineated for many personnel services. The chart shown in Figure 13-1 outlines such an hierarchy. Special consideration has been given to those services that require considerable data treatment.

personnel service area	professional level (counselor duties)	technical level (secretary duties)	unskilled level (volunteer aide duties)
testing program	1. selection of tests 2. programming of test score studies 3. counseling with pupils about scores 4. administering tests	1. ordering tests 2. paying test scoring invoices 3. posting scores on student records	1. counting out tests & answer sheets 2. alphabetizing & mailing completed answer sheets 3. inventorying & storing test supplies
student scheduling	1. counseling with students about their schedules 2. giving college & job information to students 3. designing data processing input	1. filing student schedules in cumulative folders 2. checking student records for schedule irregularities 3. preparing data processing input	1. typing & mimeographing schedule forms 2. distributing blank schedule forms to homerooms 3. post data processing output
processing transfer students	1. counseling with transfer students about emotional aspects of moving 2. giving students factual information about new places of residence	1. learning identity of transfer students 2. filing or mailing out records of transfer students	1. sending out form letter records requests 2. serving as "buddies" to incoming transfers
facilitating student taking of college admissions tests	1. counseling with student about college plans 2. giving students technical information on SAT, ACT, etc. 3. helping students prepare for tests	1. posting incoming test scores on records 2. keeping "scorecard" of different seniors & tests taken, with scores for counselor's use	1. passing out test sign-up materials & explanatory booklets 2. arranging practice sessions & pooling rides to test sites 3. putting up test posters in school halls
maintaining cumulative records	1. consulting with teachers & principal on creation of record system & its policies 2. going over each pupil's record with him during counseling	1. posting material in confidential files 2. keeping filing system current 3. checking out proper records to professionals who need to use them	1. typing basic information of forms to be placed in files, before personal information is added 2. typing & mimeographing new blank forms

Figure 13-1

Teen-agers can do much, if only given a chance.

Earlier in this book, the two major reasons pupils will volunteer without pay for aide-type duties were spelled out. They are the cognitive aspect of acquiring free training in future job skills, and the conative desire to demonstrate their ability to handle relevant responsibilities. Add to these the somewhat negative reason of escape from boredom of study halls or free time blocks, and three impelling motives for volunteering are identified. A counselor must never look upon student aides as menial workers, as they are making a top-echelon contribution when one considers that their maturity and intellectual levels are lower than the counselor's. Teen-age volunteers join the counselor and his secretary as full partners on the guidance team. Their task levels are lower only because their ages and years of schooling are less; as individuals devoted to making the guidance program go, they are equal to the counselor. If this psychological approach is followed, it will contribute greatly to the esprit de corps of student volunteer aides. They will seek to make real contributions to the guidance program because they are a part of it, with definite psychological needs being filled through their participation. Too many times, educators overlook this affective dimension and treat adolescents either impersonally or paternalistically. The counselor, more than any other faculty member, should avoid making this mistake.

Other adults will lend a hand, if asked from the proper context.

Fellow-educators—teachers, administrators, school nurse, librarian, etc.—may be asked to assist the counselor in performing certain duties, *provided that the request is relevant to the staff role of the person so asked.* For example, home room teachers certainly should help with the testing program to the extent of proctoring, supervising the passage and collection of materials, and informing pupils of their scores. After all, if testing were not taking place, they would be teaching these same students. The principal certainly should help in maintenance of pupil records, as many of the entries therein bear upon his school role to a greater extent than upon the counselor's. Similar considerations suggest themselves for other faculty members. This commonsense approach to staff involvement is a professional level consideration and must be regarded as such. It must never degenerate into a sneaky way for the counselor to take advantage of his colleagues, so that he may "goof off." After all, they have work to perform also, and if there is not a proper reason for requesting their assistance, they may not be asked.

The question of parent volunteer aides is a different colored horse indeed. Unlike fellow educators, who are paid to perform professional jobs within a school, parents have no such contractual obligation. Moreover, unlike volunteer student aides, who stand to gain job skills and psychological maturational benefits from such service, parents have little need for these things. Why, then, would a parent wish to volunteer a few hours per week as counselor's volunteer aide? What's in it for her?

Unquestionably, the motive of altruism must enter in, although cynics force us to admit that boredom and the curiosity drive are also factors. Basically, most parent-volunteers are housewives not gainfully employed. (While fathers also volunteer, their contribution is generally vocationally oriented—building a pamphlet rack for the guidance office in their home workshop, or visiting the school as a career resource specialist.) In American culture, secretarial-clerical type work is largely a feminine bailiwick, and this is what volunteer mothers generally do when helping the counselor. It's somewhat fashionable nowadays for parents to donate time to help their child's school, so the counselor shouldn't feel bashful about seeking helpers. A good way to find volunteers is to first ask the principal how he feels. Adminstrators generally have a mental list of persons who have indicated availability, or who they believe would be interested. (Principals almost always also have a list of persons whom they do not want helping in the school under any circumstances—usually with very good reason. Therefore, the counselor may save later embarrassment by gingerly and quietly inquiring of his superior.) If the principal gives his approval, but can't think of anyone, a counselor might then make quiet inquiries of parents whom he knows—and trusts. Perhaps they know of someone.

Two cautions must be observed in using parent volunteer aides: (1) The parent's own children, if attending school in the same building, must not be allowed to hang around their mother during free periods, or to seek special favors because she is an aide. (2) No parent-aide may ever be allowed to inspect the confidential files or records of any student, her own child included. This includes test scores. (Parents do have a right to know their own child's group test program scores, but the guidance office while volunteer-aiding is hardly the time or the place.)

Senior citizens are another potential source of adult volunteer help for counselors. Here again, altruism and escape from boredom are prime motivators. Some senior citizen volunteers will be former professional educators or career secretaries, hence they will be able to render a high level of service. Others, while not highly educated, have extremely insightful rapport with the young, or are unusually conscientious in performing what they are asked to do. In finding elderly volunteers, as with parents, first consult with the principal. A good next step is to inquire of clergymen, retirement home directors, and social organization heads of the school's attendance area. Here again, two cautions must be observed: (1) While most senior citizens have grown extremely tolerant over their many years, a few have become rigid. These persons may seek to indoctrinate teen-agers in a certain religious or political viewpoint. Such activity is illegal in a public school, and persons likely to attempt it may not be volunteer aides. (2) Elderly persons whose physical condition has degenerated toward senility in some aspect may appear amusing to boys and girls. Out of respect to these older persons, they should not be placed in positions of potential ridicule. Such a senior citizen who wishes to volunteer might be given a home assignment, like alphabetizing schedules or painting a pamphlet rack, so as to avoid hurt feelings all around.

A standardized guidance form system not only lightens work loads, but also escalates professionalism.

Many times, the forms that a school guidance staff uses are like Topsy—they just grew. It's suggested here that a cheap, uniform, and ingenious system may be created, in which each form fills a definite need without overlap. Some persons throw up their hands in horror at this suggestion, on the grounds that it smacks of the military-industrial complex and runs counter to the warm humanness imperative in the counseling relationship. This author would answer this very real criticism by stating that it is *how* forms are used that determines impersonality, not the mere fact they are used. Moreover, if a counselor employs a warm, empathic genuineness in his counseling, it's doubtful that his usage of forms would detract from this. After all, many of the forms in question are never used by counselees, and/or deal with various cognitive aspects of personnel services.

Each counseling staff must design its own particular forms based upon local needs. Several of the books referenced in the "For

Further Reference" section at the back of this book, in the General Guidance category, contain some representative sample forms. Ideally, teachers, administrators, students, and the counselor's secretary should share in their planning. If the district uses a color-code system, guidance forms should conform. It's also wise to allow pupils to print or mimeo the forms themselves; this helps lessen the ambiguous perception of the counseling and guidance process some may have. The following outline of a guidance form system is to be interpreted as a sample only, merely suggestive of specific forms various schools might need.

One type of guidance form system may be based upon window envelopes and full- and half-sheet stationery.

A labor-saving secretarial procedure that may easily be learned by student aides is described in the following paragraphs. Basic equipment and supplies needed are: a four-line rubber stamp bearing the designation "Guidance Office" and the school address and telephone number, a stamp pad, paper cutter, and envelopes. Standard 8½ x 11 paper is used, and four kinds of envelopes are employed: #10 window, #9 non-window, #6¾ window, and #6¼ non-window. The school mimeograph or ditto machine, or printing press, is used to reproduce forms.

All forms that circulate through the U.S. mails are full 8½ x 11 size. All forms that circulate internally within the school are half-size (5½ x 8½). Half-size forms are made by cutting full-size paper on the paper cutter. Full-size forms and letters on full-size stationery, which is merely blank paper with the rubber-stamped letterhead neatly centered at the top, are mailed out in #10 window envelopes. If the form is to be returned to the counselor, a #9 envelope is enclosed for this purpose, with the rubber stamp used to imprint the counselor's address upon it. Internally circulated forms and letters on half-sheet stationery go out in #6¾ window envelopes, and if a reply is warranted, come back in #6¼ non-window ones. Again, the half-size letterhead and return envelope address are made with the old reliable rubber stamp.

Forms are set up so that a four-line "target" for the window address is printed on them. The target's location is kept standard by use of an equal-sectioning accordion fold with all mailed forms and letters. While this procedure smacks a little of military or overly emphasized regimentation, it must be remembered that its purpose is to save labor and time without detracting from professionalism.

Therefore, it must be held uniform and simple so that student aides may readily understand and use it. All internally circulated forms bear a notation that if confidential material is enclosed the envelopes are to be sealed; if non-confidential material is inside, the envelope flap is to be merely tucked in. This system enables aides to open as much mail as possible without seeing confidential matters. All sealed U.S. and internal mail must be opened by the secretary or counselor himself.

Descriptions of some frequently used guidance forms follow. These are only cursory, as local needs always dictate specifics:

> a. Records Request—8½ x 11, mailed out to schools from which transfer pupils have come or will soon come, #9 non-window return envelope enclosed with it.
>
> b. Staff Memo—5½ x 8½, circulated internally; the "to, from, subject" type of thing; #6¼ return envelope enclosed if reply is warranted.
>
> c. Anecdotal Record—5½ x 8½, circulated internally; small size aimed at deliberate brevity; stapled in triplicate for carbon paper insertion; teacher retains copy, returns two to counselor—one for files, one for office use; return envelope always comes back sealed.
>
> d. Staff or Parent Conference Record—8½ x 11, never circulated, but used to record professional meetings and discussions; stapled in quadruplicate for carbon insertion, and given to conference partici-pants for record purposes.
>
> e. Confidential Impressions Request—5½ x 8½, circulated inter-nally; again small to encourage brevity; used to get more general and subjective data than anecdotal record; always to be returned from teachers to counselor sealed; must bear the admonition: "Circulation of this form does not necessarily mean the student named is involved in any disciplinary trouble or other difficulties."
>
> f. Class Schedule—5½ x 8½, circulated internally; stapled in quad-ruplicate (one copy to pupil, one to home room teacher, one to principal, one to counselor is typical); never sealed.
>
> g. Personal Data card—5½ x 8½, circulated internally; contains personal, but not counseling, information (typical quadruplicate distribution: principal, nurse, school secretary, counselor); sealed whenever circulated when completely filled out.

There are other forms that counselors in various school situations will wish to use. The preceding are listed more as examples than as any attempt to dictate a "best" collection to the reader. There are some forms that, in the author's opinion, are best *not* used by counselors, for various reasons. These are listed, along with reasons for recommended non-use, in the following paragraphs:

a. Interview Notes—Let each counselor "do his own thing." A form is too rigid; also, putting certain counselee communications down on paper may be most unwise.

b. Report Card—O.K. to have them, but not a guidance function. Also, many data processing companies furnish these—might as well let them do so, and save the guidance office the work!

c. Cumulative Folder—Again, fine to use in the school, but not a guidance function. Let the "pro's" print these for the school, as it's awfully hard to print on full-size card stock!

d. Test Score Report—This *is* a guidance function, but why not use the many fine print-outs and explanatory leaflets that commercial test producers furnish?

e. Health Record—This is in the nurse's bailiwick; allow her the courtesy of designing her own procedure.

f. Speech Record—Let the speech clinician, like the nurse, run her own area.

g. Guidance Essay—This is a guidance "form" all right, but a blank lined sheet of paper makes a better form for this purpose than anything printed, with the rigid structure it might connote.

THE MUNDANE REFLECTS THE THEORETICAL

Much of what has been said in this chapter has of necessity dealt with rather pedantic, matter-of-fact detail. Any description of how to obtain clerical help and create office procedures cannot avoid this. However, in setting up a hierarchy of guidance office duties and designing a series of forms, a counselor must never lose sight of the intellectual dimension, namely, his philosophy or rationale for counseling. The theoretical position from which a counselor counsels is mirrored by his non-counseling duties, especially the way he goes about practicing personnel services. It's also reflected in less professional, but equally important things—dealings with his secretary and volunteer aides, guidance office decor, and design of guidance forms. For example, a counselor practicing a non-directive philosophy would set up work roles and create forms with a minimum of structure. A trait-factorist might fashion forms upon which test scores, grades, and listed interests appear prominently. A neo-behaviorally oriented counselor would structure aides' work-roles so as to stress reinforcement of desired behaviors. An existentialist, when dealing with data processing technician, secretary, and aides, might continually stress their need to make decisions as best they can in light of the present, to do so, and to quit worrying about it. And so forth. A counselor's theoretical rationale for counseling, whatever it might be, should permeate the total guidance effort down to the humblest form or most menial office duty. When the so-called subprofessional aspects of a guidance program are looked upon in this light, they suddenly become a little more appealing. Moreover when both professional and clerical operations are based upon one rationale, a smooth, unifying influence pervades the guidance program. All duties performed—counseling, personnel services, and office work—fall logically into the proper niche, and all workers— counselor, secretary and aides—pursue their respective jobs with singularity of purpose.

FOURTEEN

Telling the Guidance Story –
PR in Action

Public Relations isn't a personnel service in the strict-
est sense of the term. However, neglect of good PR
principles has spelled big trouble for many a counselor.
There are some very simple, practical, and fully ethical
ways in which secondary school counselors may introduce public relations activities into their professional
roles. What are they, and why are they needed?

WHY PUBLIC RELATIONS?

**Counseling and personnel service successes are often not
measurable by traditional educational yardsticks.**

A counselor works primarily with individuals, while a teacher has a
basic commitment to a field of scholastic knowledge. Thus it's easier
to recognize a superior teaching performance than a counseling one.
While a teacher can point with pride to pupil achievement test scores,
science fair projects, or prize-winning themes, the counselor cannot
in turn boast of a child whose personal problem was resolved. A
principal may enter a classroom and observe a well-managed learning
environment, but he must not intrude on a counseling interview.
Parents may look with pride at the tangible "A's" on their youngster's report card, but they probably know nothing of the intangible
personality or vocational development gains he made through counseling. When publicizing achievements, a counselor must never, of
course, reveal pupil data and confidences. This leaves only half of his
professional role, i.e., personnel services, as possible fair game for
revelation. And even here, there are many types of personal informa-

tion, such as individual test scores and referral identities, that must not be told to the general public. Therefore, two obstacles make publicizing a counselor's successes difficult, namely, the intangibility of many client gains and the ethic of confidentiality.

The ignorance-ambiguity-hostility syndrome threatens guidance and counseling.

Counseling is much less understood by the lay public, and even by many professional educators, than are the traditional teaching and administrative roles. Three probable reasons for this are the relative newness of guidance in many schools, inter-school variance in counselor work-roles, and the confidentiality ethic. These three factors are unavoidable facts with which counselors must live. Psychological research has established that ignorance of something leads those who come into contact with it to consider it ambiguous. This ambiguity frequently leads to suspicion and fear of the un-known thing—or person, or process. This in turn begets hostility toward the ambiguous factor, as persons tend to form all sorts of misconceptions about its true nature. In short, people fear what they fail to understand. If guidance and counseling are to obtain full public acceptance, and counselors are to experience optimum profes-sional success, the ignorance-ambiguity-hostility syndrome must never be allowed to begin to operate. This can only be done by properly informing everyone what counseling is all about. Some persons believe counselors to be mollycoddlers of teen-agers, or snoopers into their sex lives, or "super clerks" who make out their class schedules for them. These and other misconceived stereotypes stand in the way of success for all counselors and their programs, and must be destroyed.

What can a counselor do?

If on one hand, it's impossible or unethical to tell people about counseling-personnel services, and on the other hand, fatal to the profession not to tell them, what can be done? If indeed such a dichotomous situation existed, counselors would be in grave trouble. However, there are two aspects of counseling-personnel services that do lend themselves to public information. First, while normally it is never permissible to reveal client counseling information, it's quite all right to explain to the public what counseling itself is like. For example, most lay persons confuse counseling with advising, and to set them straight violates no individual confidences. Second, certain personnel activities may ethically be publicized. Examples include visits of employers and admissions counselors to the school, visits of pupils to areas of potential employment or educational opportunities, success of students in scholarship competitions, and results of standardized achievement tests, provided that individual performances are not revealed. A counselor can come up with all kinds of positive, interesting material about the guidance program that may properly be told to the public, if he puts his mind to the task.

Who are the "publics" of school counselors?

The first step for a counselor to take in telling the guidance story is to identify his "publics." A public is a specific group of persons that have a common interest in the counselor. Because each public has a unique reason for knowing about counseling-personnel services, each is best reached by a communication slanted especially to it. There are three general categories of publics of counselors: *internal* publics, *external* publics, and *allied professionals.* Internal publics are all groups inside a school with whom counselors must work, the main ones being teachers, administrators, students, the board of education, and non-certified staff. External publics are groups outside the school that nevertheless have a bona fide interest in it. Major external publics are parents, former students, future students, employers, and the tax-paying, voting public-at-large. Allied professional publics are other helping profession members with whom a counselor in a given school must deal. They are fellow high school counselors, elementary and junior high counselors of feeder schools, counselors and personnel workers of area higher educational institutions, referral agencies, including local psychiatrists and clinical psychologists, area employment counselors and personnel managers, and the school counseling profession nationally. Each public within all three categories has a unique need for information about a specific secondary counselor and his guidance program. A counselor who sees that his publics have the proper, meaningful information they need has little to fear from ambiguity, and much to gain professionally.

SOME PR ACTIVITIES FOR COUNSELORS

External publicity informs the community via releases to local news media.

It's a good idea, with administrative approval, for a counselor to send periodic releases to local news media. Daily and weekly newspapers and radio and TV stations servicing a school district will use timely school information, provided that it is presented to them in proper journalistic format. This format is not difficult to learn; in fact, writing news copy is well within the grasp of better-ability high school seniors. A counselor can easily train a volunteer student aide in this job, provided that she is a strong English student, and a good typist. Of course, the counselor must exercise supervision to insure that no confidential material is released to news media.

Two free booklets are excellent for teaching pupils how to write, prepare, and submit news releases. They are *Publicity Handbook*, obtainable from Consumer Relations, The Sperry and Hutchinson Company, 3003 East Kemper Road, Cincinnati, Ohio 45241, and *If You Want Air Time*, obtainable from Public Relations Service, National Association of Broadcasters, 1771 "N" Street, North-West, Washington, D.C. 20006. Figure 14-1 is a sample release of a typical guidance news item suitable for media disclosure.

Occasionally, radio stations allow individuals to call in news spots, which are taped from the telephone conversation and later used as newscast fillers. A counselor should inquire of local radio news directors regarding this possibility. Sometimes a counselor or student under his supervision can utilize a taped radio spot to publicize some guidance news item. The personal touch created by hearing someone tell his own news story over the air is a potential community rapport-builder.

Internal publicity informs students and staff via a guidance newsletter.

A guidance department newsletter, issued on a weekly or bi-monthly basis, is a journalistic endeavor that student volunteers will take on with enthusiasm. Such a missive handily posts faculty and pupils on guidance activities, and may also be sent home to parents. One counselor even includes the community-at-large in newsletter circulation by leaving a supply at several cooperating local businesses.

The guidance newsletter is most easily reproduced on spirit duplicator (ditto); schools offering a graphic arts curriculum may wish to use offset printing. If duplicator or mimeo is used, the operation may be greatly simplified by limiting the newsletter to one page. Because space then becomes a problem, the use of elite type, 14-inch paper, minimal margins, and both sides of the paper tends to achieve maximum page utilization. A sample guidance newsletter

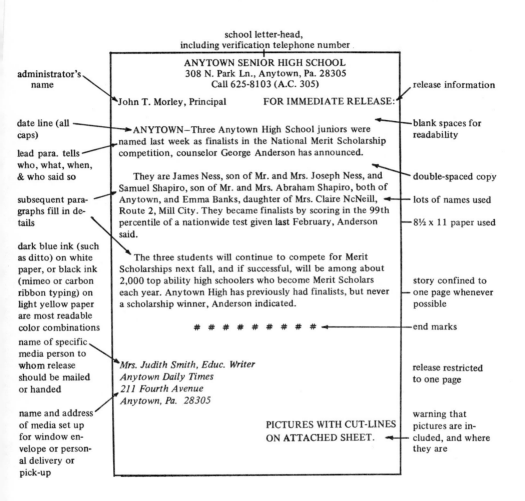

The figure shows a sample press release on school letterhead with annotations. The central document reads:

school letter-head,
including verification telephone number

ANYTOWN SENIOR HIGH SCHOOL
308 N. Park Ln., Anytown, Pa. 28305
Call 625-8103 (A.C. 305)

John T. Morley, Principal   FOR IMMEDIATE RELEASE:

ANYTOWN—Three Anytown High School juniors were named last week as finalists in the National Merit Scholarship competition, counselor George Anderson has announced.

They are James Ness, son of Mr. and Mrs. Joseph Ness, and Samuel Shapiro, son of Mr. and Mrs. Abraham Shapiro, both of Anytown, and Emma Banks, daughter of Mrs. Claire NcNeill, Route 2, Mill City. They became finalists by scoring in the 99th percentile of a nationwide test given last February, Anderson said.

The three students will continue to compete for Merit Scholarships next fall, and if successful, will be among about 2,000 top ability high schoolers who become Merit Scholars each year. Anytown High has previously had finalists, but never a scholarship winner, Anderson indicated.

# # # # # # # # #

Mrs. Judith Smith, Educ. Writer
Anytown Daily Times
211 Fourth Avenue
Anytown, Pa. 28305

PICTURES WITH CUT-LINES
ON ATTACHED SHEET.

Left-side annotations: administrator's name; date line (all caps); lead para. tells who, what, when, & who said so; subsequent paragraphs fill in details; dark blue ink (such as ditto) on white paper, or black ink (mimeo or carbon ribbon typing) on light yellow paper are most readable color combinations; name of specific media person to whom release should be mailed or handed; name and address of media set up for window envelope or personal delivery or pick-up

Right-side annotations: release information; blank spaces for readability; double-spaced copy; lots of names used; 8½ x 11 paper used; story confined to one page whenever possible; end marks; release restricted to one page; warning that pictures are included, and where they are

Figure 14-1

front page is shown in Figure 14-2. Note that the counselor has used it to communicate routine but essential information to his internal publics. A primary school typewriter has been used for headlines, a pica typewriter for second order headlines, a script typewriter for the masthead, and an elite electric for copy. Practically all school districts own at least one machine of each of these four varieties.

published weekly
by student volunteers

A.H.S. Guidance News

vol. 6, no. 29, April 23, 1972

"all the news about
C & G"

SENIOR HIGH TO ADD COUNSELOR IN FALL

12 SOPHS COMMENDED BY S.R.A. FOR N.E.D.T. SCORES

NEEDED TO MEET RISING ENROLLMENT, MORLEY SAYS

WERE IN UPPER 10% NATIONWIDE

Twelve A.H.S. sophomores scored at the 90th percentile or higher on the National Educational Development Tests last March, according to Science Research Associates of Chicago, makers of the tests.

High scorers were: Michael Anderson, Sandra Barlow, Richard Dennis, Mary Finley, Derek Karakas, Bonnie O'Sullivan, Patricia Overstreet, Hedwig Schmidt, Robert Tortorici, William Vertheimer, Polly Woods, and Betty Zuchinni.

The tests were given on a voluntary basis, and resemble the National Merit Scholarship Tests formerly taken the same day by the juniors.

SIGN-UPS FOR TRIP TO S.I.U. CAMPUS BEING URGED

Several places still remain on the the bus trip to Southern Illinois University next Friday, Mrs. Diana Johnson, counselor in charge of of the trip, has announced.

All seniors planning to attend college are eligible to take this trip, provided they bring a note from home and make up missed assignments, Mrs. Johnson said.

FIRST NATIONAL BANK PERSONNEL DIRECTOR TO VISIT A.H.S. NEXT TUES.

Mrs. Freida Phillips, personnel director of the Anytown First National Bank, will visit A.H.S. Tuesday, to talk with seniors interested in working for her institution.

I.T.E.D. SCORES NOW IN COUNSELING OFFICE

A complete score report of the Iowa Tests of Educational Development is available in the guidance office.

Students may see their counselor for an interpretation.

NEW SOUND FILMSTRIPS ARRIVE FOR INFORMATION SERVICE

Three new sound film-strips from Guidance Associates have just arrived, and have been placed in the information service viewing area, Thomas Smith, counselor, has revealed.

The strips are about careers in mechanical type jobs. They are about welding, lathe operation, and foundry work.

Anytown High will have a sixth counselor during the 1972-73 school year, principal John Morley has announced.

Another counselor is needed because of anticipated higher enrollment. This year's 8th grade class, next year's freshmen, numbers 347, while there are only 201 graduating seniors, Principal Morley pointed out. He said that he hopes to hire a lady counselor, because only two of the five present counselors are women.

GUIDANCE HELPERS TO STAGE BAKE SALE

The guidance helpers club will hold a bake sale during activity period next Friday, in the student commons.

Profits will be used to rent vocational movies, Vickie Thomas, club president said.

Figure 14-2

Community interactions add a personal touch by making the counselor well known.

No counselor ever becomes an ambiguous, little understood "boogie-man" if he or she frequently rubs shoulders with local residents. People tend to look favorably upon what is familiar, and to fear the unknown. A counselor who's known to community residents is much more apt to receive their support and approval for his programs than one who is not. Of course, each person, counselor included, is an individual, and has a constellation of unique personal traits. For this reason, a counselor seeking community interaction should choose activities commensurate with his sex, age, hobbies, and personality. Some counselors might be at home in a sportsmen's club, others in a church choir. Some might feel comfortable as a member of a mayor's study group on youth, while others may choose to interact informally while grocery shopping. Regardless of the type of shoulder rubbing a counselor selects, the main thing is to have a good word and smile for everyone. The counseling profession is predicated upon the premise that each client is a worthy individual, entitled to dignified, accepting treatment. It therefore behooves counselors to either display a similar philosophy in dealing with the general public, or run the risk of being branded hypocrites. In developing community contacts, however, one caution must be noted: a counselor must avoid becoming identified with one particular clique, be it political, social, or economic. While he should pursue interests best suited to himself, he must also be on good terms with everyone.

Guidance-sponsored events stimulate student body interest.

Commensurate with conditions in the various schools in which they work and their own interests and abilities, counselors can sponsor guidance-related pupil activities. Such events tend to build rapport and interest among students, and indirectly stimulate interest in the guidance program among the counselor's other publics. The nature of these activities will vary widely from school to school, and the following examples are intended only as general guiding suggestions.

Using a faculty committee as judges, the counselor sponsors an essay contest among students. Possible topics include: "My Future Career, and Why I Chose It," "What Teen-Agers Can Learn from

Summer Work," "How to be a True, Helping Friend," "The Secret of Popularity," etc. Contest winners receive appropriate school and news media recognition and a guidance-related prize, such as a book on work or college success.

The counselor's volunteer student aides promote a dance, bake sale, student-faculty basketball game, car-wash, etc. Proceeds are used to purchase guidance materials for pupil use, such as "how to study" workbooks, or to finance guidance-related activities, such as field trips to investigate employment or further educational opportunities.

The counselor and several student volunteers stage a program for a P.T.A., church, or civic group meeting. They demonstrate a fictitious individual and group counseling session, and report on actual personnel services, such as the school visit of a career consultant.

The art teacher and counselor co-sponsor a poster contest. Topics must have guidance themes, such as careers, further education, drug abuse, or mental health. Winners receive a prize, and their work is exhibited in the counselor's outer office.

Working with the social studies teacher, the counselor conducts a community occupational survey. Pupils interview potential employers, and compile a file of available jobs, including descriptions of duties, wages, qualifications, etc. Topics for social studies class discussion are developed from the survey, as well as job placement references for guidance. The occupational survey has great public relations potential because students interact directly with many prominent community figures on behalf of the school guidance program.

**Scholarly publications build respect for
the counselor and his district in professional circles.**

The writing of journal articles is not the exclusive province of college and university professors. Neither is authorship of articles in commercial educational magazines necessarily the prerogative of paid staff members of these publications. Moreover, even if the major scholarly journals and educational magazines were not receptive to the offerings of school counselors, there are a myriad of state level publications which are veritably crying for article manuscripts. Roughly, there are about 50 scholarly journals, 10 commercial magazines, and 200 regionally circulated journals and newsletters that are potential domestic publishers of secondary school coun-

seling-related professional articles. When elementary school counseling is added to this list, the first figure jumps to around 55, and the
second to 12. The following is a breakdown of publications:

	SCHOLARLY JOURNALS	EDUCATIONAL MAGAZINES	REGIONAL JOURNALS & NEWSLETTERS
specifically devoted to counseling & guidance	American Vocational J.	Careers Today	State A.P.G.A. publications
	Canadian Counsellor	Lovejoy's Magazine The Guidance Clinic	
	CAPS Communique		State Dept. of Education Guidance Bulletins
	CAPS Journal		
	College Board Review		
	Counselor Education & Supervision		State Guidance Assn. (N.E.A. affil.) publications
	*Elementary School G. & C.		
	Facility		
	Family Coordinator Guidance J.		
	Impact		
	Integrated Personnel Services Index		
	J. of Applied Behavioral Science		
	J. of Character Ed.		
	J. of Counseling Psych.		
	J. of the International Assn. of Pupil Personnel Workers		
	J. of the Nat. Assn. of Women Deans & Couns.		
	J. of Vocational Behavior		
	Measurement & Evaluation in Guidance		
	Nat. Catholic Guidance Conference J.		
	Personnel & Guidance J		
	Vocational Guidance Quarterly		
interested in counseling & guidance topics	American Education	Amer. School Board J.	Archdiocesan (Catholic) School Office Bulletin
	American Educational Research J.	Educate	
		*Grade Teacher	
	Changing Education	*Instructor	State Dept. of Education General Bulletins
	Child Study J.		
	Clearing House	Nations' Schools	
	Education	Scholastic Teacher	State Education Assn. (N.E.A. affil.) publications
	Educational Forum	School & Society	
	Educational Horizons	School Management	

SCHOLARLY JOURNALS (*con't*)	EDUCATIONAL MAGAZINES (*con't*)	REGIONAL JOURNALS & NEWSLETTERS (*con't*)
Educational Leader- ship Educational Record *Elementary School J. Harvard Ed. Review High School J. J. of Educational Research J. of Experimental Education J. of Educational Measurement J. of General Education J. of Secondary Education *Nat. Elementary Principal Nat. Secondary Principal Peabody J. of Education Phi Delta Kappan Record (The) Review of Educational Research School Review Today's Education	Teacher	State Federation of Teachers (A.F.T. affil.) publications

*elementary school level only

STUDENTS BENEFIT FROM HELPING
THEIR COUNSELOR PUBLICIZE HIS PROGRAM

**Pupils and their teachers appreciate enrichment
opportunities afforded by PR helping.**

Boys and girls who assist the counselor with publicity have opportunities to develop skills in English, speech, business education, and art. Writing news and feature articles and preparing photographs with captions are closely related to English composition. Needless to say, tense, spelling, case, and punctuation get a thorough workout whenever a child prepares copy for publication. English teachers welcome the added incentive to write well that preparing media copy gives students. Teachers will frequently urge pupils to volunteer for duty as counselor's helpers in order to receive such an opportunity.

Likewise, a speech teacher is usually more than happy to give a youngster tips on delivering a radio spot. The business education teacher sees valuable office skills practice coming from typing, duplicating, and mailing news releases. The art teacher welcomes the chance for her charges to exhibit their posters, or develop photography skills.

Client ego-strength is reinforced by achieving media recognition.

All normal individuals seek peer-group recognition in some manner. Teen-agers are no exception; in fact, the need for social acceptance is unusually strong during adolescence. Frequently, boys and girls who fail to win notice in such legitimate areas as scholarship, athletics, or personal popularity, seek attention in illicit ways—defying authority, wearing bizarre clothing, using drugs or alcohol. While no counselor should "bribe" clients to be "good" in return for placing their names in the newspaper, legitimately earned media mention can be a positive force for client emotional growth. This happens when a child who has earned distinction receives modest, unexpected public recognition for making his own little social contribution. For example, a tenth grader spends some free school time building an occupational monograph wall rack for the counselor's information service. This child, neither scholar nor athlete, not exceptionally popular among peers, has given of the only school-connected talent he has, wood-working ability. By mentioning his effort in one or two lines of a periodic guidance department news release, the counselor gives the boy a reward more priceless than money—social recognition and approval. Everyone wants social acceptance and the feelings of worthwhileness it engenders. Dr. William Glasser, among others, has pointed out that personality disintegration frequently results from an individual's perceptions of social unacceptance. On the other hand, Glasser maintains, the person who feels worthwhile and socially accepted is one with good mental health. A few lines in a newspaper story cannot, of course, spell the difference between psychosis and normality in a youngster's life, but journalistic recognition can be a powerful force for strengthening client perceptions of self-worth and societal participation.

Insight into possible journalism, advertising,
and photography careers results from PR helping.

The various "helper" programs described elsewhere in this book are structured to provide teen-agers with relevant vocational development experiences. This chapter's PR activities are no exception.

When children assist the counselor with publicity, it's not an "all give, no take" situation; rather, student volunteers gain experience and insights for the world of work ahead. Some potential career fields related to publicity helping are newspaper reporter, house organ or advertising copy writer, press photographer, commercial photographer, radio announcer, mail and telephone sales worker, and industrial psychology. Two types of vocational development benefits stem from PR helping—immediate and long-range. Immediate benefits are the salable skills that teen-agers acquire for use in summer and part-time jobs during high school and college. Long-range benefits are insights, whether positive or negative, for selection of a life career.

Pupils with a stake in guidance program operation become heralds of its value.

Sometimes the best public relations tools are not news releases, posters, or speeches, but satisfied customers and employees. This principle applies to a school guidance program as well as to a business operation. Boys and girls who know that their counselor has helped them are the "satisfied customers" of the guidance program. Those who have benefited from counseling and personnel services performed on their behalf can be counted upon to spread the word. Oftentimes, the attitude displayed by students toward guidance is more important than factual testimonials.

The "satisfied employees" are those pupils who enjoyed serving as counselor's helpers. All normal human beings crave the feeling of belonging that results from contributing to a larger endeavor in which they believe. This psychological phenomenon is frequently apparent in political party and church membership, and in fan behavior at athletic events. Possibly, identification with something deemed worthwhile is a natural social instinct. Throughout this book, a theme of relevancy through student participation in personnel service operation has been stressed. Those youngsters who joined directly with the counselor in running his program take with them strong positive identification feelings. Their attitudes are bound to have vast public relations impact—upon fellow students and parents in the present, and upon their own children in the future.

PERSONAL GAINS

The community notices that things are going on.

A point has been made that because much of the counselor's work must be treated with confidentiality, teachers and the general public may be unaware of what he is doing. Public relations activities, designed to acquaint various publics with the counselor and his non-confidential duties, make everyone aware that he is there, and he is busy! Public notice is not, of course, synonymous with favorable professional evaluation of counselor competence. Nevertheless, the people have a right to know how *their* tax dollars are being spent in *their* school. Parents and teachers certainly should know what personnel services are being rendered on behalf of the children in whom they have so vital an interest. The counselor who keeps his publics current with what's going on not only establishes his own public image, but also builds a more positive image of his school and his profession.

The profession recognizes a counselor's contribution.

Just as publicity techniques alert a local community to guidance program existence and help explain its nature, professional level activities inform the field of education and school counseling profession nationally and regionally of a counselor's contributions. Publication of journal and magazine articles, paper and program presentations at conventions, and participation in organizations' are three means of achieving this. Professional publications and activities promote the exchange of new ideas and research findings, from which all counselors benefit. They also enable educators to meaningfully interact in ways that further both individual careers and education in general. And most important of all, counselors who contribute professionally soon become known as leaders and authorities in their field, or in some specialized aspect of it. The fact that they have both inclination and ability to make professional contributions establishes both their individual reputations and those of their respective school districts.

Organizational membership offers several benefits in addition to the obvious ones of potential prestige through office-holding and opportunity to interact with fellow counselors at meetings. More subtly, membership provides numerous chances to meet persons from fields peripheral to school counseling. Also, it automatically places a counselor on numerous mailing lists of educational, governmental, and commercial agencies. Then too, the fact that one is a member certainly does not hurt his chances for having an article accepted for publication in an organization's journal. In fact, a few groups openly state such a preferential authorship policy. In addition, state, regional, and national conventions offer almost unlimited opportunity for a counselor to share his professional interests by presenting papers or conducting panels, demomonstrations, or other group sessions.

Some organizations of specific interest to counselors are:

LOCAL LEVEL	STATE OR REGIONAL LEVEL	NATIONAL LEVEL
city or area guidance assn.——>	state guidance association——>	Nat. Education Association
city or area personnel & guidance association————>	state personnel & guidance assn.—>	Amer. Personnel & Guidance Association
city or area A.S.C.A. chapter— >	State A.S.C.A. chapter————>	A.S.C.A.
#Phi Delta Kappa chapter———>	#Phi Delta Kappa district————>	#Phi Delta Kappa
Professional Counselors' Assn.—>	P.C.A. region—————————>	Prof. Counselors' Assn.
American Educational Research—> Assn. (informal only at local level)	American Ed. Research Assn.——> (informal only at regional level)	American Educational Research Association
Society of Individual Psy.————> chology	Society of Individual Society——>	American Society of Adlerian Psychology
———	*American Psychological Assn.——> Division 17	*American Psychological Assn. Division 17
———	**National Association of Women—>**National Association of Deans & Counselors (state meeting)	Women Deans & Counselors
———	State Vocational Association——>	National Vocational Assn.
**Delta Kappa Gamma chapter— ->	**Delta Kappa Gamma district——>**Delta Kappa Gamma	
———	Association for Measurement——> and Evaluation in Guidance (State Pers. & Guid. Assn.)	Association for Measurement and Evaluation in Guidance (Amer. Pers. & Guid. Assn.)
Diocesan Guidance Conference——————————————>National Catholic Guidance		Conference (Nat. Catholic Education Association)
———	———	International Association of Pupil Personnel Workers

   * Open only to counselors who are also qualified for A.P.A. membership
  ** Open only to counselors who are women
 *** Open only to counselors employed in Roman Catholic schools, or who are Catholics themselves
   # Open only to counselors who are men

FIFTEEN

Humanizing Counseling –
the "Other Half " of the Professional Role

The counseling relationship is at the same time both easy and difficult to define. This is because the basic underlying process and goals of all counseling are the same, yet the strategies and approaches to these are numerous and complex. Let's examine some basic considerations of counseling. . . . What's it like?

WHAT COUNSELING IS

There are two fundamental types of counseling, namely, individual or one-to-one, and group or multiple counseling. The former may be defined as a personal relationship between a counselor and client, during which the counselor helps the client help himself achieve either greater self-acceptance and understanding or modification of behavior and personality patterns, as appropriate. The latter consists of a personal relationship among a counselor and small group of clients who perceive a common interest or problems. The counselor helps group members help themselves and each other achieve either greater self-acceptance and understanding or modification of behavior and personality patterns, as appropriate. Frequently, greater appreciation of the feelings and problems of others is also a goal. Some forms of and topics for group counseling are not always advisable for in-school use.

HOW COUNSELING PROCEEDS

No two counseling relationships are the same, of course, but certain general commonalities exist. For example, almost all counseling cases pass through five generalized phases, the first and last phase not always being necessary. These stages might be termed rapport, exploration, definition, therapy, and follow-up.

During the rapport phase, a feeling of
mutual trust and concern is nurtured.

Rapport means little more than counselor and client getting to know, trust, and appreciate each other. Usually this portion of the counseling process lasts one counseling session or less, but occasionally rapport development is lengthy and difficult. In compulsorily referred cases, rapport is generally hard to achieve, while for voluntary referrals it frequently "comes easy." In group counseling, rapport may not occur for all members of a group simultaneously. In cases where a counselor has achieved rapport during previous counseling contact, the rapport stage may be completely skipped during the present relationship. Until rapport has been established, the counseling activity may not proceed further.

In the exploration phase, a counselor enables the client
to examine himself.

This second stage varies, depending upon circumstances and philosophies. In a crisis-oriented case, it consists of immediate discussion of the obvious problem at hand, while in a developmental situation, it features very general, ambiguous investigation. Counselors who follow one of the more directive, counselor-as-authority-figure strategies often prefer to engage in probing and questioning, while those more non-directively oriented prefer that the client probe himself. Some counselors have made use of a paper and pencil, client autobiographical essay type of appraisal, rather than verbal interaction, during this phase. In order for meaningful exploration to occur, client feelings of threat and insecurity must be held to a minimum, regardless of strategy or philosophy. This anxiety reduction had its beginnings during the rapport phase, or rapport wouldn't have become established. It must continue to be reinforced during exploration.

During the definition phase, the client determines and states
his principal areas of concern, and begins to decide what
he wants to do about it.

After an exploratory period, long in some cases, short in others, the client, facilitated by counselor support, arrives at the realization of three basic, sequential awarenesses. These are (a) what the problem or immediate concern is perceived to be, (b) what its likely genetic causal factors are, and (c) what course of action should be taken in light of this over-all picture. In some cases, these determinations are aided by mutually agreed upon recourse to test scores and other factual data. In all cases, however, the definition phase is fundamentally an affective process, and any use of tests or other factually oriented aids is but ancillary to the main stream of counseling. It also must be remembered that no fine lines can be drawn between exploration, definition, and therapy stages. Each phase overlaps with and dovetails into those adjacent to it.

In the therapy phase, the counselor helps the client work toward achievement of his chosen objectives.

Once the counselee has explored and defined his concerns, he must do things to attain his set goals. In some cases, this means learning to accept his limitation and live happily with a formerly troubling adversity. In other cases, it means modification of behavioral patterns so that a previously unidentified or unachievable goal is now reachable. Either way, the counselor doesn't, in fact cannot, "do the job" for the client. Rather, he provides the emotional support and occasional factual information needed by the counselee so he may help himself.

Counselor behavior during the therapy phase varies somewhat, commensurate with counselor personality and client needs. A rule of thumb for most counseling interviews is that the counselee should almost always be doing the most talking. A counselor who finds himself verbalizing excessively may unwittingly be preventing the occurrence of client gains. Some interesting research in the fields of psychiatry and clinical psychology, although conducted in the late 1940's and early 1950's, still has important ramifications for school counselors. Two investigators, Fred Fiedler and Hans Strupp, working independently, arrived at similar conclusions. They found that analysts, regardless of their theoretical orientation, gravitated toward an ideal therapeutic relationship as they became more experienced. Many persons have generalized this discovery to apply to school counseling and pastoral counseling, as well as psychiatry and clinical psychology. If this application is valid, which it may well be, it seems to mean that there is a best way to proceed during a counseling interview, at least after rapport has been established. This best way, or ideal therapeutic relationship, has been said to be both an art and a skill, in which counselors and other therapists grow in facility with experience. The specific qualities of this relationship are discussed in subsequent paragraphs.

During follow-up, care is taken that the gains already made are not eroded away.

The follow-up phase has been likened to a medical check-up shortly after the cure of a recent illness. Many times during counseling, it consists of the client's participation in a personnel service activity following counseling about it. For instance, a counselee may have engaged in extensive counseling over the problem of whether or not to attend college. Then, having resolved his problem, in this case in the affirmative, the counselee participates in various personnel services, described in detail in Chapters Three and Four, to implement his therapy phase gains. In other cases, follow-up means returning for an interview to keep the counselor, a concerned friend, posted on how things are going. After all, if he helped someone once, he'll help again when needed.

Certain counseling approaches, such as the neo-behavioral and the imaginative, utilize formal follow-up type routines as vehicles for accomplishing behavioral modification. In these approaches, a mutually agreed-upon reinforcing or reminding technique is the follow-up procedure for implementing the discoveries and decisions clarified during the therapy stage. For instance, a student who has discussed a fear of taking tests with his neo-behavioral, or S-R oriented counselor, may decide, with counselor help, to take the ACT several times to desensitize this fear. In a colloquial way, this form of follow-up may be regarded as the home work of the counseling subject. There is one circumstance where a follow-up stage may actually be undesirable. This occurs when a counselor perceives that any post-therapy effort might appear to a client as lack of trust, or "checking up." Since trust is such an important component of all counseling relationships, anything which could destroy it is to be avoided at all cost. Counselors must use their professional judgment to determine when follow-up is unwise for this reason.

THE NATURE OF COUNSELING

Certain warm personal qualities must permeate counselor behavior during all types of counseling relationships.

In the September, 1958, *Personnel and Guidance Journal*, Dr. Carl Rogers published a frequently quoted article: "Characteristics of a

Helping Relationship." This piece is just as timely today as when it appeared. Citing the Strupp and Fiedler findings, Dr. Rogers translated them into practical terms for analysts and counselors everywhere. While he was writing primarily with the non-directive school of thought in mind, the basic essential qualities of the counseling process apply equally to other theoretical positions. Rogers had one-to-one rather than group counseling in mind when he penned his landmark article. Subsequent writers—the late Fritz Perls, Merle Ohlsen, Clarence Mahler, George Gazda, James Muro, and others —have in their work more or less adapted these fundamental helping qualities to multiple counseling. The reader is strongly urged to refer to this Rogers article. Most persons who study it carefully gather the impression that an ideal helping relationship is little more than good, plain applied human decency—one person sincerely caring about another. Of course, this caring takes place upon a professional background that includes graduate education in personality dynamics and learning theory.

Three keystone properties of a good counseling relationship (there are others, but these three should be mastered first) are *empathy*, *positive regard,* and *reflection.* These terms are borrowed from the non-directive school of thought, but the counselor behaviors they define transcend all theoretical approaches. They may be exhibited in different ways by a counselor to his client, depending not only on his philosophy, but on sex and personality as well. *Empathy* means demonstration of sincere concern for the counselee's problems and feelings. It is not the same as sympathy, which implies a mutual sharing of feelings between client and counselor. "Empathy" connotes a greater emotional involvement with the client than does the word "interest," but a less intense one than does the term "sympathy." Basically, it may be said to be an expression of complete understanding, appreciation, and acceptance of client feelings, without counselor adoption of them as his own.

Positive regard demands full acceptance of and interest in the counselee, his personality and actions, as far as the counselor is emotionally able to do so. If a counselor cannot accept his client as a person, or vice versa, and the two mutually agree that this problem is insurmountable, the counselee had better see a different counselor. There is no set formula for demonstrating positive regard to a client; each person is unique and shows concern for others in different ways. One thing is certain, though: if a counselor lacks positive regard, students learn this in a hurry! Insincerity is difficult to conceal, especially from the young.

Reflection consists of restating for the counselee his feelings and concerns, so he may better focus upon them. Sometimes this means immediate repetition, other times restatement in clearer or different language, still other times recall and reverbalization of statements made earlier during the counseling relationship. Reflection serves the dual purpose of helping the counselee place his expressed concerns in perspective, and showing him that the counselor is seeking to do likewise.

**The ways in which helping, human qualities are manifested
depend on counselor personality and philosophic orientation.**

Richard Farson has advanced an ingenious hypothesis that counselor behaviors during a good helping relationship are more nearly resemblant to a woman's personality than to a man's. This is so, according to Farson, because it is more consonant with the feminine psycho-social role to take time to listen, and express feelings of concern for others' problems. After all, men, the bread-winners, often lack time to listen and psychological need to consider what's troubling someone else. When Farson first proposed that "the Counselor is a Woman," a minor philosophic controversy erupted, some authorities agreeing, others disputing his claim.

This author agrees with Farson in that the basic therapeutic process of sitting down to listen and empathize is a little more innately feminine than masculine. However, it also must be noted that empathy, positive regard, reflection, and other helping qualities are not always exhibited in a womanly manner. Some counselors communicate a very genuine acceptance of and concern for their clients in ways not too ladylike. To get a little mad or chew out a counselee doesn't necessarily destroy a counseling relationship, *as long as the expressed feelings are not judgmental of him or of his behavior.* Some of the rational approaches to counseling, to be described shortly, are actually predicated upon a rather hard-nosed demeanor. The main factor in counseling success is for a counselor to accept, trust, and listen to a counselee. Sometimes these qualities are best exhibited in rather passive, gentle, and kindly ways; other times in more active, forthright, even "rock 'em, sock 'em" ways. Each counselor must decide for himself whether to develop a quiet, somewhat reserved counseling decor, or a more forceful, tougher one. Which way to go comes naturally for every counselor as he gathers experience. The personality and life philosophy of each individual leads him to a natural counseling style. Some counselors see a place for both passive and active interview decorum in their counseling style; for them, this is no doubt the best way to proceed.

Conversation topics and their emotional depth vary greatly during most counseling interviews.

Clients must have free rein to discuss whatever concerns them during counseling. As insights are generated during the exploration and definition phases, this means that it's likely that a variety of different matters, or at least a number of facets of one central matter, will be verbalized. The counselor must be careful to allow each of these themes to be developed; many valuable leads or cues result from them. By permitting the counselee to state freely, in the absence of threat or pressure, what concerns him, a gradual uncovering of basic underlying problems occurs. Of course, there are infrequent times when a counselor perceives the shift of conversational topic to be a mild client defense mechanism or blockage. When this is so, the counselor may carefully, in a non-threatening, low pressure way, steer the counselee back on what appears to be the right track.

A gradation, often referred to as the factual-emotional continuum or line, may be used to label all client statements and expressions during counseling. (This gradation has also been called the cognitive-conative or effective-affective continuum.) This concept merely means that some counselee expressions are information giving or seeking in character, while others are highly charged with feeling and psychological meaning. For example, the high school senior discussing college choice with his counselor may one minute inquire about tuition costs, a highly factual matter. The next minute, he may relate very emotionally tinged family relations, revolving around his father's attempts to influence his selection of college and course of study. Both the cognitive and conative dimensions are essential components of the overall counseling relationship gestalt; neither may be divorced from it or from each other. A counselor must be prepared to deal with both forms of counselee expressions, as well as mixtures of the two, which lie toward the middle of the line, or continuum. Analogy may be made between this concept and a tennis ball bouncing rapidly up and down a line drawn on the court. One minute the ball (the progress of the counseling interview) is at one end of the line (factual extreme), the next minute, at the other end (emotional extreme), and often, in the middle. The directions taken during a counseling relationship, like those of a bouncing ball, are rapid and unpredictable.

Regardless of the nature or severity of a case, the fundamental counseling process remains the same.

Some persons have suggested that a basic difference exists between crisis-oriented and so-called developmental counseling. The former finds the counselor dealing with serious problems only, while the latter approach stresses his working with as many as possible, regardless of whether a serious problem is perceived. It has been said that the former procedure marshals all resources where most needed, but is oriented toward after-the-fact "cure" after trouble has occurred. The latter approach has been criticized for diluting counseling resources by applying them where less needed, but is believed in many cases to avert problems before they ever become serious.

This author takes the position that crisis-oriented and developmental counseling are two legitimate philosophies of how counselor time should be spent. There is no difference between the actual counseling relationships that occur in them. There are, of course, differences in counselor behavior during the rapport phase of counseling. When initiating counselor in a crisis-oriented case, it's often best to call a spade a spade and begin immediate consideration of the perceived serious matter. A developmental case, on the other hand, frequently opens with an explanation of why counseling will benefit the client, followed by a very general exploration phase, in which the counselee seeks to ascertain the nature of his concerns.

Personal values may be discussed whenever pertinent, but never imposed on the client, except in one rare case.

It used to be said by many authorities that counselor values, especially moral ones, were a taboo topic for counseling. This was believed to be so because anything smacking of judgment or admonition is likely to convey lack of acceptance to the counselee, and thus destroy the counseling relationship. Today's breed of student is just too sophisticated for a counselor to dare attempt concealment of his value system. Therefore, a better tack is never to freely offer one's values to a client, but to discuss them openly if they come up logically during counseling. To hide one's values or refuse to talk about them turns a counselee off much more than bringing them out in the open. Avoidance of a topic connotes lack of acceptance as much as being judgmental does. Of course, the counselor must never seek to impose his values on any client. This, rather than mere discussion of them, is what ruins a helping relationship. A good thumb rule, then, is not to bring up values, but if the subject is broached, to discuss them in a non-threatening, fully accepting way.

In one case, however, values must be imposed. This rare instance occurs whenever a counselor perceives that the life or physical well-being of someone is in jeopardy. A suicidal or homicidal client must be dissuaded from harming himself or others. Reverence for life is a universal human value, therefore its imposition is mandatory and does not connote lack of acceptance of a troubled counselee who may reject it.

THEORIES OF COUNSELING AND PSYCHO-THERAPY

The intellectual rationales underlying helping relationships are grounded in theories found in such allied fields as psychiatry, psychology, philosophy, theology, and government. Each is an idea of why counseling should work, what underlying counseling goals should be, and what the relationship of counseling to other social values is. Generally, each theory of counseling occurs in one form or another throughout all the helping professions. This author prefers to divide the many theories or approaches into eight general categories. The first seven are, in rough chronological order of their appearance upon the intellectual scene, the analytic, rational, imaginative, neo-analytic, non-directive, existential, and neo-behavioral schools of thought. The eighth viewpoint, combination eclecticism, involves a mixing or amalgamation of two or more of the other seven. Encapsulations of the eight schools of thought follow. Each is treated regarding origins, basic tenets, and important names in the field. The psychological relationship of counselor to client (superior, equal, subordinate), and time-orientation of the counseling process (past, present, future) is indicated, but in very simplified terms. The alleged strong points and limitations of the eight schools of thought are summarized.

The *analytic* school of thought began with Sigmund Freud, founder of the psychiatric field.

The analytic approach, when applied to school counseling, features less emotionally deep therapy than that done by a psychiatrist or doctoral level clinical psychologist. In this counseling strategy, the counselor, after establishing rapport, gently probes the counselee's early childhood recollections. This is done because, as Freud initially pointed out, infantile trauma, frustrations, and familial relationships have a great deal to do with shaping the personality. Persons interested in this method should familiarize themselves with basic Freudian hypotheses; the id-ego-superego personality concept and the five-stage child development (oral, anal, phallic, latent and genital) progression are good ones with which to begin. Three contemporaries of Freud—Carl Jung, Alfred Adler, and Otto Rank— also did much early writing on analytic approaches to psycho-therapy; their intellectual heirs, like Freud's, have continued research and writing on the ideas these great men began.

In school counseling, Rudolph Dreikurs has done much to apply Adler's ideas to modern settings. The Society for Individual Psychology, to which many counselors belong, is part of a modern Adlerian revival. Also worth mention here is the work of Edward Bordin. In analytic counseling systems, the therapist or counselor is an authority figure, albeit a kindly one, over the client. These systems all have a strong past orientation, due to the extreme emphasis on infantile experiences. Therapy occurs, theoretically, through the restating, talking out, and analyzing of past causes of present problems, once they are unearthed and identified. The analytic approach has been said to be on the right track regarding the importance of early childhood; empirical research has supported the contention that personality is crystallized by age three. It has been criticized as placing too much importance upon infantile sex feelings and frustrations, and upon child-parent relationships, to the exclusion of other shaping forces.

The *rational* school of thought grew as a reaction against over-emphasis upon the affective domain.

While Freud no doubt did mankind a great intellectual service, subsequent writers have carried his ideas to ridiculous extremes. The rational approaches to counseling, as the name implies, largely reject this affective emphasis, and concentrate on empirically measurable human characteristics. The earliest of these systems to appear is the trait-factor approach, begun by Frank Parsons during the first decade of the twentieth century. This counseling method places heavy emphasis upon vocational choice; test scores and other counselee data (traits) are matched against various job situations (factors) in which he may have an interest. This system seeks to copy the diagnosis-prognosis method of the medical profession, adapting it to solution of counselee problems.

Another form of rational approach is the shock-emotive and other types of marriage counseling employed by Albert Ellis. Here, couples wanting help are urged to lay their cards on the table and not worry about deep psychological concepts. The late Ed Roeber was known as a member of the communications approach to counseling; this branch stresses great faith in the ability of two persons to sit down and talk things out. Again, all that "deep stuff" isn't important, only the views and ideas of counselor and client. Another branch bearing mention—that of John Rosen—is the hardest-nosed of them all. Working chiefly with inmates of mental institutions, Rosen chews them out for not living up to their expectations, but only in a framework of complete acceptance. Other prominent rationalists include E. G. Williamson and Frederick Thorne.

In the rational school of thought, the counselor is in a superior position, psychologically, to the counselee, as he is providing him with a solution, in the manner of a teacher or doctor. The system is neither past, present, nor future oriented, but rather is all three sequentially. The data drawn from the past is synthesized during the present, so solution may affect one's future. Rationalism is alleged to provide tangible, understandable, measurable help to a client who needs it. It has been criticized as overly mechanistic, and as overlooking the complex, affective dimensions of human personality.

The *imaginative* school of thought is based upon faith.

There are two subdivisions of this approach to counseling, namely, secular and religious. The former branch seeks to build counselee ego-strength and confidence through recourse to faith in one's self; the latter hopes to do the same by stressing faith in God. The secular wing of the imaginative school of thought began (as a formal counseling theory) with the work of the early twentieth century French psychiatrist Emile Coué. The religious approach, as far as a formal procedure for self-improvement is concerned, is traceable to Mary Baker Eddy, founder of the Christian Science denomination. Of course, informal, non-organized efforts to employ the dynamics of this approach are as old as mankind itself. Certain elements of this philosophy, frequently referred to as positive thinking, often appear in methods of persons other than counselors, clinical psychologists, or psychiatrists. Examples are the football coaching of the late Vincent Lombardi and the faith healing of the Reverend Oral Roberts.

Best known contemporary exponent of the imaginative approach is the Reverend Norman Vincent Peale. His counseling strategy combines both secular and religious emphases. All positive-thinking therapies seek to first build client self-confidence through the insistence that anything (within reason) is possible as long as it is so believed. Next, the counselee selects his personal goal, and receives a counselor (or peer group, in the case of group counseling) pep talk reinforcement of this decision. Finally, a reminding procedure is agreed upon, lest the client lapse into his former behavior pattern; the wearing of religious medals or the proverbial string around one's finger are examples. Motivational signs and posters are often used to foster counselee determination; some familiar slogans are: "Every day, in every way, I'm getting better and better," "Only *you* can change you," "The Lord helps those who help themselves," "Today is the first day of the rest of your life," and so on.

In the imaginative approach, counseling begins with the counselor as superior to counselee, but terminates with the reverse being true. This is because the counselee, now a "better" man or woman, needs help from no one (save God) as long as he or she perseveres. This school of thought is very future oriented. Often cited as the advantage of the positive thinking method is the fact that determination, faith, stubbornness, or whatever you call it when used by someone convinced, is probably the most powerful motivator of all. The method is criticizable on the grounds that selection of unreachable goals may lead to later severe frustration, and that persons overly goal-directed may overlook their need for others and exhibit symptoms of conceit.

The *neo-analytic* school of thought grew from an attempt to update Freud's ideas.

During the 1930's and since, some members of the psychiatric profession, while agreeing with many Freudian theories, rebelled against others. Specifically, they objected to the heavy past emphasis in classical analytic thought, claiming that many neuroses are a function of present social forces impinging on clients. Social psychologists and others also became involved in the neo-analytic movement. Some key pioneers of this philosophy are Harry S.

Sullivan, Karen Horney, French and Alexander, Freida Reichmann, and Erich Fromm. In the school counseling field, many recent attempts to work with drop-outs, drug users, and juvenile deliquents are basically neo-analytic in character.

In neo-analytic counseling, gentle counselor probing occurs as in the analytic method, but present peer group relationships, rather than past parent-child ones, are the target. While effects of early experiences may be touched upon, their significance is relevant in terms of present counselee life-style. Coping with social forces and pressures plays a major part in this approach; client future goals are always appraised in the light of these.

In neo-analytic therapy, the counselor occupies an authority figure position at the onset of counseling, but becomes more an equal as the relationship progresses. This is because counselor and client become partners in working out the problem; each may have valuable insights and hypotheses to offer. This approach is quite present-oriented. An advantage is its emphasis upon the "now" importance of current life situations and social problems. This has high appeal to adolescent counselees. It may be criticized on the grounds that there is little agreement on what causes various social type problems— prejudice, delinquency, sexual deviance, etc.—hence one set strategy for combating them may not exist.

Non-directive **counseling, unlike other approaches, places the responsibility for charting the course of counseling upon the client.**

The non-directive school of thought, more than any other, is dominated by the reputation of one man, its founder Carl Rogers. This philosophy, first promulgated by him during the 1940's, spread like wildfire throughout the fields of school counseling, clinical psychology, and psychiatry alike during the 1950's. This rapid spread was a good thing in that it attracted great interest to counseling relationships and spawned many debates among intellectuals regarding the nature of therapy. Unfortunately, it also brought into existence a few charlatans and quacks who thought they could become professional counselors just by sitting still and periodically saying "uh-huh" to counselees—a happenstance which Rogers would condemn as much as anyone else. Other writers who have contributed to non-directivism are C. H. Patterson, Roy Grinker, and George Kelly.

In any client-centered, or non-directive counseling, the counselor never picks a discussion topic, probes, or gives advice. (He does give information, if asked by a client to do so.) Tests are never prescribed for a counselee; they could under rare circumstances be used if the counselee, on his own, asks that a test be given him. The counselor's job is to lead the client to probe himself, by serving as a fully accepting and empathetic helping friend. The counselor fosters therapeutic relationship progress by serving as a reflective mirror of client communications and feelings. Since non-directivism is based on phenomenological learning theory, the therapist's major task is to convey trust and regard of the counselee as a worthy person. This is because, in phenomenological thinking, personality problems stem from conditional acceptance of a youngster. The withholding of love by parents or of friendship by peers causes a child to alter reality by distorting or rejecting incoming perceptions. Only when a counselee is completely accepted and trusted, this theory goes, is he able to reorient reality into correct perspective—hence, the kindly, passive, positive-regarding nature of non-directive counseling.

The counselor and client are always psychological equals in non-directivism. There is no set past, present and/or future emphasis, as the orientation of the relationship goes any way the client desires. A major advantage of this school of thought is its universal basic manifestation of acceptance to all persons; there is no change in counselor behavior from case to case. A disadvantage frequently heard is that some clients, especially teen-agers, are leery of a therapist who doesn't say much or is reluctant to render value judgments. Some counselees apparently misconstrue non-directive methods as being evidence of a lack of concern or backbone, or as cover-up for counselor incompetence.

The *existential* viewpoint comes to the helping professions from the field of philosophy.

Existentialism as a philosophy formally began in the mid 19th century with the work of Soren Kierkegaard, a Danish thinker who primarily concerned himself with the constructive reform of the Lutheran Church from a layman's perspective. An interesting precursor of modern existential counseling was Jonathan Chapman (Johnny Appleseed), who toured frontier America seeking to interest people in Kierkegaard's ideas. Like the imaginative school of thought, it's subdivided into secular and religious branches. For those interested in studying underlying philosophies, the work of Atheistic French thinker Jean Paul Sartre is recommended for the former; a top source for the latter is the writing of Belgian Catholic Jesuit theologian Teilhard de Chardin. The person credited with adapting existentialism to helping relationships is Viktor Frankl, an Austrian Jewish psychiatrist who developed his theories while a Nazi death-camp inmate during World War II. His book, *From Death Camp to Existentialism,* is highly recommended. The American psychologists Gordon Allport and Rollo May played major roles in popularizing Frankl's ideas in their professional field and nation. As of this book's writing, existential counseling is one of the three "hottest brands going" among school counselors. (The other two are behavioral modification, a neo-behavioral approach, and the reality therapy of William Glasser, a combination-eclectic system.)

The basic tenets of existentialism, secular or religious branch, are that man is basically good, just because he's man. Each person must be responsible for his own decisions; being unique, he alone can properly decide for himself. Neuroses (the "problems" of counseling clients) stem basically from the inability to decide for one's self, or from dread that a "wrong" past decision has been made. Decisions must be made from a a present context only, as conditions prevalent at the moment of decision will never again exist. Some go so far as to interpret this approach as saying that each person living is the most important person in the world, as far as he is personally concerned. It follows from this thinking that an existential counselor first works to build counselee ego-strength by informing him of his importance. Next, the client is urged to make his own decisions relative to the problem at hand. Finally, he is encouraged to move forward in life, avoid worrying about his decision as it was the best one possible, and live day by day.

In existential counseling, counselor and counselee can only be equal, as each one, to be consistent with this philosophy, must see himself as important. This school of thought is very present-oriented. An advantage of the existential position is that it provides a logical rationale for leading one's life and dispelling guilt feelings over troubling past behaviors. An oft-cited disadvantage is the lack of coming to grips with man's social environment. Perhaps, for some persons, it is unnatural to behave as though they are "the most important thing in the world." Interestingly, the one person who ever lived who obviously fit that description, a man whom many existentialists, at least Catholic and Protestant ones, regard as their hero, certainly didn't act that way!

**The *neo-behavioral* school of thought is grounded
in S-R learning theory.**

Like its "competitor" of sorts, existentialism, the neo-behavioral
school of thought has been spreading rapidly throughout all the
helping professions during the past 25 years. This approach is based
upon S-R, or behavioral learning theory. There are almost as many
different forms of neo-behavioral counseling as there are practitioners. Basically, however, they all rely upon helping clients asso-
ciate some form of reward with "desirable" behavior and either the
lack of reward or some sort of punishment with "undesirable"
behavior. The theories underlying this type of counseling began with
the pioneering work of 19th Century Russian biologist Ivan Pavlov.
Experimental psychologists such as Hull, Spence, and Skinner have
worked to update and expand upon Pavlov's original discovery,
bringing S-R theory to its current advanced intellectual stage. Some
thinkers who have developed rationales for S-R therapy are Dollard
and Miller, E. J. Shoben, O. Hobart Mowrer, E. Lakin Phillips, the
Pepinskys, and Raymond Hosford. The Patterson book referenced
earlier contains a very good overview chapter on neo-behavioral
approaches. The most prominent S-R name in the school counseling
field is that of John Krumboltz.

There are two general subdivisions of the neo-behavioral school of
thought; it may, in somewhat an oversimplification, be divided into
counseling systems based upon classical conditioning and those
predicated upon operant conditioning. The former procedure
involves associating a stimulus coincidentally with a behavior for
which there otherwise would be no connection,—the most famous
example of this being Pavlov's dog, who learned to salivate when a
bell rang because it was previously rung during his dinner. The latter
method revolves around learning to repeat a certain specified action
to receive a particular reward. Here the most famous examples are no
doubt B. F. Skinner's rats, who learn to operate levers to receive
food pellets. The reader is urged to do some reading in fundamental
S-R learning theory, in order to more fully understand its application
to counseling. In addition to the terms *classical* and *operant conditioning,* the following are a few more that need be mastered for basic
understanding: *S-R bond, suprasystem, reward and punishment*
(technical usage) *reinforcement, desensitization, approach-avoidance*

gradient, reciprocal inhibition, and *successive approximations method,* to name a few key ones.

Most neo-behavioral counseling methods proceed along lines of other forms of helping relationships during rapport, exploration, and definition stages. Attention may be given to reinforcing client attitudes during these phases, however, especially those leading to enhanced ego-strength and motivation. During the therapy and/or follow-up stages, a definite strategy of positive and/or negative reinforcement is pursued, the specific nature of which varies from practicioner to practicioner. Its purpose is to alter future client behaviors. The counselor is in a psychologically superior role to the client in neo-behaviorism, because as therapist he is teaching him, sometimes even to the extent of manipulation. Of course, the counselee chooses, at least in part, the directions in which he wishes to be manipulated. This school of thought is future oriented, although some consideration must first be given the past and present. An advantage cited for neo-behaviorism is that it offers a scientifically proven process for eliminating unwanted behavior patterns and substituting new, desired ones. A frequently heard objection is that it can lead to mechanistic manipulation of counselees, smacking at times of "big-brotherism."

Combination eclecticism **is predicated upon mixing two or more of the other seven approaches in three possible ways.**

An eclectic counselor is one who uses more than one school of thought, or their component parts, as the basis for his work. There are three ways in which this may be done: (1) Some eclectics believe in using one strategy in one form of counseling case, another in another. For instance, such a counselor might apply an analytic approach to crisis-oriented cases, and a rational outlook to developmental ones. (2) Other eclectics use one approach during certain phases of the counseling relationship, then switch to different schools of thought for a later stage. For example, this type of counselor might employ non-directivism during rapport, exploration, and definition, then use neo-behavioral methods in therapy and follow-up. (3) The third form of eclectic builds his own private school of thought by amalgamating various component parts of existing standard counseling approaches. For instance, Leona Tyler has written that her counseling philosophy is drawn from the ideas of both Freud and Rogers. Some eclectics have blended personality, learning, and child development theories, as well as counseling ones, into their own private approaches to establishing helping relationships. For example, Gail Farwell has drawn upon the work of Erik Erikson and Robert Callis upon the ideas of the late A. H. Maslow, and Donald Blocker upon several developmental concepts. Also sometimes used by eclectics are the ideas of Bruner and Piaget.

A frequently encountered eclectic system, interesting because it mixes two schools of thought often said to be widely disparate, is the reality therapy of William Glasser, Los Angeles psychiatrist. Glasser, who has developed his own theory of human personality disorganization, combines this with elements of existentialism and neo-behaviorism. The reader is urged to read his books *Reality Therapy* and *Schools Without Failure,* which explain this brilliant man's theories.

The psychological position of counselor to client, and the matter of past, present, or future orientation vary, of course, in combination-eclecticism, depending upon whose system is under consideration. A reputed advantage of this philosophic position is that it enables each counselor to draw elements from other approaches which he privately feels are best for him to use. An objection often heard is that mixing approaches may really destroy the effectiveness of these parent schools of thought, as combining incompatible ingredients results in a worthless aggregate.

In summary, it might be said that all schools of thought appear to have some validity; social science has not reached the stage where counseling approaches may be empirically tested to see which is best. A certain faddishness has accompanied each intellectual position's impact upon the counseling scene. In the 1950's non-directivism spread very rapidly. It has been said by many existentialists that their movement is spreading so widely today because it's seen as reaction to two other systems. They rebel against what they consider the over-passivity of non-directivism and the over-mechanization of neo-behaviorism. Glasser's reality therapy is undoubtedly as popular as it is today because its cornerstone is the insistence that people be responsible for their actions—and this comes precisely at a time in history when buck-passing and "getting out of things" are at all-time highs in society.

DOES ANY OF IT HELP?

Hans Eysenck's research has been aimed at proving that only certain specialized forms of neo-behaviorism do anyone any good.

There are a few studies, some slipshod but others well done, that conclude that counseling neither helps nor hinders. Who knows? Maybe all this theorizing has been for naught! Two long-term follow-up studies, those of John Rothney and David Campbell, found that counseling did indeed help, but over time, non-counseled control groups "caught up" to the counseled subjects. To this author, their findings seem to suggest that counseling helps slightly on the average, and that persons not receiving any turn to other helping sources, either formally or informally. Who knows? More research on methods, theories, and effects of counseling certainly is needed!

THE GAINS OF COUNSELING

Theoretically, counseling should help clients in three ways. These potential benefit areas may be termed *informational, therapeutic*, and *placebo*. The first area of gain, *informational,* stems from the factual-cognitive-effective or what-have-you end of the counseling continuum. The counselor, as information-giver, supplies the average counselee with a good many pieces of new information during a normal helping relationship. Wage rates, college tuition costs, manners for dating behavior, etc., are examples of typical informational gains. The counselor, as helping facilitator of his clients, must be ready to provide information whenever pertinent and acceptable.

Therapeutic gains occur at the emotional-conative-affective end of the counseling relationship continuum. They are the most dramatic outcome of counseling in that their existence connotes changed behavior and personality patterns. These gains exist in two forms: (1) greater adjustment or self-acceptance, and (b) modified future behaviors. The former consists of enhanced client ability to cope with his environment and accept his limitations. The latter involves actual outward manifestation of altered behavioral responses by a counselee, along lines set for himself during counseling. Each form of therapeutic gain stems from the client himself, but is made possible by the supportive, catalytic relationship with the counselor.

"Placebo" is a term borrowed from the medical profession and first applied to counseling by C. H. Patterson. It means something of no helping value which nevertheless helps a patient because he *thinks* it has value. Whenever someone shows that he cares about another and wishes to help, e.g., the counselor-client relationship, this is bound to perk up the troubled party. Placebo gains are not to be discounted; anything which helps a counselee is worth cultivating. This author harbors no illusions; perhaps the *only* gains of some counseling relationships are placebo ones. It is hoped, of course, that major derived counseling benefits are of the informational and therapeutic variety, with placebo effect being complementary but of lesser importance. Until research finally answers this question empirically, let us hope that all three areas of potential gain come in some measure from all successful counseling encounters. At least this occurrence should be the goal of all counselers.

HUMANIZING MEANS ALL THE TIME

One of the goals of this book, as stated in the introduction, is to suggest an overall personal counselor philosophy that could permeate both counseling and practice of personnel services alike. It was suggested that such a unified outlook on the professional role would lead to greater counselor success in practicing each component of it. The kindly, accepting qualities advocated for counseling relationships adapt themselves nicely as departure points for global display of helpfulness to all. Demonstrating positive regard doesn't just happen in the guidance office during interviews; it should take place every waking moment of a counselor's entire life. Of course, each counselor's manifestation of this humanness toward others will be a little different, as personalities differ. But the feeling induced in all those with whom a counselor comes into contact will be the same—and humanity the better for it!

An example of this positive, humanizing counselor attitude is found in the life and writings of Dugald Arbuckle, noted Boston University counselor-educator. Arbuckle is known to practice what he preaches; his positive interest in his fellowmen is a constant factor, not something artificially turned on from 8:00 A.M. to 4:00 P.M. on school days. Now, fellow counselors, let us go and do likewise!

For Further Reference . . .

GENERAL GUIDANCE

Common Sense in Guidance, Homer Gammons. West Nyack, N.Y.: Parker, 1969

Contemporary Guidance Concepts and Practices, Brown & Srebalus. Dubuque, Iowa: W.C. Brown, 1972.

Counseling and Guidance in the Twentieth Century, William VanHoose and John Pietrofesa. Boston: Houghton Mifflin, 1970

The Counselor and Society, Lawrence Stewart and Charles Warnath. Boston: Houghton Mifflin, 1965

Foundations of Developmental Guidance, Harold Munson. Boston: Allyn & Bacon, 1971

Foundations of Guidance, 2nd ed., Carroll Miller. New York: Harper & Row, 1971

Foundations of Guidance and Counseling, C. E. Smith and O. G. Mink, eds. Philadelphia: J. B. Lippincott, 1969

Fundamentals of Guidance, 2nd ed., Bruce Shertzer and Shelley Stone. Boston: Houghton Mifflin, 1971

Guidance: A Developmental Approach, 2nd ed., Gail Farwell and Herman Peters. Skokie, Ill.: Rand McNally, 1967

Guidance: A Systematic Introduction, Robert Nordberg. New York: Random House, 1970

Guidance and the Emerging Adolescent, Philip Perrone, T. Antoinette Ryan, and Franklin Zeran. Scranton, Pa.: International, 1970

The Guidance Function in Education, 2nd ed., Percival Hutson. New York: Appleton-Century-Crofts, 1968

Guidance in Action: Ideas and Innovations for School Counselors, Kenneth Gutsch and Joseph Alcorn. West Nyack, N.Y.: Parker, 1970

The Guidance Process, Herman Peters. Itasca, Ill.: F. E. Peacock, 1970

Guidance Systems, Donald Blocher, B. Richard Dustin, and Willis Dugan. New York: Ronald Press, 1971

An Introduction to Counseling in the School, C. H. Patterson. New York: Harper & Row, 1971

Pupil Personnel Services, Donald Ferguson. New York: Center for Applied Research in Ed., 1963

The School Counselor, Edward C. Roeber. New York: Center for Applied Research in Ed., 1963

A Strategy for Guidance, Edward Roeber, Garry Walz, and Glenn Smith. New York: Macmillan, 1969

Techniques of Guidance, 3rd ed., Arthur Traxler and Robert North. New York: Harper & Row, 1964

Today's Guidance, Carroll Miller and George Weigel, eds. Boston: Allyn & Bacon, 1970

The Work of the Counselor, 3rd ed., Leona Tyler. New York: Appleton-Century-Crofts, 1969

SPECIFIC COUNSELOR ROLE COMPONENTS

COUNSELING

The Authentic Counselor, John Pietrofesa, George Leonard, and William Van-Hoose. Chicago: University of Chicago Press, 1971

Barriers and Hazards in Counseling, Dorothy Johnson and Mary Vestermark. Boston: Houghton Mifflin, 1970

Beyond Counseling and Therapy, Robert Carkhuff and Bernard Berenson. New York: Holt, Rinehart & Winston, 1967

Counseling and Values: A Philosophical Examination, James Peterson. Scranton, Pa.: Intext, 1970

Counseling: Group Theory and System, Daniel Fullmer. Scranton, Pa.: Intext, 1971

Counseling the Disadvantaged Youth, W. Amos and J. Grambs. Englewood Cliffs, N.J.: Prentice-Hall, 1968

Counseling: Philosophy, Theory, and Practice, 2nd ed., Dugald Arbuckle. Boston: Allyn & Bacon, 1970

The Counseling Process, Daniel Delaney and Sheldon Eisenberg. Skokie, Ill.: Rand McNally, 1971.

Developmental Counseling, Donald Blocher. New York: Ronald Press, 1966

Developmental Counseling and Therapy, Bill Kell and Josephine Burow. Boston: Houghton Mifflin, 1970

Foundations of Counseling Strategies, James Barclay. New York: Wiley, 1971

Fundamentals of Counseling, Bruce Shertzer and Shelley Stone. Boston: Houghton Mifflin, 1968

Group Counseling, Merle Ohlsen. New York: Holt, Rinehart & Winston, 1970

Group Counseling: A Developmental Approach, George Gazda. Boston: Allyn & Bacon, 1971

Group Counseling in the Schools, Clarence Mahler. Boston: Houghton Mifflin, 1969

Group Counseling: Theory and Practice, Don Dinkmeyer and James Muro. Itasca, Ill.: F. E. Peacock, 1971

Helping Relationships: Basic Concepts for the Helping Professions, Arthur Combs, Donald Avila, and William Purkey. Boston: Allyn & Bacon, 1971

Perspectives on the Group Process, 2nd ed., C. Gratton Kemp. Boston: Houghton Mifflin, 1970

Psychobehavioral Counseling and Therapy, Robert Woody. New York: Appleton-Century-Crofts, 1971

The Psychology of Counseling, Edwin Lewis. New York: Holt, Rinehart & Winston, 1970

Strategies in Counseling for Behavior Change, Samuel Osipow and W. Bruce Walsh. New York: Appleton-Century-Crofts, 1970

A Successful Approach to High School Counseling, J. Liggero. West Nyack, N.Y.: Parker, 1968

VOCATIONAL DEVELOPMENT AND INFORMATION SERVICES

Career Information in Counseling and Teaching, 2nd ed., Lee Isaacson. Boston: Allyn & Bacon, 1971

A Guide to Professional Careers, Walter Duckat. New York: Simon & Schuster (Messner Div.), 1970

The Information Service in Guidance, 3rd ed., Willa Norris, Franklin Zeran, and Raymond Hatch. Skokie, Ill.: Rand McNally, 1972

Occupational Psychology, Donald Super and Martin Bohn, Jr. Belmont, Calif: Wadsworth, 1970

Occupations and the Social Structure, Richard Hall. Englewood Cliffs, N.J.: Prentice-Hall, 1970

Personalizing Information Processes, J. W. and L. U. Hollis. New York: Macmillan, 1969

Vocational Education and Guidance, James Rhodes. Columbus, Ohio: Charles Merrill, 1970

Vocational Guidance and Career Development, 2nd ed., Herman Peters and James Hansen, eds. New York: Macmillan, 1971

FURTHER EDUCATIONAL PLANNING AND ADMISSION

Against the Odds, William Moore. San Francisco: Jossey-Bass, 1970

Barron's Profiles of American Colleges, Woodbury. New York: Barron's Educational Services, 1971

Free-Access Higher Education, Warren Willingham. New York: C.E.E.B., 1970

The Ghetto College Student, Gordon Morgan. Iowa City: American College Testing Program, 1970

Guiding the Future College Student, Jean Reiss and Mildred Fox. Englewood Cliffs, N.J.: Prentice-Hall, 1968

Higher Education: Participants Confronted, Josiah Dilley. Dubuque, Iowa: W. C. Brown, 1970

Human Resources and Higher Education, John Folger, Helen Austin, and Alan Boyer. New York: Basic Books, 1970

Lovejoy's College Guide, 11th ed., Clarence Lovejoy. New York: Simon & Schuster, 1970 (see also *Career and Vocational School Guide, Lovejoy's Scholarship Guide, Prep School Guide*)

Successful Programs and Practices for Counseling the College-Bound Student, Martin Bloom, West Nyack, N.Y.: Parker, 1969

TESTING AND MEASUREMENT

Building a School Testing Program, rev. ed., Robert Bauernfeind. Boston: Houghton Mifflin, 1969

Essentials of Psychological Testing, 3rd ed., Lee Cronbach. New York: Harper & Row, 1970

Evaluating Pupil Growth, 4th ed., J. Stanley Ahmann and Marvin Glock. Boston, Allyn & Bacon, 1971

Guidance Monograph Series (five sets), Shelley Stone and Bruce Shertzer, eds. Boston: Houghton Mifflin, continuing

Individual Mental Testing (two vols.), Allen J. Edwards. Scranton, Pa.: Intext, 1971

Personality Tests and Reviews, Oscar Buros. Highland Park, N.J.: Gryphon Press, 1970

Principles of Educational and Psychological Testing, Frederick G. Brown. Hinsdale, Ill.: Dryden Press, 1970

Psychological Testing, 3rd ed., Anne Anastasi. New York: Macmillan, 1968

Standardized Tests in Education, William Mehrens and Irvin Lehmann. New York: Holt, Rinehart & Winston, 1969

Testing Student Achievement and Aptitudes, J. Stanley Ahmann. New York: Center for Applied Research in Ed., 1962

Topics in Measurement, Dick Hagerty, Walter Dick, and Nancy Hagerty. New York: McGraw-Hill, 1971

Using Tests in Counseling, Leo Goldman. New York: Appleton-Century-Crofts, 1971

RESEARCH, INCLUDING STATISTICS

Conducting Educational Research, Bruce Tuckman. New York: Harcourt Brace Jovanovich, 1972

Handbook of Educational Research, Tyrus Hillway. Boston: Houghton Mifflin, 1969

Research in Education, 2nd ed., John Best. Englewood Cliffs, N.J.: Prentice-Hall, 1970

Research Guidelines for High School Counselors, ACES Experimental Designs Committee. New York: C.E.E.B., 1967

Research Methods in Education, William Wiersma. Philadelphia: J. B. Lippincott, 1969

Research for the Practitioner in Education, Fred P. Barnes. Washington, D.C.: National Association of Elementary School Principals, 1966

The Research Process in Education, David J. Fox. New York: Holt, Rinehart & Winston, 1969

Research and the School Counselor, Stanley Cramer, Edwin Herr, Charles Morris, and Thomas Frantz. Boston: Houghton Mifflin, 1970

Research for Tommorow's Schools, Lee Cronbach and Patrick Suppes, eds. New York, Macmillan, 1969

Statistical Methods for Behavioral Science Research, Leonard Marascuilo. New York: McGraw-Hill, 1971

Statistics for Educational Measurement, Thomas Knapp. Scranton, Pa.: Intext, 1971

Statistics: The Essentials for Research, Henry Klugh. New York: Wiley, 1970

Statistics and Measurement, 2nd ed., Lowell Schoer. Boston: Allyn & Bacon, 1971

Statistics for Problem Solving, C. Mitchell Dayton and Clayton Stunkard. New York: McGraw-Hill, 1971

Statistical Reasoning in Psychology and Education, Edward Minium. New York: Wiley, 1970

REFERRAL AND MENTAL HEALTH

Education and Mental Health, Louis Kaplan. New York: Harper & Row, 1971

The Encyclopedia of Human Behavior: Psychology, Psychiatry, and Mental Health (two vols.), Robert Goldenson. Garden City, N.Y.: Doubleday and Co., 1970

Freedom to Learn, Carl Rogers. Columbus, Ohio: Charles E. Merrill, 1969

Mental Health Book Review Index, vol. 16. New York: Research Center for Mental Health, 1971

Schools Without Failure, William Glasser, New York: Harper & Row, 1969

WORKING WITH PARENTS, TEACHERS, AND OTHER SUPPORTING PERSONNEL

Collaboration in School Guidance: A Creative Approach, Mary Sarvis and Marianne Pennekamp. N.Y.: Brunner-Mazel, 1970

Discord in Teacher-Counselor Relations, Gerald Kushel. Englewood Cliffs, N.J.: Prentice-Hall, 1967

Pupil Personnel Services in the Modern School, Dugald Arbuckle. Boston: Allyn & Bacon, 1966 (pp. 113-209)

The School Counselor as a Professional, John Pietrofesa and John Vriend. Itasca, Ill.: F. E. Peacock, 1971

Teacher's Role in Counseling, The, Mary Ligon and Sarah McDaniel. Englewood Cliffs, N.J.: Prentice-Hall, 1970

WORKING WITH SUB-PROFESSIONALS AND AIDES

Educational Manpower, James Olivero and Edward Buffie, eds. Bloomington, Ind.: Indiana University Press, 1970

Helping and Human Relations (2 vols.), Robert Carkhuff. New York: Holt, Rinehart & Winston, 1969

Using Teacher Aides, Lawrence Snow. Highland Park, N.J.: Dreier Educational Systems, 1970

PUBLIC RELATIONS, PUBLICITY, AND COUNSELOR ROLE PERCEPTION

The American School Counselor, David Armor. New York: Russel Sage Foundation, 1969

Effective Public Relations, 4th ed., Scott Cutlip and Allen Center. Englewood Cliffs, N.J.: Prentice-Hall, 1971.

Helping Counselors Grow Professionally, W. Evraiff. Englewood Cliffs, N.J.: Prentice-Hall. 1968

Lesly's Public Relations Handbook, edited by Philip Lesly. Englewood Cliffs, N.J.: Prentice-Hall, 1971

Management and Improvement Of Guidance, George Hill. New York, Appleton-Century-Crofts, 1965 (selected chapters)

Professional Problems in School Counseling Practice, Richard Dunlop, Ed. Scranton, Pa.: International, 1968 (selected chapters)

The Schools and American Society, Daniel Selakovich. Waltham, Mass.: Blaisdell, 1967

Social Foundations of Educational Guidance. Carl Weinberg. New York: Free Press, 1969

INDEX